ANNUAL EDITIO

Business Ethics 11/12

Twenty-Third Edition

EDITOR

John E. Richardson
Pepperdine University

Dr. John E. Richardson is a professor of marketing in the George L. Graziadio School of Business and Management at Pepperdine University. He is president of his own consulting firm and has consulted with organizations such as Bell and Howell, Dayton-Hudson, Epson, and the U.S. Navy, as well as with various service, nonprofit, and franchise organizations. Dr. Richardson is a member of the American Management Association, the American Marketing Association, the Society for Business Ethics, and Beta Gamma Sigma honorary business fraternity.

ANNUAL EDITIONS: BUSINESS ETHICS, TWENTY-THIRD EDITION

Published by McGraw-Hill, a business unit of The McGraw-Hill Companies, Inc., 1221 Avenue of the Americas, New York, NY 10020. Copyright © 2012 by The McGraw-Hill Companies, Inc. All rights reserved. Previous edition(s) 2005, 2008, 2009, 2011. No part of this publication may be reproduced or distributed in any form or by any means, or stored in a database or retrieval system, without the prior written consent of The McGraw-Hill Companies, Inc., including, but not limited to, in any network or other electronic storage or transmission, or broadcast for distance learning.

Some ancillaries, including electronic and print components, may not be available to customers outside the United States.

Annual Editions® is a registered trademark of The McGraw-Hill Companies, Inc.

Annual Editions is published by the **Contemporary Learning Series** group within the McGraw-Hill Higher Education division.

1 2 3 4 5 6 7 8 9 0 QDB/QDB 1 0 9 8 7 6 5 4 3 2 1

ISBN 978-0-07-352865-6
MHID 0-07-352865-X
ISSN 1055-5455 (print)
ISSN 2159-1016 (online)

Managing Editor: *Larry Loeppke*
Developmental Editor: *Dave Welsh*
Permissions Coordinator: *DeAnna Dausener*
Marketing Specialist: *Alice Link*
Senior Project Manager: *Joyce Watters*
Design Coordinator: *Margarite Reynolds*
Buyer: *Susan K. Culbertson*

Compositor: Laserwords Private Limited
Cover Images: Eric Audras/Photoalto/PictureQuest (inset); Courtesy of D. Brendan Welsh (background)

www.mhhe.com

Editors/Academic Advisory Board

Members of the Academic Advisory Board are instrumental in the final selection of articles for each edition of ANNUAL EDITIONS. Their review of articles for content, level, and appropriateness provides critical direction to the editors and staff. We think that you will find their careful consideration well reflected in this volume.

ANNUAL EDITIONS: Business Ethics 11/12
23rd Edition

EDITOR

John E. Richardson
Pepperdine University

ACADEMIC ADVISORY BOARD MEMBERS

Preface

In publishing ANNUAL EDITIONS we recognize the enormous role played by the magazines, newspapers, and journals of the public press in providing current, first-rate educational information in a broad spectrum of interest areas. Many of these articles are appropriate for students, researchers, and professionals seeking accurate, current material to help bridge the gap between principles and theories and the real world. These articles, however, become more useful for study when those of lasting value are carefully collected, organized, indexed, and reproduced in a low-cost format, which provides easy and permanent access when the material is needed. That is the role played by ANNUAL EDITIONS.

Recent events have brought ethics to the forefront as a topic of discussion throughout our nation. And, undoubtedly, the area of society that is getting the closest scrutiny regarding its ethical practices is the business sector. Both the print and broadcast media have offered a constant stream of facts and opinions concerning recent unethical goings-on in the business world. Insider trading scandals on Wall Street, the marketing of unsafe products, money laundering, and questionable contracting practices are just a few examples of events that have recently tarnished the image of business.

As corporate America struggles to find its ethical identity in a business environment that grows increasingly complex, managers are confronted with some poignant questions that have definite ethical ramifications. Does a company have any obligation to help solve social problems such as poverty, pollution, and urban decay? What ethical responsibilities should a multinational corporation assume in foreign countries? What obligation does a manufacturer have to the consumer with respect to product defects and safety?

These are just a few of the issues that make the study of business ethics important and challenging. A significant goal of *Annual Editions: Business Ethics 11/12* is to present some different perspectives on understanding basic concepts and concerns of business ethics and to provide ideas on how to incorporate these concepts into the policies and decisionmaking processes of businesses. The articles reprinted in this publication have been carefully chosen from a variety of public press sources to furnish current information on business ethics.

This volume contains a number of features designed to make it useful for students, researchers, and professionals. These include the *table of contents* with summaries of each article and key concepts in bold italics, a *topic guide* for locating articles, new Critical Thinking study questions, and an Additional Business Ethics Resources section, which can be used to further explore article topics.

The articles are organized into five units. Selections that focus on similar issues are concentrated into subsections within the broader units. Each unit is preceded by an overview that provides background for informed reading of the articles, emphasizes critical issues, and presents key points to consider that focus on major themes running through the selections.

Your comments, opinions, and recommendations about *Annual Editions: Business Ethics 11/12* will be greatly appreciated and will help shape future editions. Please take a moment to complete and return the postage-paid *article rating form* on the last page of this book. Any book can be improved, and with your help this one will continue as well.

John E. Richardson

John E. Richardson
Editor

Contents

UNIT 1
Ethics, Values, and Social Responsibility in Business

The concepts in bold italics are developed in the article. For further expansion, please refer to the Topic Guide.

UNIT 2
Ethical Issues and Dilemmas in the Workplace

The concepts in bold italics are developed in the article. For further expansion, please refer to the Topic Guide.

The concepts in bold italics are developed in the article. For further expansion, please refer to the Topic Guide.

UNIT 3
Business and Society: Contemporary Ethical, Social, and Environmental Issues

UNIT 4
Ethics and Social Responsibility in the Marketplace

The concepts in bold italics are developed in the article. For further expansion, please refer to the Topic Guide.

UNIT 5
Developing the Future Ethos and Social Responsibility of Business

The concepts in bold italics are developed in the article. For further expansion, please refer to the Topic Guide.

The concepts in bold italics are developed in the article. For further expansion, please refer to the Topic Guide.

Correlation Guide

The *Annual Editions* series provides students with convenient, inexpensive access to current, carefully selected articles from the public press. **Annual Editions: Business Ethics 11/12** is an easy-to-use reader that presents articles on important topics such as *workplace misconduct, social and environmental issues, global ethics in the marketplace,* and many more. For more information on *Annual Editions* and other *McGraw-Hill Contemporary Learning Series* titles, visit www.mhhe.com/cls.

This convenient guide matches the units in **Annual Editions: Business Ethics 11/12** with the corresponding chapters in four of our best-selling McGraw-Hill Business Ethics textbooks by DesJardins, Ghillyer, Hartman/DesJardins, and Hosmer.

Annual Editions: Business Ethics 11/12	An Introduction to Business Ethics, 4/e by DesJardins	Business Ethics Now, 3/e by Ghillyer	Business Ethics: Decision-Making for Personal Integrity & Social Responsibility, 2/e by Hartman/ DesJardins	The Ethics of Management, 7/e by Hosmer
Unit 1: Ethics, Values, and Social Responsibility in Business	**Chapter 1:** Why Study Ethics? **Chapter 2:** Ethical Theory and Business **Chapter 3:** Corporate Social Responsibility **Chapter 4:** Corporate Culture, Governance, and Ethical Leadership	**Chapter 1:** Understanding Ethics **Chapter 2:** Defining Business Ethics **Chapter 4:** Corporate Social Responsibility	**Chapter 1:** Ethics and Business **Chapter 5:** Corporate Social Responsibility	**Chapter 1:** The Nature of Moral Problems in Management **Chapter 4:** Moral Analysis and Ethical Duties
Unit 2: Ethical Issues and Dilemmas in the Workplace	**Chapter 4:** Corporate Culture, Governance, and Ethical Leadership **Chapter 5:** The Meaning and Value of Work **Chapter 6:** Moral Rights in the Workplace **Chapter 7:** Employee Responsibilities **Chapter 11:** Diversity and Discrimination	**Chapter 2:** Defining Business Ethics **Chapter 3:** Organizational Ethics **Chapter 7:** Blowing the Whistle	**Chapter 6:** Ethical Decision-Making: Employer Responsibilities and Employee Rights **Chapter 7:** Ethical Decision-Making: Technology and Privacy in the Workplace	**Chapter 1:** The Nature of Moral Problems in Management
Unit 3: Business and Society: Contemporary Ethical, Social, and Environmental Issues	**Chapter 10:** Business' Environmental Responsibilities **Chapter 12:** International Business and Globalization	**Chapter 2:** Defining Business Ethics **Chapter 9:** Ethics and Globalization	**Chapter 5:** Corporate Social Responsibility **Chapter 9:** Business and Environmental Sustainability	**Chapter 3:** Moral Analysis and Legal Requirements
Unit 4: Ethics and Social Responsibility in the Marketplace	**Chapter 8:** Marketing Ethics: Product Safety and Pricing **Chapter 9:** Marketing Ethics: Advertising and Target Marketing	**Chapter 3:** Organizational Ethics **Chapter 8:** Ethics and Technology **Chapter 10:** Making it Stick: Doing What's Right in a Competitive Market	**Chapter 5:** Corporate Social Responsibility **Chapter 8:** Ethics and Marketing	**Chapter 2:** Moral Analysis and Economic Outcomes
Unit 5: Developing the Future Ethos and Social Responsibility of Business	**Chapter 4:** Corporate Culture, Governance, and Ethical Leadership **Chapter 10:** Business' Environmental Responsibilities	**Chapter 10:** Making it Stick: Doing What's Right in a Competitive Market	**Chapter 3:** Philosophical Ethics and Business	**Chapter 6:** How Can a Business Organization Be Made Moral?

Topic Guide

This topic guide suggests how the selections in this book relate to the subjects covered in your course. You may want to use the topics listed on these pages to search the Web more easily.

On the following pages a number of websites have been gathered specifically for this book. They are arranged to reflect the units of this Annual Editions reader. You can link to these sites by going to www.mhhe.com/cls

All the articles that relate to each topic are listed below the bold-faced term.

Internet References

The following Internet sites have been selected to support the articles found in this reader. These sites were available at the time of publication. However, because websites often change their structure and content, the information listed may no longer be available. We invite you to visit www.mhhe.com/cls for easy access to these sites.

Annual Editions: Business Ethics 11/12

General Sources

Center for the Study of Ethics in the Professions
http://ethics.iit.edu

Sponsored by the Illinois Institute of Technology, this site links to a number of world business ethics centers.

GreenMoney Journal
www.greenmoneyjournal.com

The editorial vision of this publication proposes that consumer spending and investment dollars can bring about positive social and environmental change. On this website, they'll tell you how.

U.S. Department of Labor
www.dol.gov

Browsing through this site will lead to a vast array of labor-related data and discussions of issues affecting employees and managers, such as the minimum wage.

U.S. Equal Employment Opportunity Commission (EEOC)
www.eeoc.gov

The EEOC's mission "is to ensure equality of opportunity by vigorously enforcing federal legislation prohibiting discrimination in employment." Consult this site for facts about employment discrimination, enforcement, and litigation.

Wharton Ethics Program
http://ethics.wharton.upenn.edu/

The Wharton School of the University of Pennsylvania provides an independently managed site that offers links to research, cases, and other business ethics centers.

UNIT 1: Ethics, Values, and Social Responsibility in Business

Association for Moral Education (AME)
www.amenetwork.org/

AME is dedicated to fostering communication, cooperation, training, and research that links moral theory with educational practices. From here it is possible to connect to several sites of relevance in the study of business ethics.

Business for Social Responsibility (BSR)
www.bsr.org

Core topic areas covered by BSR are listed on this page. They include Corporate Social Responsibility; Business Ethics; Community Investment; the Environment; Governance and Accountability; Human Rights; Marketplace; Mission, Vision, Values; and finally Workplace. New information is added on a regular basis. For each topic or subtopic there is an introduction, examples of large and small company leadership practices, sample company policies, links to helping resources, and other information.

Enron Online
www.enron.com/corp/

Explore the Enron website to find information about Enron's history, products, and services. Go to the "Press Room" section for Enron's spin on the current investigation.

Ethics Updates/Lawrence Hinman
http://ethics.sandiego.edu/index.html

This site provides both simple concept definitions and complex analysis of ethics, original treatises, and sophisticated search engine capability. Subject matter covers the gamut, from ethical theory to applied ethical venues.

Institute for Business and Professional Ethics
http://commerce.depaul.edu/ethics/

Sponsored by DePaul College of Commerce, this site is interested in research in the field of business and professional ethics. It is still under construction, so check in from time to time.

National Center for Policy Analysis
www.ncpa.org

This organization's archive links lead you to interesting materials on a variety of topics that affect managers, from immigration issues, to affirmative action, to regulatory policy.

Open Directory Project
http://dmoz.org/Business/Management/Ethics

As part of the Open Directory Project, this page provides a database of websites that address numerous topics on ethics in business.

Working Definitions
www.workingdefinitions.co.uk/index.html

This is a British, magazine-style site devoted to discussion and comment on organizations in the wider social context and to supporting and developing people's management skills.

UNIT 2: Ethical Issues and Dilemmas in the Workplace

American Psychological Association
www.apa.org/homepage.html

Search this site to find references and discussion of important ethics issues for the workplace of the 1990s, including the impact of restructuring and revitalization of businesses.

International Labour Organization (ILO)
www.ilo.org

ILO's home page leads you to links that describe the goals of the organization and summarizes international labor standards and human rights. Its official UN website locator can point you to many other useful resources.

UNIT 3: Business and Society: Contemporary Ethical, Social, and Environmental Issues

National Immigrant Forum
www.immigrationforum.org

The pro-immigrant organization offers this page to examine the effects of immigration on the U.S. economy and society. Click on the links to underground and immigrant economies.

Internet References

Workopolis.com
http://sympatico.workopolis.com

This Canadian site provides an electronic network with a GripeVine for complaining about work and finding solutions to everyday work problems.

United Nations Environment Programme (UNEP)
www.unep.ch

Consult this UNEP site for links to topics such as the impact of trade on the environment. It will direct you to useful databases and global resource information.

United States Trade Representative (USTR)
www.ustr.gov

This home page of the U.S. Trade Representative provides links to many U.S. government resources for those interested in ethics in international business.

UNIT 4: Ethics and Social Responsibility in the Marketplace

Business for Social Responsibility (BSR)
www.bsr.org/

BSR is a global organization that seeks to help companies "achieve success in ways that respect ethical values, people, communities, and the environment." Links to Services, Resources, and Forum are available.

Total Quality Management Sites
www.nku.edu/~lindsay/qualhttp.html

This site points to a variety of interesting Internet sources to aid in the study and application of Total Quality Management principles.

U.S. Navy
www.navy.mil

Start at this U.S. Navy page for access to a plethora of interesting stories and analyses related to Total Quality Leadership. It addresses such concerns as how TQL can improve customer service and affect utilization of information technology.

UNIT 5: Developing the Future Ethos and Social Responsibility of Business

International Business Ethics Institute (IBEI)
www.business-ethics.org/index.asp

The goal of this educational organization is to promote business ethics and corporate responsibility in response to the growing need for transnationalism in the field of business ethics.

UNU/IAS Project on Global Ethos
www.ias.unu.edu/research/globalethos.cfm

The United Nations University Institute of Advanced Studies (UNU/IAS) has issued this project abstract, which concerns governance and multilateralism. The main aim of the project is to initiate a process by which to generate jointly, with the involvement of factors from both state- and nonstate institutions in developed and developing countries, a global ethos that could provide or support a set of guiding principles for the emerging global community.

Additional Resources

The following business ethics sites have been selected to support the articles found in this reader. These sites were available at the time of publication. However, because websites often change their structure and content, the information listed may no longer be available. We invite you to visit *www.mhhe.com/cls* for easy access to these sites.

Annual Editions: Business Ethics 11/12

Contents

- Articles/Publications
- Cases/Case Studies
- Corporate Codes of Ethics
- Professional Organizations and Associations
- Resources and Resource Centers

Articles/Publications

Business Corporate Ethics
www.washingtonpost.com/ac2/wp-dyn/NewsSearch?st=
Business%20Corporate%20Ethics&

Business Corporate Ethics is a special report outlining recent corporate scandals involving ethics violations compiled by the *Washington Post.* Breaking news features, Enron updates, WorldCom activities, accounting probes, as well as timelines and analysis are posted.

Business Ethics Forum
www.managementlogs.com/business_ethics.html

The focus of this blog is designed for those "interested in promoting ethical business practices, moral behavior and responsible management in corporations and institutions." Free membership is required to participate in the discussions.

Business Ethics Newsletter
www.iese.edu/aplicaciones/news/index.asp?lang=en

Joan Fontrodona and Roberto García Castro edit this newsletter that is affiliated with the IESE Business School at the University of Navarra (Spain). The goal of the Business Ethics Newsletter is to highlight certain stories featuring business ethics that have appeared recently in the media.

Business Ethics: Resources for Educators
An article featured on the SocialFunds.com site discusses the top 100 companies that made the Business Ethics' Best Corporate Citizens List for 2009; can be found at www .socialfunds.com/news/article.cgi/2652.html

BusinessWeek Online
www.businessweek.com

BusinessWeek Online allows you to search for articles dealing with ethics in business. Use their search feature to retrieve current articles covering a variety of ethical dilemmas affecting the business world including information about the Enron, Tyco, and WorldCom scandals.

Corporate Ethics
www.pbs.org/newshour/bb/business/ethics

This online special report featured on the program *NewsHour with Jim Lehrer* covers some of the recent scandals that have been hitting the business world. Links to stories discussing some of the corporations affected by the controversies, online forum resources and background reports dating back to 1995 are included.

Ethics Resource Center (ERC)
www.ethics.org

An extensive list of articles dealing with business ethics and related issues can be found in the section, Organizational Ethics Articles: Business at www.ethics.org/resources/ nr_oearticles.cfm?NavCat=Business.

Financial Scandals
www.ex.ac.uk/~RDavies/arian/scandals

Financial Scandals is a site created by Roy Davies that covers some of the "greatest" scandals of all times. The site is divided into 8 sections and is designed for a broad audience, from business executives interested in business ethics issues to financial history enthusiasts.

Fortune.com
www.fortune.com

Fortune.com has numerous articles discussing ethics and ethical issues in the corporate world. Type "ethics" in the site's search feature to retrieve the latest articles.

A Question of Ethics
www.informationweek.com/825/ethics.htm

As companies move into the e-business arena, new ethical issues arise. This timeless *Informationweek.com* article from February 19, 2001, discusses topics such as compromising customer privacy for advertising gain and trust concerns between employers and employees. Links to other e-business ethics articles can also be found at this site.

Case Studies

Babson Business College: Business Ethics Program
http://roger.babson.edu/ethics/index.htm

The Babson Business Ethics Program is designed to integrate ethics into businesses and business education. Numerous resources are available including the following:

- **Case Studies**
  http://roger.babson.edu/ethics/business.htm

Carnegie Mellon: Ethics Teaching Materials
http://ba.gsia.cmu.edu/ethics/teaching.htm

This site, developed by the Center for International Corporate Responsibility, provides links to the role of ethics instruction in B-school, case studies, tutorials, and business scandal articles. Academic resources, membership organization information, and other ethical materials are also available.

Additional Resources

CasePlace.org
www.caseplace.org

CasePlace.org is a free service for business faculty and students offered by Aspen Institute's Initiative for Social Innovation through Business (Aspen ISIB). Cases and topics for discussion are posted at this site, and the cases are searchable by topic or discipline.

Case Studies: Analyses
http://businessmajors.about.com/cs/casestudies/index.htm?once=true&iam=dpile&terms=+IT++case++stud

About.com's collection of case studies is presented at this site. A few are links to sites related to business ethics or related topic areas.

Inc.comGuide: Case Studies in Business Ethics
www.inc.com/partners/intel/case-studies.html#content

Editors at Inc.com select the resources found at this site. Case studies covering ethical topics such as environmental challenges, getting involved in the community, and making global connections can be found in this section of their site.

Other Inc.com guides can be found at www.inc.com/home/.

Institute for Global Ethics (IGE)
www.globalethics.org

IGE is an organization dedicated to promoting "ethical behavior in individuals, institutions, and nations through research, public discourse, and practical action." Numerous resources and articles are provided on the IGE site. The following is an example of a section of this site containing useful materials:

Institute of Business Ethics (IBE)
www.ibe.org.uk

The goal of the Institute of Business Ethics (IBE) is to "encourage high standards of corporate and business behavior and the sharing of best practice." Sections of this site to note are Codes of Conduct and News/Resources. The Codes of Conduct section provide links on how to develop a code, what types of information should be included, and links to companies with codes. Latest news dealing with business ethics and links to external sites like the Caux Rountable (www.cauxroundtable.org) and the Institute for Global Ethics (www.globalethics.org) can be found in the News/Resources section. IBE was established in 1986 and strives to be the "leader in knowledge and practice of corporate business ethics." The development of the IBE site was a joint effort by the Open University and the Institute of Business Ethics and sponsored by the Foundation for Business Responsibilities. It is designed to be an online information center for academics and students interested in business ethics. The case study section is an example of resources found at this site.

Markkula Center for Applied Ethics
www.scu.edu/ethics

The Markkula Center for Applied Ethics was founded in 1986 and has grown into one of the most active university applied ethics centers in the U.S. It is based at Santa Clara University and was initially funded by an endowment by Linda and A. C. "Mike" Markkula Jr. Articles, cases, briefings and dialogue in all areas of applied ethics can be found at this online center. Case studies specifically addressing the issue of business ethics can be found at:

- **Business Ethics: Cases**
  www.scu.edu/ethics/practicing/focusareas/cases.cfm?fam=BUSI

Corporate Codes of Ethics

Baxter Healthcare: Working with Integrity
www.baxter.com/doingbusiness/customers/index.html

Baxter Healthcare works to create an environment that fosters the development of "conscientious ethically-minded people who are committed to integrity, honesty and fairness." The company's "Working with Integrity" document outlines global business practices standards, compliance issues, their bioethics policy, and position statement on bioethics and other ethics resources.

Boeing
www.boeing.com

Boeing has a long and diverse history, and ethics is a central component of the company's mission. The Ethics and Business Conduct Committee has been charged with the oversight of the ethics program at Boeing, and the following are some ethics resources available at its site.

- **Code of Conduct**
  www.boeing.com/companyoffices/aboutus/ethics/code_of_conduct.pdf
- **Ethics and Business Conduct Program**
  www.boeing.com/companyoffices/aboutus/ethics/pro3.pdf
- **Ethics Policies and Procedures**
  www.boeing.com/companyoffices/aboutus/ethics/epolicy.htm
- **Values**
  www.boeing.com/companyoffices/aboutus/ethics/integst.htm

Cadbury Schweppes: Ethical Business Practices
www.cadbury.com/ourresponsibilities/Pages/ourresponsibilities.aspx

A section of the business principles that guide employees at Cadbury Schweppes addresses ethical issues. Areas covered as part of the company's ethical practices include communications, confidentiality, conflict of interest, gifts, and inside information.

Codes of Ethics Online Business
http://ethics.iit.edu/codes/business.html

Illinois Institute of Technology's Center for the Study of Ethics in the Professions developed this online collection of codes on the Web, and it has grown out of the Center's Library of codes that resides in its vertical file. In addition to subject specific codes, like ones for business, resources for authoring a code, case studies, and other information can be found at this site.

Creating a Code of Ethics
www.ethicsweb.ca/codes

Chris MacDonald, PhD, Philosophy Department, St. Mary's University (Halifax, Canada) has put together this site with links to resources to assist individuals and groups in writing a code of ethics. He discusses why organizations and institutions should even have a code and provides guidance in writing one. He also provides links to essays on ethics, sample codes and contacts for ethics consultants.

Additional Resources

MacDonald has also worked on several other ethics sites including EthicsWeb at www.ethicsweb.ca.

Hewlett-Packard (HP)
www.hp.com/hpinfo/globalcitizenship/csr/ethics.html

This ethics page outlines the HP values, standards, and guidelines for responsible conduct of business.

IBM: Business Conduct Guidelines
www.ibm.com/investor/corpgovernance/cgbcg.phtml

IBM has created a very detailed set of guidelines designed to facilitate ethical conduct within the company. This 5-section document is broken down into several subcategories by topic.

Johnson & Johnson: Our Credo
www.jnj.com/our_company/our_credo/index.htm

Johnson & Johnson is not guided by a mission statement that hangs on the wall of the corporation. Instead, a one-page "Credo" guides the actions of the company. A link to the history of the "Credo" is also available.

Microsoft: Mission & Values
www.microsoft.com/mscorp

Microsoft CEO, Steve Ballmer, presented the company's mission, vision, and values in June 2002, and that information is provided on this site.

Occidental Petroleum Corporation: Code of Business Conduct
www.oxy.com/SiteCollectionDocuments/code_of_business_conduct.pdf

This document outlines Occidental Petroleum Corporation's guidelines for administering and enforcing the Code of Business Conduct and the company's compliance requirements with applicable laws and ethical standards.

Rite Aid: Code of Ethics and Business Conduct
www.riteaid.com/www.riteaid.com/w-content/images/company/governance/code_of_ethics.pdf

The purpose of this 18-page code is to "reinforce and enhance Rite Aid's commitment to an ethical way of doing business." It outlines how Rite Aid puts the company's values and obligations to work. The document also addresses Rite Aid's responsibility to associates, responsibility to the corporation, competing with integrity, interacting with the government, and implementing the code.

Sara Lee: Global Business Practices
www.saralee.com/AboutSaraLee/GlobalBusinessPractices.aspx

In September 1997, Sara Lee introduced their Global Business Practices program as a way of conveying the company's values and beliefs to their employees. Over 100 Business Practice Officers currently oversee this ethics program in every unit and department operated by Sara Lee.

ServiceMaster: Code of Conduct
http://corporate.servicemaster.com/overview_conduct.asp

The ServiceMaster Code of Conduct outlines policies, values, and regulations must be followed by every employee at the company. This 33-page document addresses topics such as responsibilities in the workplace, customer relationships, and conflicts of interest.

Weyerhaeuser: Business Conduct
www.weyerhaeuser.com/citizenship/businessconduct

Weyerhaeuser is one of the largest owners and producers of softwood and hardwood lumber and lumber products in the world. The company has a "reputation for conducting business honestly and with integrity," and they expect the highest level of ethical and professional conduct from their employees. All employees receive copies of Weyerhaeuser's Code of Ethics and Business Conduct document, plus they must attend ethics training on a regular basis.

Williams-Sonoma, Inc.: Corporate Values
www.williams-sonomainc.com/careers/corporate-values.html

This brief overview outlines the values that Williams-Sonoma strives to uphold in order to help the company succeed in "enhancing the quality of life at home." The company's commitment to its people, customers, quality, shareholders and ethical sourcing are addressed.

Professional Organizations and Associations

American Finance Association (AFA)
www.afajof.org/default.shtml

Initial planning for the organization that is now AFA began in December 1939 in Philadelphia, PA. AFA is a professional association that deals with financial economic issues and promotes knowledge related to this area.

Better Business Bureau (BBB): Promoting Fairness and Integrity in the Marketplace
www.bbb.org

In 1912, the very first BBB was founded, and today, this system is supported by 250,000 local business members throughout the world. The goal of the Better Business Bureau is to "promote and foster the highest ethical relationship between businesses and the public through voluntary self-regulation, consumer and business education, and service excellence."

Business for Social Responsibility (BSR)
www.bsr.org

BSR, a global, non-profit organization works to "create a just and sustainable world by working with companies to promote more responsible business practices, innovation and collaboration." It strives to help members be successful and operate successful businesses while upholding the highest ethical standards of professional behavior. Links to free reports on a variety of issues plus other resources are available at this site.

The Caux Roundtable
www.cauxroundtable.org

The Caux Roundtable is an organization comprised of senior business leaders from around the world, including Europe, Japan, and North America. These leaders are individuals who "believe that business has a crucial role in developing and promoting equitable solutions to key global issues." One document provided on this site that serves as a guide to all businesses interested in responsible conduct is "The Principles for Business."

The Center for Ethics, Capital Markets and Political Economy
www.iath.virginia.edu/cecmpe

This center is a nonprofit organization that was established in 1994. It is designed to be an arena to foster discussion and a resource center for ethics information for "persons who believe that moral concerns should be taken into account in economic and political thinking." Services provided by the Center include sponsoring a working paper series, offering seminars, publishing "Ethics behind the News," and providing other research materials.

Additional Resources

The Defense Industry Initiative (DII) Business Ethics and Conduct

www.dii.org

DII is a "consortium of U.S. defense industry contractors which subscribes to a set of principles for achieving high standards of business ethics and conduct." Links to ethics training resources plus other resources of interest can be found at this site.

Ethics and Compliance Officer Association (ECOA)

www.theecoa.org/AM/Template.cfm?Section=Home&Template=/Templates/TemplateHomepage/EthicsComplianceOfficerAssociation_1510_20070109T133141_LayoutHomePage.cfm

ECOA was founded in 1992 and currently has over 800 members including the ethics officers from over half of the Fortune 100 companies. Resources available on the site include the 2000 EOA Member Survey, educational centers, government-related organizations and links to ethics programs for companies like Honda, Sara Lee, and Lockheed Martin.

European Business Ethics Network (EBEN)

www.eben-net.org

The formation of EBEN, a nonprofit organization founded in Brussels in 1987, was considered to be a significant step in recognizing business ethics as an important area of research. Links to ethics organizations, university programs and other research institutions are provided.

Financial Executives International (FEI)

www.financialexecutives.org/eweb/startpage.aspx?site=_fei

FEI was founded in 1931 and is considered to be the "professional association of choice for corporate financial executives." This organization strongly encourages all its members to practice the highest level of professional and ethical conduct.

Financial Planning Association (FPA): Code of Ethics

www.fpaforfinancialplanning.org/AboutFPA/CodeofEthics

Seven principles make up the Code of Ethics for FPA, and they are designed to guide members in the practice of professional ethics in the field of financial planning. The formation of FPA came about on January 1, 2000, as the result of the merger of the International Association for Financial Planning (IAFP) and the Institute of Certified Financial Planners (ICFP).

The Kennedy Institute of Ethics

http://kennedyinstitute.georgetown.edu

Georgetown Business Ethics Institute is located at Georgetown University and offers, through its Library and Information Services site, links to aid researchers in their quest for more information concerning business ethics topics.

Institute for Business, Technology & Ethics (IBTE)

www.ethix.org

IBTE was founded in 1998 to study the connections and relationships between business, ethics, and technology. The mission of this organization is to "promote good business through appropriate technology and sound ethics." Sections of the IBTE website to note are the Tools for Better Business and the Ethics Forum.

Institute for Global Ethics (IGE)

www.globalethics.org

IGE is an organization dedicated to promoting "ethical behavior in individuals, institutions, and nations through research, public discourse, and practical action." Numerous resources and articles are provided on the IGE site.

Institute of Business Ethics (IBE): Code of Ethics

www.ibe.org.uk

IBE believes that companies should uphold the highest standards of behavior and professional conduct. This organization "broadcasts" its mission through conferences, consultations, publications, and business ethics training programs. The IBE code of ethics section of the website goes beyond stating its code. It also provides tips on how to make codes effective, information on content included in a code of ethics policy, and links to various company codes of ethics.

The Society for Business Ethics (SBE)

www.societyforbusinessethics.org

SBE was founded in 1980 and is an international organization dedicated to the academic study of business ethics. The Ethics Links section of its site provides access to other associations and resource centers.

The Society of Corporate Compliance and Ethics

www.corporatecompliance.org/index.htm

The Society of Corporate Compliance and Ethics (SCCE) is a nonprofit organization that "exists to champion compliance standards, corporate governance and ethical practice in the business community and to provide the necessary resources for compliance and ethics professionals and others who share these principles." Membership opportunities and information about SCCE events are listed on this site. Resources, such as newsletters, books, and training kits (some for fee) are also available.

Resources and Centers

BELL: The Business Ethics Links Library

http://libnet.colorado.edu/Bell/frontpage.htm

Gene Hayworth, University of Colorado at Boulder, has created and continues to maintain a site designed to be a starting point for those seeking information regarding corporate ethics and social responsibility. Visitors to the site may select a topic or enter a search term. The following four categories are also available:

1. Academic organizations

2. Ethics organizations

3. Online ethics sources

4. Online ethics publications

Business Ethics

http://bubl.ac.uk/link/b/businessethics.htm

BUBL Link is a mega "catalog" of Internet resources covering various academic subject areas. An extensive section on business ethics has been compiled at this site. Resources include applied business materials, articles about financial scandals, and centers of research for business ethics.

Center for Business Ethics (CBE)

www.stthom.edu/Schools_Centers_of_Excellence/Centers_of_Excellence/Center_for_Business_Ethics/About/Index.aqf

The Center for Business Ethics (CBE) is housed on the campus of Bentley University and has been in operation

Additional Resources

since 1976 under the direction of W. Michael Hoffman. CBE is designed to be a forum for business ethics, and it provides specialized training and educational programs for businesses and their employees. Since CBE's founding, it has sponsored 10 major conferences on the topic of ethical business conduct.

Center for Ethics and Business
www.ethicsandbusiness.org/indexlo.htm

Loyola Marymount University (Los Angeles, CA) is the home of the Center for Ethics and Business. The Center acts as a forum for discussing ethical business decisions and dilemmas, including the costs and rewards of operating ethically. Numerous links to ethics programs, centers, and other tools designed to help people deal with ethical dilemmas are presented.

Center for Integrity in Business
www.spu.edu/depts/sbe/cib

Business ethics scandals making the news lately have increased the demand for business ethics educational programs and other programs designed to develop ethical business leaders. The Center for Integrity in Business at the School of Business & Economics at Seattle Pacific University has outlined 4 services: **1)** instigating and facilitating an ongoing dialogue; **2)** initiating and supporting a stream of empirical research; **3)** designing and conducting leadership development workshops and executive coaching sessions; **4)** educating and informing a broader audience. Resources available at this site include articles on current issues, instructional resources, and links to other ethics centers.

Complete Guide to Ethics Management
www.mapnp.org/library/ethics/ethxgde.htm

Carter McNamara, a business consultant in the Minneapolis/St. Paul region, has developed this free guidebook to help leaders and managers deal with the ethical issues that occur in everyday situations. The resources outlined in this online "book" include 10 myths about business ethics, ethics tools, and guidelines for managing ethics in the workplace.

E-Ethics Center
www.e-businessethics.com

The goal of the E-Ethics Center at Colorado State University is to "create a virtual community of organizations and individuals that share best practices in the improvement of business ethics." Much of the information found at the Center's website has been provided by businesses, nonprofit organizations, government agencies, and other academic institutions. The case studies and ethics links sections listed below are merely two of the resource areas at this site.

- **Business Ethics Case Studies**
  www.e-businessethics.com/case.htm

- **Ethics Links**
  www.e-businessethics.com/links.htm

Ethical Business: The Search for Research
www.eldis.org/go/topics/resource-guides/corporate-responsibility

This ELDIS (Electronic Development and Environmental Information System) guide provides links to case studies, social and environmental standards, resources for informing shareholders and consumers, and more.

The Ethics Classroom
www.ethicsclassroom.info

The Ethics Classroom at Kansas State University (KSU) is designed to act as an "interactive forum" for local business leaders and government officials and to be a resource for KSU students taking ethics-related courses. This online classroom provides links to case studies, Internet resources, and ethic poll results.

Ethics on the World Wide Web: Business
http://commfaculty.fullerton.edu/lester/ethics/business.html

Ethics on the World Wide Web is a site designed by the School of Communications at California State University, Fullerton. The annotated list includes links to ethics centers, institutes, and organizations.

Google Directory: Business Ethics
http://directory.google.com/Top/Business/Management/Ethics

Google Directory offers a rather large, annotated compilation of links to sites related to business ethics.

Markkula Center for Applied Ethics
www.scu.edu/ethics

The Markkula Center for Applied Ethics was founded in 1986 and has grown into one of the most active university applied ethics centers in the U.S. It is based at Santa Clara University and was initially funded by an endowment by Linda and A. C. "Mike" Markkula Jr. Articles, cases, briefings, and dialogue in all areas of applied ethics can be found at this online center. Resources specifically addressing the issue of business ethics, such as the case study section, can be found at:

- **Business Ethics: Cases**
  www.scu.edu/ethics/practicing/focusareas/cases.cfm?fam=BUSI

Online Ethics Center: Ethics in Business
http://temp.onlineethics.org/topics/business.html

The Online Ethics Center was established in the fall of 1995 under a grant from NSF, and its mission is to provide resources "useful for understanding and addressing ethically significant problems that arise" in the work environment. The Ethics in Business section addresses several issues such as ethics in a corporate setting, conflict of interest, intellectual property, and employees who are entrepreneurs on corporate time.

Open Directory: Business Management Ethics
http://dmoz.org/Business/Management/Ethics

Open Directory claims to be the "largest, most comprehensive human-edited directory on the Web." This annotated collection includes links to business ethics publications, resource centers, forums, codes of ethics, and more.

Prudential Business Ethics Center
www.pruethics.rutgers.edu

The Prudential Business Ethics Center is housed at Rutgers University, and it is focused on the theory and practice of ethical behavior in business. The mission of the Center is to "help create social capital as well as prosperity for the business and professional communities of New Jersey." Services offered by the Center include providing speakers, supporting ethics courses and publications, conducting case competitions for students, providing consulting services to area businesses, and surveying the ethical attitudes of those in the New Jersey business community.

Additional Resources

SOSIG: Professional and Business Ethics

www.sosig.ac.uk/roads/subject-listing/World-cat/proethic.html

SOSIG, the Social Science Information Gateway, is part of the UK Resource Discovery Network. The goal of this gateway is to provide high-quality business and other social science resources to students, faculty, and researchers. An extensive array of resources is arranged by type of resources for easier access.

Yahoo! Directory: Business Ethics and Responsibility

http://dir.yahoo.com/Business_and_Economy/Ethics_and_Responsibility

This Yahoo! category has site listings for centers, institutes, and publications. Its Categories section has links to related topics such as corporate accountability, socially responsible investing, sweatshops, and whistleblowing.

The Zicklin Center for Business Ethics Research

www.zicklincenter.org

The Carol and Lawrence Zicklin Center at the Wharton School, University of Pennsylvania, was established in 1997 to conduct leading-edge research on business ethics. Research focus areas include global business ethics, corporate governance, social contracts, deception, disclosure, bribery, and corruption. The Research Links section of the site includes information on associations, publications and other ethics-related materials.

UNIT 1

Ethics, Values, and Social Responsibility in Business

Unit Selections

Learning Outcomes

- Do you believe that corporations are more socially responsible today than they were 10 years ago? Why or why not?

- In what specific ways do you see companies practicing social responsibility? Do you think most companies are overt or covert in their social responsibility activities? Explain your answer.

- What are the economic and social implications of "management accountability" as part of the decision-making process? Does a company have any obligation to help remedy social problems, such as poverty, urban decay, and pollution? Defend your response.

- Using recent examples of stock, financial, and accounting debacles, discuss the flaws in the U.S. financial system that allow companies to disregard ethics, values, and social responsibility in business.

Student Website

www.mhhe.com/cls

Internet References

Association for Moral Education (AME)
www.amenetwork.org
Business for Social Responsibility (BSR)
www.bsr.org
Enron Online
www.enron.com/corp
Ethics Updates/Lawrence Hinman
http://ethics.sandiego.edu/index.html
Institute for Business and Professional Ethics
http://commerce.depaul.edu/ethics
National Center for Policy Analysis
www.ncpa.org
Open Directory Project
http://dmoz.org/Business/Management/Ethics
Working Definitions
www.workingdefinitions.co.uk/index.html

Ethical decision making in an organization does not occur in a vacuum. As individuals and as managers, we formulate our ethics (that is, the standards of "right" and "wrong" behavior that we set for ourselves) based upon family, peer, and religious influences; our past experiences; and our own unique value systems. When we make ethical decisions within the organizational context, many times there are situational factors and potential conflicts of interest that further complicate the process.

Decisions do not only have personal ramifications—they also have social consequences. Social responsibility is really ethics at the organizational level, since it refers to the obligation that an organization has to make choices and to take actions that will contribute to the good of society as well as the good of the organization. Authentic social responsibility is not initiated because of forced compliance to specific laws and regulations. In contrast to legal responsibility, social responsibility involves a voluntary response from an organization that is above and beyond what is specified by the law.

The nine selections in this unit provide an overview of the interrelationships of ethics, values, and social responsibility in business. The essays in this unit offer practical and insightful principles

© Ingram Publishing/Getty Images

and suggestions to managers, enabling them to approach the subject of business ethics with more confidence. They also point out the complexity and the significance of making ethical decisions.

Thinking Ethically
A Framework for Moral Decision Making

MANUEL VELASQUEZ ET AL.

Moral issues greet us each morning in the newspaper, confront us in the memos on our desks, nag us from our children's soccer fields, and bid us good night on the evening news. We are bombarded daily with questions about the justice of our foreign policy, the morality of medical technologies that can prolong our lives, the rights of the homeless, the fairness of our children's teachers to the diverse students in their classrooms.

Dealing with these moral issues is often perplexing. How, exactly, should we think through an ethical issue? What questions should we ask? What factors should we consider?

The first step in analyzing moral issues is obvious but not always easy: Get the facts.

The first step in analyzing moral issues is obvious but not always easy: Get the facts. Some moral issues create controversies simply because we do not bother to check the facts. This first step, although obvious, is also among the most important and the most frequently overlooked.

But having the facts is not enough. Facts by themselves only tell us what *is*; they do not tell us what *ought* to be. In addition to getting the facts, resolving an ethical issue also requires an appeal to values. Philosophers have developed five different approaches to values to deal with moral issues.

The Utilitarian Approach

Utilitarianism was conceived in the 19th century by Jeremy Bentham and John Stuart Mill to help legislators determine which laws were morally best. Both Bentham and Mill suggested that ethical actions are those that provide the greatest balance of good over evil.

To analyze an issue using the utilitarian approach, we first identify the various courses of action available to us. Second, we ask who will be affected by each action and what benefits or harms will be derived from each. And third, we choose the action that will produce the greatest benefits and the least harm. The ethical action is the one that provides the greatest good for the greatest number.

The Rights Approach

The second important approach to ethics has its roots in the philosophy of the 18th-century thinker Immanuel Kant and others like him, who focused on the individual's right to choose for herself or himself. According to these philosophers, what makes human beings different from mere things is that people have dignity based on their ability to choose freely what they will do with their lives, and they have a fundamental moral right to have these choices respected. People are not objects to be manipulated; it is a violation of human dignity to use people in ways they do not freely choose.

Of course, many different, but related, rights exist besides this basic one. These other rights (an incomplete list below) can be thought of as different aspects of the basic right to be treated as we choose.

- *The right to the truth*: We have a right to be told the truth and to be informed about matters that significantly affect our choices.
- *The right of privacy*: We have the right to do, believe, and say whatever we choose in our personal lives so long as we do not violate the rights of others.
- *The right not to be injured*: We have the right not to be harmed or injured unless we freely and knowingly do something to deserve punishment or we freely and knowingly choose to risk such injuries.
- *The right to what is agreed:* We have a right to what has been promised by those with whom we have freely entered into a contract or agreement.

In deciding whether an action is moral or immoral using this second approach, then, we must ask, Does the action respect the moral rights of everyone? Actions are wrong to the extent

The Case of Maria Elena

Maria Elena has cleaned your house each week for more than a year. You agree with your friend who recommended her that she does an excellent job and is well worth the $30 cash you pay her for three hours' work. You've also come to like her, and you think she likes you, especially as her English has become better and you've been able to have some pleasant conversations.

Over the past three weeks, however, you've noticed Maria Elena becoming more and more distracted. One day, you ask her if something is wrong, and she tells you she really needs to make additional money. She hastens to say she is not asking you for a raise, becomes upset, and begins to cry. When she calms down a little, she tells you her story:

She came to the United States six years ago from Mexico with her child, Miguel, who is now 7 years old. They entered the country on a visitor's visa that has expired, and Maria Elena now uses a Social Security number she made up.

Her common-law husband, Luis, came to the United States first. He entered the country illegally, after paying smugglers $500 to hide him under piles of grass cuttings for a six-hour truck ride across the border. When he had made enough money from low-paying day jobs, he sent for Maria Elena. Using a false green card, Luis now works as a busboy for a restaurant, which withholds part of his salary for taxes. When Maria Elena comes to work at your house, she takes the bus and Luis baby-sits.

In Mexico, Maria Elena and Luis lived in a small village where it was impossible to earn more than $3 a day. Both had sixth-grade educations, common in their village. Life was difficult, but they did not decide to leave until they realized the future would be bleak for their child and for the other children they wanted to have. Luis had a cousin in San Jose who visited and told Luis and Maria Elena how well his life was going. After his visit, Luis and Maria Elena decided to come to the United States.

Luis quickly discovered, as did Maria Elena, that life in San Jose was not the way they had heard. The cousin did not tell them they would be able to afford to live only in a run-down three-room apartment with two other couples and their children. He did not tell them they would always live in fear of INS raids.

After they entered the United States, Maria Elena and Luis had a second child, Jose, who is 5 years old. The birth was difficult because she didn't use the health-care system or welfare for fear of being discovered as undocumented. But, she tells you, she is willing to put up with anything so that her children can have a better life. "All the money we make is for Miguel and Jose," she tells you. "We work hard for their education and their future."

Now, however, her mother in Mexico is dying, and Maria Elena must return home, leaving Luis and the children. She does not want to leave them because she might not be able to get back into the United States, but she is pretty sure she can find a way to return if she has enough money. That is her problem: She doesn't have enough money to make certain she can get back.

After she tells you her story, she becomes too distraught to continue talking. You now know she is an undocumented immigrant, working in your home. What is the ethical thing for you to do?

This case was developed by Tom Shanks, S.J., director of the Markkula Center for Applied Ethics. Maria Elena is a composite drawn from several real people, and her story represents some of the ethical dilemmas behind the immigration issue.

This case can be accessed through the Ethics Center home page on the World Wide Web: www.scu.edu/Ethics/. You can also contact us by e-mail, ethics@scu.edu, or regular mail: Markkula Center for Applied Ethics, Santa Clara University, Santa Clara, CA 95053. Our voice mail number is (408) 554-7898. We have also posted on our homepage a new case involving managed health care.

that they violate the rights of individuals; the more serious the violation, the more wrongful the action.

The Fairness or Justice Approach

The fairness or justice approach to ethics has its roots in the teachings of the ancient Greek philosopher Aristotle, who said that "equals should be treated equally and unequals unequally." The basic moral question in this approach is: How fair is an action? Does it treat everyone in the same way, or does it show favoritism and discrimination?

Favoritism gives benefits to some people without a justifiable reason for singling them out; discrimination imposes burdens on people who are no different from those on whom burdens are not imposed. Both favoritism and discrimination are unjust and wrong.

The Common-Good Approach

This approach to ethics presents a vision of society as a community whose members are joined in the shared pursuit of values and goals they hold in common. This community comprises individuals whose own good is inextricably bound to the good of the whole.

The common good is a notion that originated more than 2,000 years ago in the writings of Plato, Aristotle, and Cicero. More recently, contemporary ethicist John Rawls defined the common good as "certain general conditions that are . . . equally to everyone's advantage."

In this approach, we focus on ensuring that the social policies, social systems, institutions, and environments on which we depend are beneficial to all. Examples of goods common to all include affordable health care, effective public safety, peace among nations, a just legal system, and an unpolluted environment.

Appeals to the common good urge us to view ourselves as members of the same community, reflecting on broad questions concerning the kind of society we want to become and how we are to achieve that society. While respecting and valuing the freedom of individuals to pursue their own goals, the common-good approach challenges us also to recognize and further those goals we share in common.

The Virtue Approach

The virtue approach to ethics assumes that there are certain ideals toward which we should strive, which provide for the full development of our humanity. These ideals are discovered through thoughtful reflection on what kind of people we have the potential to become.

Virtues are attitudes or character traits that enable us to be and to act in ways that develop our highest potential. They enable us to pursue the ideals we have adopted.

Honesty, courage, compassion, generosity, fidelity, integrity, fairness, self-control, and prudence are all examples of virtues.

Virtues are like habits; that is, once acquired, they become characteristic of a person. Moreover, a person who has developed virtues will be naturally disposed to act in ways consistent with moral principles. The virtuous person is the ethical person.

In dealing with an ethical problem using the virtue approach, we might ask, What kind of person should I be? What will promote the development of character within myself and my community?

Ethical Problem Solving

These five approaches suggest that once we have ascertained the facts, we should ask ourselves five questions when trying to resolve a moral issue:

- What benefits and what harms will each course of action produce, and which alternative will lead to the best overall consequences?
- What moral rights do the affected parties have, and which course of action best respects those rights?
- Which course of action treats everyone the same, except where there is a morally justifiable reason not to, and does not show favoritism or discrimination?
- Which course of action advances the common good?
- Which course of action develops moral virtues?

This method, of course, does not provide an automatic solution to moral problems. It is not meant to. The method is merely meant to help identify most of the important ethical considerations. In the end, we must deliberate on moral issues for ourselves, keeping a careful eye on both the facts and on the ethical considerations involved.

Critical Thinking

1. Describe briefly each the five approaches to solving ethical dilemmas.
2. Set up a table for the five approaches and show how each approach would address The Case of Maria Elena.

This article updates several previous pieces from *Issues in Ethics* by **Manuel Velasquez**—Dirksen Professor of Business Ethics at SCU and former Center director—and **Claire Andre,** associate Center director. "Thinking Ethically" is based on a framework developed by the authors in collaboration with Center Director **Thomas Shanks, S. J.,** Presidential Professor of Ethics and the Common Good **Michael J. Meyer,** and others. The framework is used as the basis for many Center programs and presentations.

Business Ethics
Back to Basics

With business news dominated in recent years by some spectacular examples of ethical malfeasance, confidence in the business world has been shaken. Never mind that the Enrons of the world are actually few and far between. No business or organization can afford even a suspicion of unethical behavior and must take proactive steps to ensure that no suspicions arise. Ethical behavior begins at the top with actions and statements that are beyond reproach and ambiguity. Managements may want to follow an eight-point action list presented here for establishing a strong ethical culture and also a decision checklist when ethical dilemmas loom. Sterling reputations are valuable business assets: they are earned over time but can be lost almost overnight.

WILLIAM I. SAUSER, JR.

Introduction

Enron, Arthur Andersen, Tyco, ImClone, Martha Stewart, WorldCom, Global Crossing, Merrill Lynch, Rite-Aid, Qwest, Adelphia, Kmart, HealthSouth—the list of formerly respected businesses (and business leaders) being charged with breaches of ethical conduct seems to be growing by the day. This is having adverse effects on our economic well-being, on investor confidence, and on the perceived desirability of pursuing business as a respectable calling.

Commenting on the ethical crisis in business leadership, Eileen Kelly (2002) observed, "Recently a new business scandal seems to surface each day. The current volatility of the market reflects the apprehension, the sense of betrayal, and the lack of confidence that investors have in many large corporations and their managements" (p. 4). Marcy Gordon (2002), reporting on a speech by United States Securities and Exchange Commissioner Paul Atkins, noted, "The string of accounting failures at big companies in the last year has cost U.S. households nearly $60,000 on average as some $5 trillion in market value was lost."

Accounting failures are not the only ethical concerns facing modern business organizations. The Southern Institute for Business and Professional Ethics (2002) lists on its website an array of issues that put pressures on business enterprises. These include the globalization of business, work force diversification, employment practices and policies, civil litigation and government regulation, and concerns about environmental stewardship. The institute (on the same website) concluded, "Despite such powerful trends, few managers have been adequately equipped by traditional education to recognize, evaluate, and act upon the ethical dimension of their work."

Columnist Malcolm Cutchins (2002), an emeritus professor of engineering at Auburn University, summed up the problem concisely: "We have seen the effect of not teaching good ethics in business schools. If we continue to neglect the teaching of good principles on a broad scale, we all reap the bad consequences."

Business Ethics

Ethics has to do with behavior—specifically, an individual's moral behavior with respect to society. The extent to which behavior measures up to societal standards is typically used as a gauge of ethicality. Since there are a variety of standards for societal behavior, ethical behavior is often characterized with respect to certain contexts. The Ethics Resource Center says, "*Business Ethics* refers to clear standards and norms that help employees to distinguish right from wrong behavior at work" (Joseph, 2003, p. 2). In the business context, ethics has to do with the extent to which a person's behavior measures up to such standards as the law, organizational policies, professional and trade association codes, popular expectations regarding fairness and rightness, plus an individual's internalized moral standards.

Business ethics, then, is not distinct from ethics in general, but rather a subfield (Desjardins, 2003, p. 8). The subfield refers to the examination and application of moral standards within the context of finance; commerce; production, distribution, and sale of goods and services; and other business activities.

It can be argued that an ethical person behaves appropriately in all societal contexts. This may be so, in which case one might prefer the term "ethics in business" to "business ethics." The distinction is subtle, but serves as a reminder that morality may be generalized from context to context. Adam Smith, for example, saw no need for ethical relativism when it comes to business. "It is impossible to determine just how business became separated from ethics in history. If we go back to Adam Smith, we find no such separation. In addition to his famous book on business and capitalism, *The Wealth of Nations*, Adam Smith also wrote *The Theory of Moral Sentiments*, a book about our ethical obligations to one another. It is clear that Smith believed that business and commerce worked well only if people took seriously their obligations and, in particular, their sense of justice" (Bruner, 1998, p. 46).

May (1995) echoed this important point: "The marketplace breaks down unless it can presuppose the virtue of industry, without which goods will not be produced; and the virtues of "honesty and integrity, without which their free and fair exchange cannot take place."

Standards of Behavior

The law (including statutory, administrative, and case law) is an important and legitimate source of ethical guidance. Federal, state, and local laws establish the parameters (Fieser, 1996), and violation of the law is almost always considered unethical (with the possible exception of civil disobedience as a mechanism for putting the law itself on trial). Pursuing business outside the law is regarded as an obstructionist approach to business ethics (Schermerhorn, 2005, p. 75). Such an individual would almost certainly be labeled unethical.

A second important source of authority is organizational policies, which are standards for behavior established by the employing organization. Typically they are aligned with the law (which takes precedence over them) and spell out in detail how things are done. All employees are expected to adhere to organizational policies. It is very important that managers at the highest level set the example for others by always working within the law and the policies of the organization.

Another important source of ethical guidance is the code of behavior adopted by professional and trade associations. These codes are often aspirational in nature and frequently establish higher standards for behavior than the law requires. Members of a profession or trade association typically aspire to meet these higher standards in order to establish and uphold the reputation of a profession or trade.

These social mores, based on commonly held beliefs about what is right and wrong and fair and unfair, can be powerful determinants of a person's reputation. Behavior that—in the strictest sense—meets legal requirements, organizational policies, and even professional standards may still be viewed by the general public as unfair and wrong (Krech, Crutchfield, and Ballachey, 1962).

A fifth set of standards reflects the individual conscience. Coleman, Butcher and Carson (1980, p. Glossary IV) define "the conscience" as "the functioning of an individual's moral values in the approval or disapproval of his or her own thoughts and actions," and equate it roughly with the Freudian concept of the superego. Highly ethical business leaders typically have moral standards that exceed all four of the lesser standards just listed. These values, learned early in life and reinforced by life's experiences, are internalized standards often based on personal, religious or philosophical understandings of morality (Baelz, 1977, pp. 41–55).

Ethical Dilemmas

An ethical dilemma is a situation where a potential course of action offers potential benefit or gain but is unethical, in that it violates one or more of the standards just described. Behaviors violating laws are, by definition, illegal as well as unethical. The key question for the business leader when presented with an ethical dilemma is: "What to do?" Behavior determines a person's ethical reputation, after all. Ethical leadership is exhibited when ethical dilemmas are resolved in an appropriate manner.

Here is a sampling of some ethical dilemmas that frequently rise in the business setting. Many of these behaviors are illegal as well as unethical.

- Providing a product or service you know is harmful or unsafe
- Misleading someone through false statements or omissions
- Using insider information for personal gain
- Playing favorites
- Manipulating and using people
- Benefiting personally from a position of trust
- Violating confidentiality
- Misusing company property or equipment
- Falsifying documents
- Padding expenses
- Taking bribes or kickbacks
- Participating in a cover-up
- Theft or sabotage
- Committing an act of violence
- Substance abuse
- Negligence or inappropriate behavior in the workplace.

Poor Ethical Choices

Why do people sometimes make poor choices when faced with ethical dilemmas? One set of reasons has to do with flaws of *character*. Such character defects include malice (intentional evil); sociopathy (lack of conscience); personal greed; envy, jealousy, resentment; the will to win or achieve at any cost; and fear of failure. There are also flaws in *corporate culture* that lead even good people to make poor ethical judgments. Weaknesses in corporate culture include indifference, a lack of knowledge or understanding of standards on the part of employees; poor or inappropriate incentive systems; and poor leadership, including the use of mixed signals such as:

- I don't care how you do it, just get it done.
- Don't ever bring me bad news.
- Don't bother me with the details, you know what to do.

- Remember, we always meet our financial goals somehow.
- No one gets injured on this worksite . . . period. Understand?
- Ask me no questions, I'll tell you no lies.

Such statements by managers to their subordinates too often imply that unethical behaviors that obtain the intended results are acceptable to the organization. While it may be difficult—other than through termination or other sanctions—to rid the organization of employees with character flaws, correcting a poor organizational culture is clearly a matter of leadership.

Establishing a Strong Ethical Culture

Business leaders who wish to take proactive measures to establish and maintain a corporate culture that emphasizes strong moral leadership are advised to take the following steps:

1. **Adopt a code of ethics.** The code need not be long and elaborate with flowery words and phrases. In fact, the best ethical codes use language anyone can understand. A good way to produce such a code is to ask all employees of the firm (or a representative group) to participate in its creation (Kuchar, 2003). Identify the commonly-held moral beliefs and values of the members of the firm and codify them into a written document all can understand and support. Post the code of ethics in prominent places around the worksite. Make certain that all employees subscribe to it by asking them to sign it.

2. **Provide ethics training.** From time to time a leader should conduct ethics training sessions. These may be led by experts in business ethics, or they may be informal in nature and led by the manager or employees themselves. A highly effective way to conduct an ethics training session is to provide "what if" cases for discussion and resolution. The leader would present a "real world" scenario in which an ethical dilemma is encountered. Using the organization's code of ethics as a guide, participants would explore options and seek a consensus ethical solution. This kind of training sharpens the written ethical code and brings it to life.

3. **Hire and promote ethical people.** This, in concert with step four, is probably the best defense against putting the business at risk through ethical lapses by employees. When making human resources decisions it is critical to reward ethical behavior and punish unethical behavior. Investigate the character of the people you hire, and do your best to hire people who have exhibited high moral standards in the past. Remember that past behavior is the best predictor of future behavior, so check references carefully. Formal background investigations may be warranted for positions of fiduciary responsibility or significant risk exposure. Base promotional decisions on matters of character in addition to technical competence. Demonstrate to your employees that high ethical standards are a requirement for advancement.

4. **Correct unethical behavior.** This complements step three. When the organization's ethical code is breached, those responsible must be punished. Many businesses use progressive discipline, with an oral warning (intended to advise the employee of what is and is not acceptable behavior) as the first step, followed by a written reprimand, suspension without pay, and termination if unethical behavior persists. Of course, some ethical lapses are so egregious that they require suspension—or even termination—following the first offense. Through consistent and firm application of sanctions to correct unethical behavior, the manager will signal to all employees that substandard moral behavior will not be tolerated.

5. **Be proactive.** Businesses wishing to establish a reputation for ethicality and good corporate citizenship in the community will often organize and support programs intended to give something back to the community. Programs that promote continuing education, wholesome recreation, good health and hygiene, environmental quality, adequate housing, and other community benefits may demonstrate the extent to which the business promotes concern for human welfare. Seeking and adopting best practices from other businesses in the community is also a proactive strategy.

6. **Conduct a social audit.** Most businesses are familiar with financial audits. This concept can be employed in the context of ethics and corporate responsibility as well. From time to time the leader of the business might invite responsible parties to examine the organization's product design, purchasing, production, marketing, distribution, customer relations, and human resources functions with an eye toward identifying and correcting any areas of policy or practice that raise ethical concerns. Similarly, programs of corporate responsibility (such as those mentioned in step five) should be reviewed for effectiveness and improved as needed.

7. **Protect whistle blowers.** A whistle blower is a person within the firm who points out ethically questionable actions taken by other employees—or even by managers—within the organization. Too often corporate whistle blowers are ignored—or even punished—by those who receive the unfortunate news of wrongdoing within the business. All this does is discourage revelation of ethical problems. Instead the whistle blower should be protected and even honored. When unethical actions are uncovered within a firm by one of the employees, managers should step forward and take corrective action (as described in step four). Employees learn from one another. If the owners and managers of a business turn a blind eye toward wrongdoing, a signal is sent to everyone within the firm that ethicality is not characteristic of that organization's culture. A downward spiral of moral behavior is likely to follow.

8. **Empower the guardians of integrity.** The business leader's chief task is to lead by example and to empower every member of the organization to demonstrate the firm's commitment to ethics in its relationships with suppliers, customers, employees, and shareholders. Turn each employee of the firm, no matter what that individual's position, into a guardian of the firm's integrity. When maliciousness and indifference are replaced with a culture of integrity, honesty, and ethicality, the business will reap long-term benefits from all quarters.

A Checklist for Making Good Ethical Decisions

A business leader who takes seriously the challenge of creating a strong ethical culture for the firm must, of course, make good decisions when faced personally with ethical dilemmas. Here is a checklist a manager might wish to follow:

1. Recognize the ethical dilemma.
2. Get the facts.
3. Identify your options.
4. Test each option: Is it legal, right, beneficial? Note: Get some counsel.
5. Decide which option to follow.
6. Double-check your decision.
7. Take action.
8. Follow up and monitor decision implementation.

Number six is key: Double-check your decision. When in doubt consider how each of the following might guide you. Take the action that would allow you to maintain your reputation with those on this list you believe adhere to the highest ethical standards: Your attorney, accountant, boss, co-workers, stakeholders, family, newspaper, television news, religious leader, and Deity.

How would you feel if you had to explain your decision—and your actions—to each of these? If you would not feel good about this, then it is quite likely that you are about to make a poor decision. Double check your decision in this manner before you take any action you may later regret.

Conclusion

A firm's reputation may take years—even decades—to establish, but can be destroyed in an instant through unethical behavior. That is why it is so important for business leaders to be very careful about the things they say and do. Taking the time and effort to establish and maintain a corporate culture of morality, integrity, honesty, and ethicality will pay important dividends throughout the life of the firm. While taking ethical shortcuts may appear to lead to gains in the short term, this type of corporate strategy almost always proves tragic in the longer term.

Every business leader will be faced at one time or another with an ethical dilemma. Many face even daily temptations. How

the leader manifests moral integrity when faced with ethical dilemmas sets the tone for everyone else in the organization. This is why it is so important to "walk the talk" by making good ethical decisions every day. Understanding and applying the concepts presented in this article will enable you, as a business leader, to create and maintain an ethical corporate culture in your business. As Carl Skoogland, the former vice president and ethics director for Texas Instruments, recently advised, if you want to create an ethical business, you must *know what's right, value what's right, and do what's right* (Skoogland, 2003).

References

Baelz, P. (1977). *Ethics and belief.* New York: The Seabury Press.
Bruner, R. F., Eaker, M. R., Freeman, E., Spekman, R. E., and Teisberg, E. O. (1998). *The portable MBA, 3rd ed.* New York: Wiley.
Coleman, J. C., Butcher, J. N., and Carson, R. (1980). *Abnormal psychology and modern life, 6th ed,* Glenview, IL: Scott Foresman.
Cutchins, M. (2002, November 20). Business ethics must be taught or we all pay. *Opelika-Auburn News,* p. A4.
Desjardins, J. (2003). *An introduction to business ethics.* Boston: McGraw-Hill.
Fieser, J. (1996). Do businesses have moral obligations beyond what the law requires? *Journal of Business Ethics, 15,* 457–468.
Gordon, M. (2002, November 18). Accounting failures cost $60,000 on average, SEC commissioner says. *Opelika-Auburn News,* p. C4.
Joseph, J. (2003). *National business ethics survey 2003: How employees view ethics in their organizations.* Washington, DC: Ethics Resource Center.
Kelly, E. P. (2002). Business ethics—An oxymoron? *Phi Kappa Phi Forum, 82*(4), 4–5.
Krech, D., Crutchfield, R. S., and Ballachey, E. L. (1962). Culture. Chapter 10 in *Individual in society* (pp. 339–380). New York: McGraw-Hill.
Kuchar, C. (2003). Tips on developing ethics codes for private companies. *GoodBusiness, 2*(3), pages unnumbered.
May, W. F. (1995). The virtues of the business leader. In M. L. Stackhouse, D. P. McCann, S. J Roels, and P. N. Williams (Eds.), *On moral business* (pp. 692–700). Grand Rapids, MI: Eerdmans.
Schermerhorn, J. R., Jr. (2005). *Management, 8th ed.* New York: Wiley.
Skoogland, C. (2003, October 16). *Establishing an ethical organization.* Plenary address at the Conference on Ethics and Social Responsibility in Engineering and Technology, New Orleans, LA.
The Southern Institute for Business and Professional Ethics. (2002). *The certificate in managerial ethics.* Retrieved August, 14, 2002, from www.southerninstitute.org.

Critical Thinking

1. Differentiate between business ethics and ethics in general.
2. Which of the areas of ethical dilemma identified in this article have you encountered most frequently? Provide an example from your own work or school experience.

DR. SAUSER is Associate Dean for Business and Engineering Outreach and Professor of Management at Auburn University. His interests include organization development, strategic planning, human relations in the workplace, business ethics, and continuing professional education. He is a Fellow of the American Council on Education and the Society for Advancement of Management (SAM). In 2003, he was awarded the Frederick W. Taylor Key by SAM for his career achievements.

From *SAM Advanced Management Journal,* No. 2, 2005, pp. 1–4. Copyright © 2005 by Society for Advancement of Management. Reprinted by permission.

Integrating Ethics into the Business Curriculum: The Northern Illinois University Initiative

LINDA J. MATUSZEWSKI PHD, CPA AND PAMELA A. SMITH PHD, CPA

Both business and academic leaders have an interest in ensuring that the next generation of managers has a solid ethical foundation. To accomplish this goal, Northern Illinois University (NIU) has formed an innovative Ethics Task Force (ETF) representing faculty and staff across the College of Business (COB), and five corporate sponsors. The result of this partnership is a program designed to systematically integrate ethics into the COB curriculum. The five program components are: an ethics handbook, faculty support activities, external corporate sponsors, a program coordinator, and an assessment system.

Formation of the ETF resulted from partnering with business leaders to develop a relevant, credible and integrated ethics curriculum. Business leaders encouraged the college to treat ethics as a business fundamental rather than discussing it in an abstract philosophical manner. Additionally, the Ethics Education Task Force of the Association to Advance Collegiate Schools of Business (AACSB) recommended in 2004 that member schools and their faculty "renew and revitalize their commitment to ethical responsibility." In 2007 the AACSB emphasized the need to include in the business curriculum learning experiences in ethical understanding and reasoning abilities, as well as ethical and legal responsibilities in organizations and society. To accomplish these objectives, the ETF designed a five-part framework referred to as the BELIEF initiative—Building Ethical Leaders using an Integrated Ethics Framework.

The first component of this framework is a handbook that provides a consistent and standardized foundation to all students in the college and serves as a resource throughout their course work and in their careers. Entitled *Ethics Handbook: Building Ethical Leaders,* it is distributed to students in their first semester, junior-level business core course. The purpose of the handbook is not to teach students how to be ethical, but rather to help them recognize ethical dilemmas, make decisions, and take action. To reinforce the relevance of this topic to students, the handbook states that they will need to make decisions with ethical ramifications very early in their careers. Throughout the handbook, students are encouraged to see themselves as decision makers who must choose a course of action that has significant ethical implications.

The handbook includes information about the conceptual foundations of ethical decision-making, including personal values. In addition, it contains practical applications of ethics principles, plus common scenarios illustrating unethical conduct. The book presents the heart of the entire BELIEF initiative—a seven-step decision-making guide:

Step 1: Determine the facts and state the problem.
Step 2: Identify the stakeholders.
Step 3: Identify relevant factors.
Step 4: Develop a list of 3–5 options.
Step 5: Assess options using various "tests."

    a. *Harm test:* Does this option do less harm than the alternatives?

    b. *Legality test:* Is this option legal?

    c. *Precedence test:* Does this option set precedence, which, while the outcome in this fact pattern is not problematic, this option under another fact pattern could cause a dramatically different outcome?

    d. *Publicity test:* Would I want my choice of this option published in the newspaper?

    e. *Defensibility test:* Could I defend my choice of this option before a Congressional committee or a jury of my peers?

    f. *Mom test:* What would my Mom say if she learned of this option?

    g. *Reversibility or "Golden Rule" test:* Would I still think the choice of this option good if I were one of those adversely affected by it? How would I want to be treated?

    h. *Virtues test:* What would I become if I choose this option?

    i. *Professional test:* What might my profession's ethics committee say about this option?

j. *Peer or colleague test:* What do my peers or colleagues say when I describe my problem and suggest this option as my solution?

k. *"How does it make me feel?" test:* This is your conscience. How does this option make you feel physically or emotionally? Are you able to sleep?

l. *Organization test:* What does the organization's ethics officer or legal counsel say about this?

Step 6: Make a tentative choice.

Step 7: Review steps 1–6.

The second component of the BELIEF initiative is the support of faculty activities such as workshops, conferences, and speakers. The goal is to reinforce the integration of ethics throughout the curriculum by providing faculty with the encouragement and training needed to effectively utilize the decision-making guide and handbook in ethics-related assignments in their courses. An annual *Ethics Day* devoted to increasing student awareness of the initiative provides an opportunity to bring in nationally recognized speakers to address ethics topics. It also recognizes the COB Student Honor Code, and formally acknowledges corporate sponsors.

The initiative's third component is the support of corporate sponsors who provide funding, credibility, and endorsement to the BELIEF initiative. Corporate sponsorship emphasizes the importance and relevance of ethics to students. Funds provided by the sponsors support the printing of the handbook, faculty developmental activities, guest lectures on business ethics topics, and personnel to coordinate and champion the initiative. The sponsors also connect this effort to the real world by providing speakers and resources that reinforce the importance of ethics in the business world.

The fourth component of the initiative is a coordinator to champion the BELIEF program going forward. The fifth component is the regular assessment of its effectiveness through student surveys and other yet to be completed methods to provide input for continuous improvement.

It should be emphasized that this BELIEF initiative to integrate ethical concepts and their application into course work throughout the curriculum is not NIU's only ethics strategy. It supplements, but does not supplant the ethical objectives being achieved through other campus programs. These include awareness of the NIU COB Student Code of Ethics and the Accountancy Student Honor Pledge and Code of Conduct, (discussed in "Accountancy Students Develop a Unique Code of Ethics" in *Strategic Finance*, August 2004).

The introduction to the Student Code of Ethics reads: As a student at Northern Illinois University's College of Business, I understand that it is my duty to behave in a courteous and ethical manner at all times. The attitudes and habits I develop as a student form the core of my professional behavior. As such, I will set an example of the highest caliber for those that work with me. To promote these behaviors within the student body, I will use the principles of honesty, respect, integrity, and professionalism as my academic and professional guide.

To increase students' familiarity with codes of conduct generally, students are provided with URL links and encouraged to go to the websites of professional organizations in accountancy, finance, management, marketing, and operations management and information systems to find the text of professional codes of conduct, such as the IMA's Statement of Ethical Professional Practice. In addition, URL links to the codes of ethics for each corporate sponsor are provided. All of these links are included in the handbook

In conclusion, we believe the use of a cross-functional Ethics Task Force to develop the initiative and on-going support activities have helped ensure the BELIEF initiative has high visibility and broad support. We believe that this initiative is an effective way to integrate ethics-related learning objectives across all departments in the COB. We believe our approach to developing and spreading a consistent ethical climate within the COB is also applicable to other organizations and would be pleased to provide additional details about the initiative to those wishing them.

Critical Thinking

1. Consider an ethical dilemma that you have faced in the past and submit it to the various "tests" proposed in step 5. Did your decision "pass" the test?

LINDA J. MATUSZEWSKI, PhD, CPA, is an assistant professor in the Accountancy Department and PAMELA A. SMITH, PhD, CPA, is the KPMG Professor of Accountancy, both at Northern Illinois University. Dr. Matuszewski can be reached at *lmatus@niu.edu.* CURTIS C. VERSCHOOR is the Ledger & Quill Research Professor, School of Accountancy and MIS, and Wicklander Research Fellow in the Institute for Business and Professional Ethics, both at DePaul University, Chicago. He is also a Research Scholar in the Center for Business Ethics at Bentley College, Waltham, MA. His e-mail address is *curtisverschoor@sbcglobal.net*

Building an Ethical Framework

10 questions to consider in encouraging an ethical corporate culture.

THOMAS R. KRAUSE AND PAUL J. VOSS

Although we are now several years into the new and landmark regulatory environment that mandates an organizational culture of ethical conduct, there remains little guidance on how to get there. Many companies are engaged in a scramble to create a paper and electronic trail to ward off prosecution, rather than in a well-designed effort to promote or govern the culture of their organizations. While procedure is essential, the lesson we have learned from organizational change efforts is that leadership, rather than rules, finally determines behaviors and their outcomes.

This article suggests 10 primary questions every executive should ask—and expect to have answered thoroughly and well—in order to initiate a culture that encourages and sustains ethical conduct. These questions are meant to be asked and answered among leaders themselves, as well as with employees throughout the organization.

1. What is the relationship between ethics and other performance metrics in the company?
The relative cost of preventing a protracted ethical dilemma or full-fledged scandal is exponentially lower than the costs associated with fixing ethical problems. For example, see "The Cost to Firms of Cooking the Books," by J. Karpoff, D. Lee and G. Martin, forthcoming in *The Journal of Financial and Quantitative Analysis,* for a study of the substantial costs in fines and lost market value to almost 600 firms subject to SEC enforcement before the enactment of the Sarbanes-Oxley Act. Current research demonstrates that ethical companies are more competitive, profitable and sustaining than unethical companies. The challenge for the ethical leader is to find that connection and reveal it to the organization.

2. Have we, as required by the 2004 federal sentencing guidelines, offered ethics training for all of our employees? Does the training provide more than rote introduction of the company's code of conduct?
Ethics training comes in all shapes and sizes, with the most successful moving from theory to practice and from the conceptual to the real. Companies must first settle on an ethical vocabulary, define terms and establish core values. Live case studies can then help leadership and management "solve" relevant ethical dilemmas, both real and hypothetical.

3. What is the relationship between exercising sound ethics and retaining great talent?
Fortune magazine's annual list of the top 100 companies to work for contains a wide variety of companies with no obvious common denominator. Salary, benefits, career opportunities, location and profession all vary. What they do have in common is trust between employee and employer. Ethical behavior with and among employees, then, can lay the groundwork for attracting and retaining the best talent.

4. Have we conducted a "risk assessment" to determine our exposure to major ethical damage? What is our potential Enron?
While each company may have its unique "ethical nightmare," most companies face similar ethical exposures (e.g., to theft and accounting irregularities). Companies must examine the potential hazards of perverse incentives (e.g., compensation based 100 percent on financial goals) and the various "unintended consequences" of policy, procedures and protocols. Companies can reduce or eliminate adverse incentives by never rewarding, intentionally or unintentionally, improper behavior.

Research literature identifies several characteristics predictive of ethical outcomes: management credibility, upward communication, perceived organizational support, procedural justice and teamwork.

---

5. How can we be proactive in the area of ethics, culture and corporate citizenship?
Leaders need to own and shape the culture as much as they manage, for example, quality initiatives. Research literature identifies several characteristics predictive of ethical outcomes: management credibility, upward communication, perceived

organizational support, procedural justice and teamwork. Well-tested diagnostic tools allow leaders to measure these characteristics and specific behaviors that foster the culture desired.

6. What tone should executive leadership set regarding ethics, integrity and transparency?

Setting an example is just one part of the executive leadership's responsibility. What leaders say, think and feel affects the tone as much as their actions. Mistrust, cynicism or indifference from topmost leaders can erode others' loyalty to the organization, to its mission, to employees and to shareholders. Left unchecked, this tone from the top can also potentially push ethical leaders out the door.

7. What does management need from the board of directors and senior leadership to enhance and buttress corporate ethics?

Employees who see the governing board and executive leadership as unconcerned will discount any directives about ethics that come from them. Consistency and authenticity from the board and executive leadership play a signal role in establishing an ethics initiative. At a minimum this means providing a reasonable budget of time, talent and money.

8. Who is driving ethics and compliance in the company?

The recent American Management Association report *The Ethical Enterprise* (2006) shows that ethical companies do not happen by accident. Companies need to designate internal drivers who move along the discussions, training and initiatives, producing ethical outcomes.

9. Do we have consistency of message between and among the board, the CEO, the senior executive team and the associates in terms of ethics and culture?

We all need to be on the same page, but finding the proper tone and guidance can be tricky. Establishing a common vocabulary can help with this process. For example, what does it mean to act unethically? What is an ethical dilemma? Who were Aristotle, Plato and Machiavelli, and how can they help provide a vocabulary for our company? What ethical model do we want to follow? What can we do to make it stick?

10. What roadblocks now discourage ethical conversations and the implementation of ethical practices, procedures and protocols?

Most people want to act with ethics and integrity, "to do the right thing." Yet our current approach to ethical conversation often does not advance our thinking or practice past our own perspectives. The object of dialogue, as advocated by physicist David Bohm, is "not to analyze things, or to win an argument, or to exchange opinions. Rather, it is to suspend your opinions and . . . to listen to everybody's opinions, to suspend them, and to see what all that means. . . . And if we can see them all, we may then move more creatively in a different direction." (For more information, see "On Dialogue," Ojai, Calif.: David Bohm Seminars, 1990.)

> **Most people want . . . "to do the right thing." Yet our current approach to ethical conversation often does not advance our thinking past our own perspectives.**

Starting the Conversation

Asking these 10 questions at board meetings, in leadership team meetings, and in the course of day-to-day interactions with employees engenders a climate that leads, over time, to zero tolerance for ethical lapses and impropriety. They also help executives assure their own diligence and oversight of ethical risks and threats, and deliver on their promise to employees, shareholders, customers and the community at large.

Critical Thinking

1. Which three of these 10 questions do you think are the most important? Why?
2. Add one more question to those necessary for designing an ethical corporate culture.

Thomas R. Krause, PhD is author of several books and Chairman and Co-founder of Behavioral Science Technology, Inc. (BST), an international performance solutions consulting company. He focuses on executive leadership development and coaching for clients including NASA, BHP Billiton and the FAA. **Paul J. Voss,** PhD is Ethics Practice Leader with BST. An author, scholar and lecturer, Dr. Voss' clients include Home Depot, the FBI lab, General Electric and Russell Athletics.

From *CRO,* May/June 2007, pp. 34–35. Copyright © 2007 by CRO Corp., LLC. Reprinted by permission.

Moral Management Methodology/Mythology: Erroneous Ethical Equations

Andrew Sikula, Sr.

After nearly 50 years of studying, researching, and writing about business ethics, I prefer to use the concept of *moral management* instead of the term *business ethics.* Moral management refers to a state of ethical excellence and the practice and the implementation of the moral maximization principle (Sikula, 1989). Moral morass refers to the absence of moral maximization and the presence of "anything goes" ethics and values. I do not distinguish between ethics and morals, although some authors envision ethics as having a societal or cultural nature and morals as more personal or individual values. Both ethics and morals represent an authoritative and widely accepted code of good, right, and proper conduct. Ethics and morals involve pure, righteous, honorable, and virtuous behavior.

Moral Maximization

Moral maximization manifests itself as behaviors, actions, and decisions that result in the greatest enhancement of individual and collective human rights, human freedoms, human equity, and human development (Sikula, 1992). Human rights involve just claims, prerogatives, powers, privileges, and entitlements that people inherently possess as a result of birth. Human rights include life, property, safety, work, education, voting, due process, and privacy. Human freedoms involve personal exemptions and immunities from controls and restraints. Human freedoms include liberty, speech and expression, religious worship, peaceful assembly, petition, travel, pursuit of happiness, and leisure/rest (Sikula, 1992). Human equity involves human fairness and human justice and consists of human equality items including equal employment opportunity, and human variety components such as affirmative action, minority mentoring, and community mirroring. Human development in this context represents bringing humanity to a more advanced or effective state and causing it to grow and expand individually and collectively. Human development dimensions include

self-respect, internal accord, prosperity, security, recognition, companionship, health, and achievement.

Why Not Business Ethics?

I prefer to talk and write about moral management instead of business ethics for several reasons. Many people jokingly refer to the phrase "business ethics" as an oxymoron. Such attitudes incorrectly conclude that business practices will not prove ethical and that ethical actions cannot survive in a business-oriented setting.

Cultural Conditions

The world has increasingly become more secular and less spiritual. At all levels of education, we find certain beliefs and values taught with content and emphases that often are quite different from those which were commonly learned in generations past. For some, humankind rather than God now represents a central focus, and evolution has replaced creationism in most elementary and secondary courses teaching biology, science, geology, anthropology, and other subjects. We teach concepts focused on human achievement and self-actualization. This paradigm shift has caused more moral morass than ethical and/or educational enlightenment.

Moral Math

In the 10 equations discussed below, I seek to capture the essence of current culture and our contemporary educational systems. The moral math described summarizes common beliefs held by the general public. Despite the general population's belief in the relationships, I regard them as falsehoods and believe that promoting them will cause a continuation in the decline of individual and societal morality. With the goal of enhancing and expanding moral management, I have framed this set of moral mathematics as "erroneous" ethical equations. Progress toward ethical excellence can only occur by seeing past these popular misconceptions. Admittedly, doing so represents a minority perspective in today's world. Nonetheless, the highest levels of ethical excellence and moral management can only occur by going against the grain and taking the high road instead of the path more commonly trod.

Erroneous Ethical Equations
1. Change = Progress
One misconception hammered into the heads of the populace states that change equals progress. Seeking change for the sake of change almost always proves detrimental to both individuals and institutions. Even carefully planned and programmed changes may have negative rather than positive effects. In actuality, most changes bring about both positive and negative repercussions, although not to the same degree or magnitude.

Undoubtedly, change proves inevitable and a constant. Many schools teach students to uncritically accept the notion that all change represents advancement or progress. More appropriately, we should view change as cyclical—sometimes improving and at other times worsening conditions or situations—and then later eventually reversing itself. This proves true of the weather, the stock market, and people's health, but also applies generally to interpersonal relationships, which can logically extend to international trade. Pendulums swing back and forth, and so do the positive and negative consequences of change.

One makes moral management progress by evaluating potential change and its probable consequences. Some change occurs inevitably, but much of it flows in a discretionary and controllable manner. Seek to avoid changes which hinder ethical excellence. One commonly finds courses taught about the Management of Change, and/or Crises Management to help anticipate and control environmental upheavals. Anger Management seminars help individuals to deal with the consequences of changes that generate discomfort. Ethical executives must manage change so that as much as possible of it leads to progress instead of regression.

2. Pay = Performance
Another commonly accepted lie holds that people's pay links closely and directly to their performance. From the lowest levels to the top echelons of business, this ethical equation is erroneous. Examples of CEOs who receive bonuses even though their companies are losing money abound in the press. The fact remains that positions and pay levels often flow from connections to family members and friends. In addition to such networking, the general state of the economy also exerts a major force in determining pay raises. Only in jobs involving sales and/or piecework does pay directly connect to performance.

Not just annual increments, but even more important, initial employment and position advancement result more from personal networking than job performance. This has become most obvious in the United States where today small businesses increasingly supply the majority of jobs in the modern workforce. And the smaller the enterprise, the more important connections become, and the less validity applies to the pay equals performance assumption.

Moral managers must recognize the current falsehood of this equation and try to make this moral math truth rather than fiction. Effort and reward need to become more closely related if we expect ethical excellence to advance. Paying people based upon networking or who you know rather than merit creates problems in morals, mores, and morale.

3. Legality = Morality
Another cognitive mistake commonly believed by the general public incorrectly holds that legality and morality are identical or the same. Laws represent majority opinion and they vary widely over time and by location. What stands as legal in one jurisdiction may violate the law in another. Prostitution and gambling provide illustrative examples. Local and national laws change over time, for example, highway speed limits and drinking ages. Legality stands at the very bottom of the morality food chain. Yet many people believe they practice morality simply by not breaking legal ordinances.

Morality represents a much higher ethical standard than merely following the law. Some expert theologians have argued that laws represent relative values set by man, whereas morals constitute absolute values dispensed by God. Legal behavior usually proves moral, and moral conduct almost always proves legal. However, exceptions exist. Many protesters cite capital punishment as legal, but not moral, or note that allowing the homeless to sleep in public parks may violate statutes while qualifying as a moral necessity.

Following the letter of the law does not automatically determine or verify one's ethical standing. Acting as a moral person often involves going above and beyond legal minimum requirements. In addition, one's ethical standards should lead to the same choices in private as in public. The moral manager's challenge involves acting morally and ethically in all aspects of one's personal/private and professional/public life and helping society move from a condition of moral decadence to a state of moral development and ethical excellence (Sikula, 1996).

4. Mankind = Like-Kind
Another factor causing the deterioration of ethics involves the failure to recognize mankind as different from other forms of animals and living creatures and creations. Humans differ from other life forms not only because of a greater intellectual capacity but also and especially because of a highly developed spiritual component. We find ourselves in this erroneous mental state and condition today because

we have removed God from most classrooms and have permitted the teaching of inaccurate versions of evolutionary theory.

Humans will not make moral management progress unless they think of themselves as different from plants and other animals and life forms. Humanity has three critical relevant parameters: physical, mental, and spiritual. Today, many people seem overly focused on health and the physical dimension. In addition, many people have difficulty distinguishing between the mental and the spiritual aspects of humankind. Mental refers to one's intellect, and spiritual issues involve values, ethics, and morals that flow from emotional connections. We can write a related erroneous ethical equation as

$$\text{Mental} = \text{Spiritual}$$

The human mental parameter differs from the human spiritual dimension, and moral managers must have the ability to distinguish between the two if they hope to make progress toward ethical excellence. Moral managers address spiritualism in the workplace. Religion represents a part of culture and is often a primary individual motivational factor. Yet many business and educational institutions not only do not deal with this subject but also go out of their way to avoid it. God, religion, and spiritualism represent important human concerns for most individuals, and effective teachers of commerce and education should learn to integrate such concerns into the lives and learnings of their constituents.

5. I'm OK = You're OK

In the late 1960s, a psychiatrist named Thomas Harris (1967) wrote *I'm OK—You're OK,* which remains popular today. This book described a theoretical approach to human relations called "transactional analysis." Many people believe that in order to respect themselves and everyone else, they must accept anything and everything that others assert. This anything goes attitude has led to a deterioration of societal ethics and values.

If people believe they are OK, they will make no effort to improve themselves, especially in the spiritual realm. The old Puritan concept that all people are sinners has been cast away and replaced by this newer feel good philosophy. Similarly, the belief in original sin has migrated to a neutral clean slate. The idea that people make mistakes and need repentance has become replaced in American culture with the concepts of self-actualization and achievable sainthood.

In order to advocate moral management, I teach that I'm not OK—you're not OK. I teach that all people have imperfections and suffer from ethical lapses. We all make mistakes consciously or unconsciously. I explain that one's conscience does not always provide a correct guide or determinant of ethical action. Some people lack an internal moral compass. The first steps of healing this problem involve getting past denial and into acceptance. Knowing that you can improve your ethical behavior represents the first step toward achieving ethical excellence.

6. Belief in God = Ethical Behavior

A sixth erroneous ethical equation revolves around the often very strongly held conviction that an ethical person must believe in God. The flip side of this mistaken creed holds that a person who does not believe in God can not be ethical.

We all know people who go to church, mosque, or synagogue and claim that they believe in God, yet treat people disrespectfully all week long. We all have acquaintances who avow atheism and yet consistently treat people kindly and serve others humanely at all times The key to moral management involves a desire followed by actions resulting in continuous ethical improvement which can be undertaken no matter what religion (if any) one professes and/or practices.

7. Facts = Truth

We frequently hear that facts speak for themselves. In truth, facts never speak for themselves and they always need interpretation. We can analyze all data and information from a number of different perspectives. This moral math equation simply asserts that we should analyze all figures within a reality context and given certain accurate assumptions. Some have joked that figures don't lie, but liars figure.

Two people can witness the same accident and come up with varying at-fault conclusions. At any moment in time, experts analyzing the same data offer divergent predictions about the stock market, employment, and/or the direction of interest rates. Lawyers know that you can get expert witnesses to attest to anything you want while looking at the identical evidence examined also by the opposing attorney. Such behavior often involves ethical or unethical practices above and beyond just the biased interpretation of numbers and data.

8. Self-Interest = Community Interest

The uncontrolled pursuit of self-interest does not lead to optimal outcomes for a community or society at large. Business pursuing self-interest leads to greed, undeserved power, and exploited workers. Pure capitalism assumes the perfectly free flow of goods, services, information, labor, and capital. Such never occurs in the real world. An unfettered market economy does not exist in reality.

I do not advocate communism, socialism, or fascism. I believe in and support capitalism and free markets. But I believe also that government has a role and that societies have a duty to help the less fortunate. I also believe that individuals and institutions need both internal and external controls or else some form of abusive behavior evolves. If the pursuit of self-interest equaled the best interests of communities and societies, all countries would become dictatorships. But increasingly the world has recognized the advantages of democracy over central control.

Oddly enough, today's pursuit of self-interest comes at the same time when individuals also tend to assume less and less responsibility for themselves and others (Petersen, 2002). We increasingly live in a welfare state where people have an entitlement mentality. In some states and countries, almost as many people live on governmental assistance as engage in gainful employment. A victim mentality often accompanies self-interest and lack of individual and social responsibility, resulting in a litigious society where the American dream of success through one's efforts has given way to a strong desire to win the lottery or to prevail in a law suit against some person or organization with deep pockets.

Rushworth Kidder and others recognize that both the pursuit of self-interest and community interest constitute noble goals. This eighth erroneous equation represents an ethical dilemma since two ethically acceptable choices exist rather than a moral temptation situation with one good and another evil alternative. In this situation, Kidder, I, and most other ethics experts believe that community interest takes higher priority than self-interest (Kidder, 1995).

9. Perception = Reality

Our American educational system focuses on the development of the individual. Self-esteem, self-actualization, self-control, and other individual centered foci form the behavioral goals. The system teaches that our unique individual opinions and preferences have critical importance and highest priority. Having it our way, voicing our opinions with e-mail, text messages, cell telephone calls, and blogs, have become the way of the world. We learn that our perspective matters most, even if it differs from majority opinion. This focus makes us feel good, but telling people that their singular perception of reality matters most is a lie.

Contrary to popular opinion, individual perceptions do not always reflect objective reality. You may look in the mirror each morning and envision a physically attractive person. Others may not agree. How you perceive activity or an event may not correspond with objective reality. Some individuals may believe that they are fat or skinny, but an accurate scale can tell them otherwise. A related corollary erroneous ethical equation adds to the confusion, that being

Seeing = Believing

Most people think that seeing is believing. Every magician and most wise people know otherwise. We see what we want to see—and we hear what we want to hear. Individuals rationalize their own actions and the behavior of others. "Seeing is believing" is false because "believing is seeing" is true. What you believe determines your perception of events. A person filters and interprets stimuli using a learned set of values and assumptions, which may or may not prove objectively true, accurate, and trustworthy.

Psychological and marketing theories and practices have helped to bring about this ethical erroneous equation. Marketing professionals use this ploy in attempts to sell unneeded

goods, conveniences, luxuries, services, and insurances. Certain images and impressions may carry decision making weight, but they often prove inaccurate, misleading, and without merit.

Moral managers must remain responsive to both reality and perceptions of reality. Individuals must learn to value the opinions of others, not just their own. Consumers must become less egocentric if they hope to make intelligent buyer choices. Recognizing one's ethical roles at home or work and in society can help people to not become delusional with false hopes and dreams. Moving toward ethical excellence means to better recognize differences between a perception of reality and the world as it actually exists.

10. Different Culture = Different Ethics

Many people believe that different cultures have different ethics. However, many authors today have identified a set of global ethics that cross cultures and exist around the world.

Understanding of this equation hinges on the proper definition of ethics. At the start of this article, I defined ethics as a universal code of good, right, and proper conduct. Yes, cultures and nations vary in their languages, customs, and traditions, but ethics, properly defined, extend worldwide in nature and content and are global in setting and context. Educator Herbert Spencer (1861) is widely quoted having said that "morality knows nothing of geographical boundaries or distinctions of race." This Spencer quotation also presents an opportunity to state another corollary erroneous ethical equation, specifically

Ethnic Diversity = Ethic Diversity

Some of the confusion on this point appears semantic and lies in the similar spellings of ethnic and ethic. Another part of the problem arises because diversity often focuses on variety and distinctions among races of people. Ethnic diversity enriches society, ethic diversity does not. Today, diversity often has an expanded meaning, and related concepts of pluralism, multiculturalism and inclusion encompass age, gender, sexual orientation, handicapped status, and other human traits. Human characteristics can vary, but moral standards and ethical benchmarks should not.

Rushworth Kidder (1994) identified the following eight global values: love, truthfulness, fairness, freedom, unity, tolerance, responsibility, and respect for life. Thomas Donaldson (1989) presented 10 fundamental international rights: physical movement, property ownership, no torture, fair trial, nondiscrimination, physical security, speech and association, minimal education, political participation, and subsistence. William Bennett (1993) listed 10 virtues: self-discipline, compassion, responsibility, friendship, work, courage, perseverance, honesty, loyalty, and faith. Michael Josephson (2002) listed 10 global ethics: trustworthiness, honesty, integrity, promise keeping, loyalty, respect for others, responsibility, fairness, caring, and citizenship. Finally, the Parliament of the World's Religions (1993) came up with eight global-ethic items: nonviolence (love), respect for life, commitment, solidarity, truthfulness, tolerance, equal rights, and sexual morality. Although these five citations have slightly different lists, they assert and display notable similarities.

Organizational Behavior Implications

So what can managers and leaders do to improve organizational performance if such false beliefs pervade society? Ten warnings and recommendations on how to create an affirmative moral management milieu despite various erroneous ethical beliefs in today's working world follow.

1. Do Not Rely Solely on Numbers to Make Decisions

One needs data to make good decisions, but an overreliance on numbers for problem solving can lead to organizational mistakes. Human factors become more important than numerical figures in humane solutions to problem solving. People can gather and interpret numbers to prove anything they so desire.

2. Act as a Positive Person

Spend time building people up rather than tearing them down. Always remember that people resist change and resent criticism. Moral managers look for ways to help not harm others.

3. Treat All People with Human Respect and Dignity

Effective leaders get the best from all personnel from low levels through the upper echelons and in-between. Contributions from each and every employee affect the quality of goods and services produced by a company. All individuals have both intrinsic and extrinsic worth and value to contribute to enterprise.

4. Stress Teamwork Not Individualism

Developing an ethical environment involves working as a team rather than always trying to get ahead individually. Looking out for only oneself at the expense of others takes away from group productivity. Working as a team involves more effort but brings greater satisfaction than attempting to accomplish something alone.

5. Emphasize Creative Reasoning Not Critical Thinking

We have too many critics and devil's advocates today. People have been overly taught to critique the behavior of others and to question all authority figures. Seek to replace criticism with creative reasoning and an entrepreneurial spirit.

6. Avoid Groupthink

Going along with the crowd does not bring about improved organizational behavior. Majority opinions usually do not represent creative answers to especially difficult questions. Groups work well for brainstorming but not for selecting superior solutions to unique opportunities.

7. Think and Act Long Run Rather Than Short Term

Moral managers and ethical executives plan ahead more than they worry about past or present conditions. Many people have difficulty looking beyond a 6-month time horizon. Business people must force themselves to think beyond quarterly results and lead organizations looking several decades ahead.

8. Act in an Environmentally Friendly Manner

Hard-goods manufacturers as well as service providers must operate in an environmentally protective manner. Having ethical concerns means doing one's best to preserve the world for future generations.

9. Implement a Multiple-Stakeholder Perspective

Companies must demonstrate concern about the values and priorities of all of their stakeholders—not just their stockholders. These include customers, employees, suppliers, and immediate community residents.

10. Seek Higher Ethical Ground

Developing a moral management milieu involves moral maximization and choosing the best ethical alternative from among various choices. One can avoid problems with erroneous ethical equations by always taking the high road and seeking elevated ethical ground on which to stride and stand.

References

Bennett, W. J. (1993). *The book of virtues: A treasury of great moral stories.* New York: Simon & Schuster.

Donaldson, T. (1989). *The ethics of international business.* New York: Oxford University Press.

Harris, T. A. (1967). *I'm OK—You're OK.* New York: HarperCollins.

Josephson, M. (2002). *Making ethical decisions.* Los Angeles: Josephson Institute of Ethics.

Kidder, R. M. (1994). *Shared values for a troubled world: Conversations with men and women of conscience.* San Francisco: Jossey-Bass.

Kidder, R. M. (1995). *How good people make tough choices.* New York: Simon & Schuster.

Parliament of the World's Religions. (1993). *Toward a declaration of a global ethic.* Chicago: Council for the Parliament of the World's Religions.

Petersen, V. C. (2002). *Beyond rules in society and business.* Cheltenham, UK: Edward Elgar.

Sikula, A. F. (1989). *Moral management: Business ethics*. Dubuque, IA: Kendall/Hunt.

Sikula, A., Sr. (1992). *Management in America: Crises in ethics*. Bend, OR: Daniel Spencer.

Sikula, A., Sr. (1996). *Applied management ethics*. Chicago: Richard D. Irwin.

Spencer, H. (1861). *Education: Intellectual, moral and physical*. London: W. J. Johnson.

Critical Thinking

1. Which of the 10 erroneous ethical equations speaks most powerfully to you? Provide an example.

ANDREW SIKULA, Sr., Marshall University, One Marshall Drive, Lewis College of Business, Huntington, WV 25755. E-mail: sikula@marshall.edu.

Create a Culture of Trust

Take 10 actions to cultivate a spirit of reciprocity.

NOREEN KELLY

C reating a culture of trust starts at the top. Leaders are responsible for creating a culture of shared values and meaning, promoting ethical behavior, and looking after their brand and reputation.

Edgar Schein, an expert on culture, states: "Culture defines leadership. Leaders should be conscious of culture; otherwise, it will manage them."

As guardians of culture, leaders need to live the values. Enron's espoused "values" of respect, integrity, communication and excellence, meant nothing. In a values-based organization, a leader's actions and behaviors align with stated values and beliefs. The leaders at Google, #1 on the list of the *100 Best Companies to Work For,* figured out the formula that works for them: treat people with respect, support their creative endeavors, and adhere to the motto of "Don't be evil."

Another basis for trust is the belief that you, as a leader, are acting in an ethical manner and promoting ethical ideas and practices. Culture plays a greater role than formal ethics and compliance programs when it comes to preventing unethical behaviors. Even after Enron and other scandals and enactment of Sarbanes-Oxley, few leaders have changed their culture to be one where ethical violations are simply not tolerated. This change can only come from the top, and leaders must involve employees at all levels.

Leaders must adopt an enterprise-wide cultural approach to ethics that extends beyond a compliance mentality. By creating a strong ethical culture, shaped by ethical leadership and values, you dramatically reduce misconduct. A well-implemented ethics and compliance program and a strong ethical culture greatly reduce ethics risk.

Reputation is a company's most important asset and a critical factor in earning and creating trust. Based on actions rather than words, reputation is about staying true to who you are. Companies that set high aspirations through their branding and marketing need to live up to that promise. When a gap exists between who a company is and who they say they are, an environment of distrust is created.

In promoting social responsibility, leaders must do right by employees. While protecting the environment, supporting the community, and adopting socially responsible practices are all important, leaders should be first committed to their own employees.

10 Actions Cultivate Trust

To cultivate a culture of trust, follow 10 actions:

1. *Live the values.* Match actions with words. Walk the talk. Live up to the values you espouse. Inspire people through leading by example. Practice and promote alignment with the values daily and send clear signals about what the values are. Make ethics a priority. Model ethical behavior and support those who uphold standards.

2. *Tell the truth.* Be honest. Get rid of hidden agendas. Be simple, straightforward, and consistent. Admit what you don't know when asked a question, and promise to find out. Share what you know, when you know it. If you don't know, say so. If you can't tell, say so.

3. *Communicate, communicate, communicate.* Encourage open communication. Keep employees informed and address issues when you observe them. Create a dialogue. Listen. Engage and involve people at the grassroots of a project or decision when possible. Value people's input and opinions. Communicate the importance of ethics and integrity, along with shared vision and values. Provide clear and consistent communication to key stakeholders.

4. *Be in integrity.* Make good on your promises and commitments. Be realistic. Don't overpromise. Do what you say you're going to do. Take responsibility for your actions and act ethically.

5. *Be authentic.* Engage in honest conversations. Be credible. Be who you say you are. Demonstrate company values through thoughts, words, intentions and actions. Bring words and actions into alignment.

6. *Be accountable.* Admit mistakes. Hold yourself accountable for your actions, words, and decisions to your employees and customers.

7. *Be transparent.* Be visible. Disclose information as needed. Clearly communicate facts to build trust and credibility with stakeholders.

8. *Respect the individual.* Promote mutual trust and respect. Be inclusive. Show empathy. Acknowledge and honor people's feelings and concerns.

9. *Share information.* Keep employees informed and address issues when they are observed. Note that decisions may change, and provide timely feedback. Involve people at the grassroots level of a project or decision whenever possible. Involve those who are or could be affected. Sharing of information within and between teams creates dialogue, promotes cooperation, and helps build community over time.

10. *Do the right thing.* Much evidence supports the impact of values, ethics and reputation on the bottom line: Values driven companies are the most successful. Companies that fail to look after the reputation aspects of performance ultimately suffer financially. Companies that are great places to work are more financially successful. Organizations with high trust benefit from increased profitability, market value, and lower costs.

Beyond bottom-line implications, leaders should create a culture of trust simply because it's the right thing to do. Adam Smith, author of *The Theory of Moral Sentiments* (1759), believed that virtues like trust, fairness and reciprocity are vital for the functioning of a market economy. Consider the high costs of breaking trust, risking reputation, and sacrificing ethical standards.

Creating a trust culture takes commitment and action. Trust begets trust. Trust sustains trust and repairs lost trust.

Leaders who choose to trust, value, respect, and empower their people are rewarded with motivated and productive people and greater profitability. Leaders who communicate openly and honestly create mutual trust, bolster credibility and engage their people.

Move away from fear-based values toward positive values, and create connections and conversations that maintain trust. In a spirit of reciprocity, participation, dialogue and hope, a culture of trust can be achieved.

Critical Thinking

1. From your perspective, what is the most important value to be encouraged in the workplace?

2. How does trust support and sustain successful businesses?

NOREEN KELLY is president of Trust Matters. Call 312.988.7562, email noreen@noreenkelly.com. Visit www.noreenkelly.com.

Building Trust
How the Best Leaders Do It

Stephen M. R. Covey

Trust is Declining everywhere—in our personal relationships and in our culture and organizations. Only half of employees trust their senior managers and leaders, and only 28 percent believe CEOs are a credible source of information.

We are now experiencing a crisis of trust and confidence in the financial markets. This compels us to ask: Is there a measurable cost to low trust? Is there a tangible benefit to high trust? And how can leaders build trust and reap the benefits of high trust?

Most leaders don't know how to quantify the costs of low trust or measure the gains of high trust. For many, trust is intangible. They don't know how to assess the trust level or how to improve it. Yet, the costs of low trust are very real—and often staggering.

One estimate put the cost of complying with federal rules and regulations—put in place due to lack of trust—at $1.1 trillion (11 percent of the gross domestic product). The average American company loses 6 percent of its annual revenue to fraudulent activity. We see similar effects for the other disguised low-trust "taxes" as well.

When trust is low, in a company or relationship, it places a hidden "tax" on every transaction—every communication, interaction, strategy, and decision is taxed, bringing speed down and driving costs up. *Distrust doubles the cost of doing business and triples the time it takes to get things done!*

Leaders who are trustworthy and operate with high trust experience the opposite of a tax—a "dividend" that is like a performance multiplier, enabling them to succeed in their communications, interactions, and decisions, and to move with incredible speed. *High-trust companies outperform low-trust companies by 300 percent!*

The ability to create, grow, extend, and restore trust among stakeholders is *the* critical competency of leadership. Fortunately, engendering trust is a competency that can be learned and applied. You can get good at it, measure it, improve it. You can't be an effective leader without mutual trust. As Warren Bennis notes, "Leadership without mutual trust is a contradiction in terms."

How Can Leaders Build Trust?

Job 1 of any leader is to inspire trust. Trust is confidence, born of character and competence. Character includes your integrity, motive, and intent. Competence includes your capabilities, skills, results, and track record.

With the focus on ethics, the character side of trust is now the price of entry in the global economy. However, the differentiating (and often ignored) side of trust—competence—is equally essential. You might think a person is sincere, even honest, but you won't trust that person fully if he or she doesn't get results. And the opposite is true. A person might have great skills and talents and a good track record, but if he or she is not honest, you won't trust that person either.

The best leaders frame trust in economic terms. In a low-trust culture, leaders can expect negative economic consequences. Everything takes longer and costs more because of the steps people need to take to compensate for the low trust. When these costs are counted, leaders recognize how low trust becomes an economic matter.

The dividends of high trust can also be quantified, enabling leaders to make a compelling business case for building trust, even making the building of trust an explicit objective. Like any other goal, building trust should be focused on, measured, and tracked for improvement. It must be clear that trust matters to managers and leaders, that it is the right thing to do, and the smart economic thing to do. One way to do this is to make an initial baseline measurement of trust, and then to track improvements over time.

The *trust transformation* starts with building credibility at the personal level. The foundation of trust is your personal credibility. Your reputation is a reflection of your credibility, and it precedes you in any interaction or negotiation. High credibility and a good reputation enable you to establish trust fast—speed goes up, cost goes down.

I see four *Cores of Credibility* that work in tandem—Integrity, Intent, Capabilities, and Results. You can build a culture of high trust by clarifying what constituents want and what you can offer them. Then practice behaviors that build trust. Next, extend trust to your organization. The combination of that credibility and behavior and alignment results in a culture of high trust.

For example, Warren Buffett, the trusted CEO of Berkshire Hathaway, completed an acquisition of McLane Distribution (a $23 billion company) from Wal-Mart in record time. The deal was made with one two-hour meeting and a handshake. In 30 days, it was completed. High trust yields high speed and low cost.

Behaviors of High-Trust Leaders

Effective leaders use 13 behaviors to build and maintain trust: Talk straight, show respect, create transparency, right wrongs, show loyalty, deliver results, get better, confront reality, clarify expectation, practice accountability, listen first, keep commitments, and extend trust first. When you adopt these behaviors, you make deposits into your "trust accounts." However, these behaviors need to be balanced (i.e., *talk straight* needs to be balanced by *show respect*). Any behavior, pushed to the extreme, becomes a liability.

You can always boost your *self-trust* (the confidence you have in yourself—in your ability to set and achieve goals, to keep commitments, to walk your talk), and your *relationship trust* (the ability to create and increase the trust accounts you have with others and to inspire trust in others).

The job of a leader is to extend trust first—not a blind trust but a smart trust with clear expectations and strong accountability. Trust determines the quality of our relationships, communication, projects, ventures, services, and products. It changes the quality of present moments and alters the trajectory and outcome of future moments. Nothing is as fast as the speed of trust.

Critical Thinking

1. What can an organizational leader do to build trust?
2. What is the bottom line impact of trust on organizational sustainability?

Stephen M. R. Covey is the CEO of CoveyLink Worldwide 801-756-2700 and the author of *The Speed of Trust: The One Thing That Changes Everything.*

The Ethical Employee

MICHELE COMPTON

Was it the fall of Enron that started the wave? Or did political malfeasance create the tide? Whatever the instigating event, the issue of ethics in the workplace shows no sign of abating. In fact, the terms "ethics" and "ethical behavior" have quickly become part of mainstream vocabulary.

If you type "ethics" into a Google search, more than 119 million entries are available for your review. In 2002, the Associated Press reported a national scramble on the part of business schools to beef up their ethics programs in business courses.

In the midst of the mad dash to add ethical guidelines to human resource manuals, it's difficult to define exactly what ethics means to the everyday worker.

Top-Down

There are many definitions for ethics: a system of moral principles; the rules of conduct recognized; the rightness and wrongness of certain actions. But there is only one clear, consistent guideline for incorporating ethical practices in the workplace. Ethical conduct starts at the top.

Fraud, stealing, lying and cheating are obvious infringements. However, if a CEO fails to support philanthropic events but expects employees to comply, that's also a mistake.

"Ethics and values are communicated through stories and examples from the top down," says Judy Suiter, member of the McIntosh Chapter in Peachtree City. Ga., and owner of the Competitive Edge, Inc., an organization that provides instructional, assessment and performance-enhancing assistance to companies.

In many cases, a well-versed, memorized and shared mission statement is as far as some employers go toward instituting an ethics policy. But in the case of ethical behavior, the minimum is no longer enough.

According to an article from the publication *Business 2 Business,* ethics begins with the employer. "Ethical employers want to ensure that their employees are above reproach but they must provide them more than lip service to what conduct they will tolerate. Tarnished by shady behavior in the executive suite, many once-solid companies are struggling to regain the confidence of their employees and customers. Management must do more than talk the talk. They must walk the walk."

According to the most recent National Business Ethics Survey by the Ethics Resource Center, companies can add an ethical element to their business with a few, simple additions to their regular best practices, including:

- Make ethics a priority;
- Set a good example of ethical conduct;
- Keep commitments;
- Provide information about culture and compliance;
- Consider ethics in decision-making; and
- Talk about ethics in the workplace.

Businesses that take the time to make ethics a priority will see their good work reflected in their employees.

Businesses that take the time to make ethics a priority will see their good work reflected in their employees.

"Companies that are true to their values have employees that demonstrate those values, through areas such as customer relations and community involvement," says Judy. "We are facing one of the largest labor shortages in U.S. history. How companies treat employees will mean everything."

Don't Swim with the Sharks

They say imitation is the highest form of flattery. So whether you are a business owner, manager or office employee, if you toe the ethical line, others will follow. For the everyday worker, this may be a littler harder to define. You don't cheat, lie on your time sheet or misuse company funds; you've got a great head start. But what about ethics by association?

In the latest trend in ethical evaluation, employers are looking at more than just illegal practices. How you conduct yourself with co-workers in the office also speaks to your ethical views.

One of the quickest ways to put your ethics into question is to participate in the company rumor mill. Family-owned or Fortune 100, every company has one. Usually there are one or two people who have their finger on the pulse of the latest gossip. Co-workers seem to flock to their office to revel in the latest misfortune.

Rumor mills are hard for companies to deter. But corporate giants such as Texas Instruments, which has long been a company known for promoting ethical behavior, establish guidelines for how to quell gossip.

According to TI's website. "Malicious rumors and gossip attack the spirit of the individual and attempt to divide us into groups. The ethical workplace that we strive to build at TI is based on trust, honesty, candor, and teamwork and has no place for the malicious games that people play."

To dispel the urge to rumor, the company issued the following guidelines:

1. "When you pass information, casually or not, do so in a manner that ensures that the message heard by those listening is as accurate as possible. Avoid insinuations, quibbling, and half-truths.
2. If you are not sure of the information's accuracy, don't repeat it.
3. If it is a case of obvious rumor spreading or malicious gossiping, try to stop it in an appropriate manner such as interrupting the speaker and questioning the source of information. Let it be known that you do not approve of such activity.
4. Seek help from co-workers, team members, supervisor, manager or Human Resources—whatever is appropriate to stop the rumor mill."

Knowing how to avoid the water-cooler chat is just one way employees can defend their ethics. However, business cultures are becoming just as popular a skill set. Companies used to hire using skill and personality typing to assess compatibility. In some cases, an ethics assessment has replaced that paradigm.

"Companies are incorporating hiring assessments to reveal behavior styles that could compliment or contrast with the company's cultural and ethical styles," says Judy. "This enhances or even replaces the personality typing that has been used in the past."

Employees have to do more than sign a contract to adhere to company ethics policies: they have to be ready to demonstrate their commitment.

Swimming in the Mainstream

Ethics has taken such a mainstream position that even volunteer organizations are creating a Code of Ethics to which members must adhere.

In fact, the American Business Women's Association was nominated for the 2006 Stanley C. Pace Ethics and Leadership Award from The Ethics Resource Center (ERC) Fellows Program, for its concerted effort to offer more business ethics training to its members through such programs as the "ABWA Extreme Makeover: Ethics and ABWA Groups."

At the end of the day, ethics is really about people—how we treat each other and expect to be treated in return.

At the end of the day, ethics is really about people—how we treat each other and expect to be treated in return.

So while it is important to know and follow company guidelines, how an employee interacts with fellow employees—or how a member supports a fellow member—says more than a single negative behavior.

Tom Peters, author of *In Search of Excellence* (Harpers & Row, 1982), once wrote. "High ethical standards—business or otherwise—are above all, about treating people decently. To me (as a person, business person and business owner) that means respect for a person's privacy, dignity, opinions and natural desire to grow, and people's respect for (and by) co-workers."

Critical Thinking

1. What can a company do to defuse the power of the "rumor mill"?
2. Describe an incident in an organization in which you have worked or that you have read about where the CEO or a manager has served as a role model for appropriate ethical behavior.

UNIT 2

Ethical Issues and Dilemmas in the Workplace

Unit Selections

Learning Outcomes

- What ethical dilemmas do *managers* face most frequently? What ethical dilemmas do *employees* face most often?

- What forms of gender and minority discrimination are most prevalent in today's workplace? In what particular job situations or occupations is discrimination more widespread and conspicuous? Why?

- Whistleblowing occurs when an employee discloses illegal, immoral, or illegitimate organizational practices or activities. Under what circumstances do you believe whistleblowing is appropriate? Why?

- Given the complexities of an organization, where an ethical dilemma often cannot be optimally resolved by one person alone, how can an individual secure the support of the group and help it to reach a consensus as to the appropriate resolution of the dilemma?

Student Website

www.mhhe.com/cls

Internet References

American Psychological Association
www.apa.org/homepage.html
International Labour Organization (ILO)
www.ilo.org

LaRue Tone Hosmer, in *The Ethics of Management,* lucidly states that ethical problems in business are truly managerial dilemmas because they represent a conflict, or at least the possibility of a conflict, between the *economic performance* of an organization and its *social performance*. Whereas the economic performance is measured by revenues, costs, and profits, the social performance is judged by the fulfillment of obligations to persons both within and outside the organization.

Units 2 to 4 discuss some of the critical ethical dilemmas that management faces in making decisions in the workplace, in the marketplace, and within the global society. This unit focuses on the relationships and obligations of employers and employees to each other as well as to those they serve.

Organizational decision makers are ethical when they act with equity, fairness, and impartiality, treating with respect the rights of their employees. Organizations' hiring and firing practices, treatment of women and minorities, tolerance of employees' privacy, and wages and working conditions are areas in which it has ethical responsibilities.

The employee also has ethical obligations in his or her relationship to the employer. A conflict of interest can occur when an employee allows a gratuity or favor to sway him or her in selecting a contract or purchasing a piece of equipment, making a choice that may not be in the best interests of the organization. Other possible ethical dilemmas for employees include espionage and the betrayal of secrets (especially to competitors), the misuse of confidential data, the theft of equipment, and the abuse of expense accounts.

The articles in this unit are broken down into seven sections representing various types of ethical dilemmas in the workplace. The initial article in the first section examines some of the legal consequences resulting when identity theft occurs in the workplace. The next article describes how office romance is coming out of the closet. The last article in the subsection points out that as the proportion of single and childless employees increases, so do complaints of unfairness in employers' benefits and policies.

In the subsection entitled **Organizational Misconduct and Crime,** the articles scrutinize the causes and the ramifications

© Plush Studios/Getty Images

of governmental and educational misconduct and the circumstances where small businesses are most vulnerable to fraud.

The selection under **Sexual Treatment of Employees** takes a close look at how men are now making harassment claims and examines the complex social issues faced by professional women in South Korea.

The reading in the **Discriminatory and Prejudicial Practices** section considers the impact of older workers in the workforce.

In the next subsection entitled **Downsizing of the Work Force,** articles reflect on the consequences and effects of downsizing and supplies an example of a factory that was able to survive in the midst of rampant economic pressure to close.

The selections included under the heading **Whistleblowing in the Organization** disclose why some businesses that once feared whistleblowers are now finding new ways for employees to report wrongdoing and analyzes the ethical dilemma and possible ramifications of whistleblowing.

In the last subsection, **Handling Ethical Dilemmas at Work,** some cases and organizational settings are presented for the reader to wrestle with ethical dilemmas.

Employers Are Stung with a Hefty Price When Employees Suffer an Identity Theft

Stephanie Shapson Peet, Esq.

Worried about having your vital personal information stolen, and anxious to know how to protect yourself against identity thieves?

Well, you'd better be.

According to the Federal Trade Commission, identity theft has been the number one complaint for the past eight consecutive years. Keep in mind one's identity involves much more than credit. A person's identity includes many parts—vital personal information such as Social Security numbers, driver's license numbers, dates of birth, home addresses, email passwords and ATM information—that are exchanged constantly in everyday life, well outside the boundaries of the credit system. Millions of personal data records are traded for profit on the Internet by people who will use these records for suspicious or illegal activities.

If you have not already been a victim of identity theft, chances are at least one of your friends, family members or co-workers has been victimized.

An employer's vulnerability is even greater. An employer could be held liable for any identity theft that occurs within the workplace—even if the employer did not fraudulently use its employees' personal information.

It's the frightening . . . and expensive . . . truth. Happily, you can protect yourself and your employees from becoming a victim; you can minimize your company's risk of liability. If, that is, you know how.

How Does Identity Theft Occur in the Workplace?

Identity theft is the misuse or fraudulent use of an individual's personal information. The bait drawing such crime to the workplace includes personnel files, benefits data, and payroll and tax records—all of which typically reside in the Human Resources department and can be a goldmine for identity thieves. If these files get into the wrong hands, employers can face considerable legal and economic repercussions.

For example, a Michigan jury awarded employees $275,000 after it found that their union neglected to safeguard their Social Security and driver's license numbers. How often does identity theft really happen? A lot. According to a September 2002 report by TransUnion, one of the nation's three credit bureaus, the number one underlying source of identity fraud is theft of employer records.

What Are My Legal Obligations to Protect against ID Theft?

Given the likelihood of liability when employees' files are misused or mishandled, the federal government and some states have created new duties for employers, making them responsible for safeguarding personal information. For example:

- **Federal Government:** As of June 1, 2005, the FTC amended the Fair and Accurate Credit Transactions ("FACT") Act to promulgate a "Disposal Rule" that requires all employers in the U.S., regardless of size, to shred or effectively destroy all documents and electronic files containing personal information derived from a consumer report before discarding them.

  Although the Disposal Rule applies to consumer reports and the information derived from consumer reports, the FTC encourages those who dispose of any records containing a consumer's personal or financial information to take similar protective measures.

- **Arizona:** Beginning January 1, 2009, Arizona Revised Statutes § 44-1373.02 will bar employers and others from using or printing more than five (5) numbers that are reasonably identifiable as being part of a Social Security number.

- **California:** California Civil Code § 1798.81.5 requires businesses that own or license personal information about California residents to implement and maintain reasonable security procedures to protect the information from unauthorized access, use or disclosure. The term "personal information" includes an individual's first name or first initial and last name, in combination with a Social Security number, driver's license number, California identification card number, account number, or credit or debit card number.

Additionally, as of January 1, 2008, California Labor Code § 226(a) requires employers to display no more than the last four (4) digits of the employee's Social Security number on the employee's wage statement.

- **Maryland:** Companion bills H.R. 56 and S.B. 280 bar employers from posting, displaying or printing Social Security numbers and/or requiring people to transmit their Social Security numbers over the Internet. Also, House Bill 388, Laws 2006 prohibits employers from printing an employee's Social Security number on wage payment documents, including attachments to the wage payment check, a notice of direct deposit of an employee's wage or a notice of credit to a debit card or card account.
- **Michigan:** The Social Security Number Privacy Act (Mich. Comp. Laws Ann. § 445.81 et seq.) prohibits employers and others from using more than four digits of a Social Security number and from sending anything through the mail on which a Social Security number is visible from the outside of the envelope. The law also requires any company that obtains Social Security numbers in the course of business to create, and publish in its employee handbook, a privacy policy that ensures their confidentiality, prohibits unlawful disclosure, limits access to that information, mandates procedures for disposal and establishes penalties for violations.
- **Nebraska:** Beginning September 1, 2008, L.B. 674, Laws 2007 will prohibit employers from posting displaying or otherwise making available more than four digits of an employee's Social Security number.
- **Oklahoma:** 40 Oklahoma Statutes Annotated § 173.1(A) prohibits employers from: (1) publicly posting or displaying in any manner an employee's Social Security number; (2) printing the employee's Social Security number on any card required for the employee to access information, products or services provided by the employer; (3) requiring an employee to transmit his or her Social Security number over the internet, unless the connection is secure or the Social Security number is encrypted; (4) requiring an employee to use his or her Social Security number to access an internet website, unless a password or unique personal identification number is also required to access the website; (5) printing the Social Security number on any materials that are mailed to the employee, unless otherwise required by state or federal law. Social Security numbers may be included in applications and forms sent by mail, including documents sent as part of an application or enrollment process, or to establish, amend or terminate an account, contract or policy, or to confirm the accuracy of social security numbers.

What Should I Do?

Thankfully, employers are not helpless in the fight against identity theft. By complying with state and federal statutes and following these simple dos and don'ts, your company can protect its employees and minimize the risk of identity theft and liability.

Do:

- Keep personnel files and all personal data in secure, locked cabinets.
- Make sure only appropriate personnel have access to confidential information.
- Utilize an electronic monitoring system which allows employers to observe who is attempting to access electronically stored confidential information.
- Carefully screen all employees who have access to personal data and conduct background checks when you hire new HR staff.
- Create and publish an identity theft policy which provides instruction on how to handle, secure and destroy appropriate files and encourages employees to report any identity theft crimes to management.
- Provide information to employees about protecting personal items and areas, such as purses, wallets, laptops, desks and lockers.

Don't:

- Never leave original documents or facsimiles in all-access photocopiers.
- Do not include employees' Social Security numbers on paychecks or timecards.
- Do not use Social Security numbers as a reference number of any kind.
- Avoid sending Social Security numbers in the mail.
- Do not transmit Social Security numbers over the internet without the use of encryption technology.
- Do not require employees to access the company website with a Social Security number without password protection or other authentication technology.

Critical Thinking

1. What is identity theft? In what situations can it happen in the workplace?
2. How can employers protect the identities of their employees?

STEPHANIE SHAPSON PEET is an attorney with the Philadelphia- based law firm of Obermayer Rebmann Maxwell & Hippel LLP. She is a member of the firm's Labor Relations & Employment Law Department. Ms. Shapson Peet represents management in a wide variety of employment matters, including federal court, state court and administrative proceedings involving Title VII, the Age Discrimination in Employment Act, the Americans With Disabilities Act, the Family and Medical Leave Act, Section 1981, Section 1983 and common law claims involving breach of contract and wrongful discharge. Her phone number is 215-665-3060 and her e-mail address is stephanie.shapsonpeet@obermayer.com.

For Office Romance, the Secret's Out

SUE SHELLENBARGER

Like a growing number of young couples, Nathan Shaw and Maiko Sato met at the office, in a Cisco Systems training program for new recruits. They dated openly as fellow employees for a couple of years.

And when Mr. Shaw was looking for a novel way to propose marriage, he picked the office as the setting. He engaged his boss as a co-conspirator. During a date with Ms. Sato one evening, his boss phoned Mr. Shaw on the pretext of asking him to stop by the office to test some teleconferencing gear.

As Ms. Sato gamely tried to help with the "test," Mr. Shaw guided her to the engagement ring he had hidden, then flipped a flashing slide onto her teleconferencing screen: "Say yes!" After a moment of stunned silence, she did. The two married in 2008 and remain happily co-employed at Cisco's San Jose, Calif., campus.

Office romance is coming out of the closet. More than any other time during my 19 years of writing this column, the workplace has become a place for courtship. Some 67% of employees say they see no need to hide their office relationships, up from 54% in 2005, says a CareerBuilder survey of 5,231 employees released Tuesday.

In the past, "the Baby Boomers kept office romance secret" amid fears of career damage or reprisal, says Helaine Olen, co-author with Stephanie Losee of *Office Mate,* a book on the topic. Now, amid growing openness about sexuality and greater equality between the sexes, she says, singles "are saying, 'Why is anybody even bothering to keep this secret at all?'"

That doesn't mean all the old rules have changed. Affairs when one or both partners are married are still taboo. Nor is it OK to snuggle up behind the copier with your latest crush. Employers still expect even the most out-there workplace couples to behave professionally.

Dating your boss or subordinate is generally out of bounds, too. Court rulings in recent years have broadened employers' exposure to sexual-harassment lawsuits, making this a more sensitive issue. A growing minority of employers have written policies requiring employees to disclose any romantic relationships to a superior and allowing the employer to separate the partners at work, says Manesh Rath, a Washington, D.C., employment lawyer.

Beyond that, though, employers realize that trying to stamp out office romance is like standing in front of a speeding train. "The office keeps coming up as No. 1" in surveys as the best place to meet a mate, leading bosses to conclude that they "have to be cool about it," says Janet Lever, a professor of sociology at California State University, Los Angeles, and a longtime researcher on office romance.

To Stacie Taylor, who has been dating a co-worker for 3½ years, finding a significant other at the office seems logical. "People spend so much of their time working that it's unavoidable," says Ms. Taylor, 37, a professional development coordinator at Zoot Enterprises, a Bozeman, Mont., technical-services provider. Her boyfriend, Cary Costello, 29, a project manager, adds, "If you're around a bunch of like-minded people who have similar interests, it's bound to happen."

But office romances can have a negative spillover effect on co-workers. At Slingshot, a Dallas interactive-advertising agency, one pair of co-workers who started dating were equals on the job and behaved appropriately in the office, says Owen Hannay, chief executive. Nevertheless, when they started going out to lunch with each other every day, co-workers on their seven-person team "felt excluded, and it created a lot of negativity." The daters have left the company, Mr. Hannay says.

Other couples take great pains to prevent fallout from their romance. Shortly after Erica Toth and Brian Carnevale started dating, colleagues in their open, 18-person office figured it out. But the couple bent over backward to keep their relationship from affecting others at the Rochester, N.Y., office of Text 100, a technology public-relations firm. They asked to be assigned to different projects, says Mr. Carnevale, 31, an account director.

When new employees joined the firm, Ms. Toth, 28, an account manager, would tell them about their dating relationship, she says, adding, "if for some reason you are concerned, let your manager know." And if she slipped up and called Mr. Carnevale "Honey" over lunch, he quickly corrected her. The couple also limit their conversation based on "what would my co-workers want to hear?" Ms. Toth (now Ms. Carnevale) says. After dating for three years as co-workers, they married and are now expecting their first child.

Some employers, especially those with a lot of young workers, are taking a more neutral stance on office romance. Cisco's dating policy, for example, "does not encourage or discourage consensual relationships in the workplace." Relationships between supervisors and subordinates, however, are "frowned upon" and may result in a transfer or reassignment, the policy says.

This leaves young couples who are peers to navigate the office fishbowl on their own. When co-workers Michelle Walters and Ryan Scholz started dating, Mr. Scholz, a production manager for

GMR Marketing, New Berlin, Wis., tried at first to act in meetings as if their relationship didn't exist. But he has since relaxed and become more casual about it, and both have gotten used to kidding from co-workers, says Ms. Walters, a project manager.

GMR Chief Executive Gary Reynolds says the event-marketing company doesn't have a written dating policy because its 500 employees handle it fine without one. He says, "Why try to mandate behavior and develop policy when you don't need it?"

The biggest pitfall of office romance may be its potential for messy breakups; 67% of 493 employers surveyed in 2006 by the Society for Human Resource Management cited as a significant problem the possibility of retaliation by spurned or disappointed lovers, up from 12% in 2001.

The best vaccination against a bad ending is "a long corporate courtship," says GMR's Mr. Scholz. He adds, "Keep it light and fun at first," getting to know each other at lunch or group outings, a strategy that enabled him and Ms. Walters to learn a lot about each other before they started dating. Then if it doesn't work out, "you have basically just broken up with your lunch buddy."

Indeed, many young office daters are taking things slowly—reverting to painstaking relationship-building because they know their livelihoods are at risk. "People have this notion that these relationships are scuzzy meetings in the supply closet, or Christmas-party affairs. In fact, it's just the opposite," the author

Ms. Olen says. "The office has become the last bastion of old-fashioned courting."

Jonathan Wolf met Emily Gudeman online when they were co-workers in different offices at a San Mateo, Calif., Internet-marketing concern, collaborating on a software product. They got to know each other through instant-messaging, phone calls and photos. Ms. Gudeman says Mr. Wolf gave her good advice on dealing with co-workers, and "he was really, really funny" on instant messages. After four months of remote communication, says Mr. Wolf, now a product manager for Bazaarvoice, Austin, Tex., "I had this virtual crush on this girl."

After meeting—and mindful of the risks of office romance—they took several months to get acquainted before they started dating. "We had a true courting, where we had to sit on the front porch and just talk to each other" online and by phone, says Ms. Gudeman. Eventually she transferred to his office, where the pair worked side-by-side for another year. Although both have since moved on to separate new employers, their five-year relationship is still going strong.

Critical Thinking

1. What organizational rules should govern the behavior of co-workers who are dating?
2. What words of caution would you have for co-workers who are dating? For the company that employs them?

Are You Too Family Friendly?

As the proportion of single and childless workers increases, so do complaints of unfairness in employers' benefits and policies.

SUSAN J. WELLS

Single employees' inner resentment about married peers' family needs can surface innocently enough.

Thomas Harpointner, chief executive officer of AIS Media Inc., recalls the time an employee of his Atlanta-based technology company left work early on Halloween to go trick-or-treating with his children.

"It did raise a few eyebrows," he says, "and some people poked fun about it." Half of AIS Media's employees are unmarried.

Harpointner got the message.

"We realized that this was no joke—it was a real issue," he says. "If someone needs an afternoon off, it shouldn't matter what the reason is. And if one employee gets the privilege, then everyone should—and we should make it a policy," he concluded.

Harpointner did just that, along with attractive enhancements to a set of employee-friendly—not solely family-friendly—benefits that apply to everyone equally and strive to reward everyone fairly by matching employees' individual priorities, "regardless of their lives or career stages, personal situations, whatever," he says.

More employers, and their HR leaders, would be wise to do the same. According to the latest available U.S. Census Bureau data, the nation grows more unmarried with each passing year.

The Shifting Majority

Unmarried and single U.S. residents numbered 92 million in 2006, making up 42 percent of all people 18 and older. That's up from 89 million, or 41 percent, in 2005. Sixty percent of the unmarried and single adult men and women in 2006 had never been married, up from 50 percent in 1970. Another 25 percent were divorced, and 15 percent were widowed.

Slightly more than one in four households, 26 percent, consisted of a person living alone in 2006, up from 17 percent in 1970. And of the nation's 114 million households in 2006, 47.3 percent were headed by unmarried individuals. That figure fluctuates around 50 percent; it hit 50.3 percent in 2005, for instance.

Essentially, more people live together, marry at older ages or not at all, and rear children in cohabiting or solo-parent households, says David Popenoe, professor of sociology emeritus at the New Brunswick, N.J., campus of Rutgers University. Popenoe is founder and co-director of the National Marriage Project, a non-partisan research organization at the school.

His July 2007 report, *The Future of Marriage in America,* tracks a decline of nearly 50 percent in the annual number of marriages per 1,000 unmarried adult women from 1970 to 2005. It also notes the rise in households without minor children. In 1960, for example, nearly half of all households had children under 18. By 2000, the portion had fallen to less than a third. In a few more years, it's projected to drop to a quarter, according to the report.

These trends contribute to a burgeoning movement to promote singles' rights, with a growing number of advocacy organizations becoming more vocal about what they perceive as unfair treatment by employers, government and society.

The Backlash

Nicky Grist, executive director of the 9,200-member Alternatives to Marriage Project Inc. (AtMP), a nonprofit advocacy organization in Brooklyn, N.Y., insists that the census data should make policy-makers and corporate decision-makers question and address some longtime, commonly held beliefs.

Marital status simply isn't a meaningful or reliable indicator of what's really going on in employees' lives.

"More of the workforce is going to be single, unmarried or childless—or some combination," she says. "Employers—especially now—need to recognize that marital status isn't a defining characteristic of the workplace any longer. It simply isn't a meaningful or reliable indicator of what's really going on in employees' lives."

The trends reignite some of the work/life backlash that first greeted employers' widespread adoption of "family-friendly" benefits decades ago.

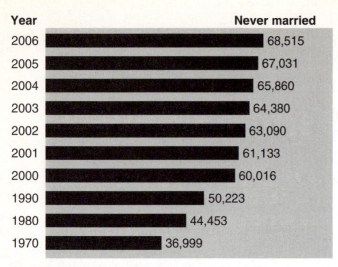

Year	Never married
2006	68,515
2005	67,031
2004	65,860
2003	64,380
2002	63,090
2001	61,133
2000	60,016
1990	50,223
1980	44,453
1970	36,999

Americans Who Have Never Married, 1970–2006. Total men and women in the U.S. population in thousands.

Source: U.S. Census Bureau, Current Population Survey, 2006 Annual Social and Economic Supplements (released March 2007), and earlier reports.

While 88 percent of 1,909 employees surveyed this spring by staffing and recruitment firm Adecco USA of Melville, N.Y., said they admire working parents' ability to "do it all" when it comes to work and family, 36 percent of men and women said parents' flexibility at work negatively affected team dynamics, and 31 percent said employee morale suffered. Working men ages 35 to 44 reported an even greater negative perception: 59 percent of them said flexibility for working mothers caused resentment among co-workers.

Fueling the Tension

What causes this workplace unease to boil over? Childless singles feel put upon, taken for granted and exploited—whether because of fewer benefits, less compensation, longer hours, mandatory overtime, or less flexible schedules or leaves—by married and child-rearing co-workers.

"The overall assumption tends to be that if you're single, you have nothing better to do—or nothing that qualifies as more important than what your married co-workers have to do—and so you're going to have to pick up what the rest of the workforce can't or won't," explains Bella DePaulo, PhD., a visiting professor of psychology at the University of California-Santa Barbara, and author of *Singled Out: How Singles are Stereotyped, Stigmatized, and Ignored, and Still Live Happily Ever After* (St. Martin's Press, 2006).

On her website, DePaulo collects experiences and complaints from single employees regarding all kinds of perceived work and benefits inequities—and she finds they're frustrated.

"If a single worker complains to a boss or co-worker about such things, they say they often get a hostile response," she says. "No one wants to be unfair—but when the issue's brought out into the open, it's obviously hitting a nerve with both parties."

Even policies dealing with office perks meant to foster employee relations can backfire. For example, DePaulo recalls an annual department picnic at a previous teaching job. Every employee was asked to pay a flat fee—no matter whether they were single or were bringing a spouse and five kids. Although the policy was unfair to singles, effectively causing them to subsidize colleagues' families, confronting the problem without sounding insensitive was a challenge, she says.

Fostering a Singles-Friendly Environment

Wendy Casper, PhD., assistant professor of management in the College of Business Administration, University of Texas at Arlington, has researched single employees' perceptions of how their organizations support their work/life balance in comparison to employees with families.

In a study of 543 singles without children published in the June 2007 issue of the *Journal of Vocational Behavior,* Casper and her colleagues documented that singles viewed more inequity in benefits policies and work/life support from their employers than did employees with families.

"Singles are more in tune with these perceptions than marrieds are," she says. "And company decision-makers, who may have greater access to work/life policies themselves, may not be as intuitive or sensitive to their single employees' views."

As part of the research, Casper identified five measures of a "singles-friendly culture." Social inclusion, equal work opportunities, equal access to benefits, equal respect for nonwork life and equal work expectations are the key, defining characteristics that employers should address, assess and evaluate, the researchers suggest.

They also point to evidence that nonmonetary and more informal elements of employee relations may be as important to equalizing the varied needs of the singles workforce.

"The social inclusion factor had much greater consequences than the other issues did in terms of driving a backlash," says Casper. "Social inclusion plays a big role: When single employees have a sense of attachment and feel more supported at work, it tends to lead to greater retention, productivity and job performance."

Casper speculates that single and childless workers have stronger needs for workplace social inclusion because their relationships and overall sense of community are more likely to be connected to their jobs.

Technology company Texas Instruments Inc. numbers among the employers who have made an effort to increase such inclusive strategies.

To help new employees connect, for example, it started a support group in its IT Services division five years ago. The group sponsors professional development, with "lunch and learn" programs, seminars and mentoring; networking, with happy hours and other events; social events such as WhirlyBall, movies and bowling; and community services such as volunteering and charitable outreach.

Since then, there has been interest among Texas Instruments' other business groups in forming "New Employee Initiative" groups. "It can mean a lot to have a peer group within the company," says Betty Purkey, manager of work/life strategies at the Dallas-based company.

Online Resources

See the online version of this article at www.shrm.org/hrmagazine/07October for links to:

- A U.S. Census Bureau fact sheet on singles' demographics.
- Census Bureau data on marital status and living arrangements.
- The Center for Work/Life Law Employer Resource Center.
- Equal Employment Opportunity Commission guidance on caregiver discrimination and a Q&A for employers.
- An *HR Magazine* article on caregiver discrimination.
- A SHRM Online article on ensuring equal treatment for parents and non-parents.
- A SHRM research paper on work/life balance.
- A sidebar on benefits preferences among employees.
- A listing of singles advocacy groups.

Creating a Wider View

To encourage a sense of equality among all demographic groups, more company officials take a wider view of the benefits and work/life programs they provide—with an eye toward diversity, flexibility, neutrality and choice.

"The buzzword shouldn't be 'family-friendly,' " says social psychologist DePaulo. "It should be 'employee-friendly' or 'life-friendly.' "

Indeed, many employers already have renamed their benefits "work/life" or "personal benefits" or have simply gotten rid of the distinction, she notes.

Some employers move to types of benefits that level the playing field by offering something for everyone.

For instance, 70 percent of 326 HR executives surveyed in 2006 by CCH and Harris Interactive said their organizations offer paid-time-off programs bundling vacation, sick and personal leave into one bank of time off that employees can manage more flexibly. In addition, 37 percent of 590 HR professionals polled for the Society for Human Resource Management's 2007 Benefits Survey said their companies offer flexible or cafeteria-benefits plans allowing employees to choose from a variety of benefits and designate a set amount of money to pay for the benefits. These types of plans can allow for different lifestyles without rewarding employees having larger families with more benefits for the same job, for example.

Yet unequal access to employer-sponsored health insurance remains one of the top complaints of many unmarried workers with partners, including AtMP members, says Grist.

According to research by the Human Rights Coalition (HRC), a Washington, D.C., civil rights organization, a majority of *Fortune* 500 companies provided benefits to same-sex domestic partners in 2006. Since then, 17 more companies have added the benefits, bringing the total to 267—or 53 percent of *Fortune* 500 companies, the HRC says.

But while same-sex benefits have been more widely adopted among large organizations, opposite-sex domestic-partner coverage generally has seen slower adoption. In fact, all unmarried couples are still significantly less likely to have health insurance than married people, according to a 2006 study by The Williams Institute on Sexual Orientation Law and Public Policy at the University of California-Los Angeles Law School.

"We found that 20 percent of people in same-sex couples are uninsured, compared with only 10 percent of married people or 15 percent of the overall population," says M.V. Lee Badgett, the institute's research director and co-author of the study. "Unmarried heterosexuals with partners are even worse off, with almost one-third uninsured."

This results in a continuing health-benefits gap for unmarried employees who may be in committed relationships or have other family members they'd like to cover but can't, says Grist. "Access to domestic-partner coverage depends on the definition of your relationship—and whether it's legally recognized," she says. "There's not a clear, legal status that currently describes a lot of these interdependent relationships." Only a few states currently recognize unmarried relationships.

Wayne Wright, PhD., and his partner of eight years, Madeline Holler, fell into that gap two years ago after relocating to Southern California from St. Louis. He had accepted a job as an assistant professor of philosophy at a state university. It was his understanding, he says, that his new job's benefits package included coverage for domestic partners—a perk that he and Holler had enjoyed at his previous employer.

Shortly after their move, however, "our 'unmarriage' began to unravel," Holler says.

It wasn't until orientation for new faculty members, Wright says, that he learned that his employer's domestic-partner coverage applied only to same-sex couples—a distinction that wasn't initially described.

And with the first $400 health insurance premium coming due to continue coverage under COBRA for Holler, Wright felt they had no choice, he says. He booked a hotel room in Las Vegas for the following weekend, and he and Holler were married at the celebrated drive-through on the Strip called The Little White Wedding Chapel.

While they hold no grudges and are secure in their relationship, Wright and Holler also say they felt powerless over what should be a personal life decision. "We absolutely felt forced to do it," Wright says.

Ending Special Deals and Stigma

While companies continue to diversify their benefits, some employers strive to custom tailor the entire employment relationship—including responsibilities, scheduling, workload and benefits—in an effort to end perceived tensions between employee groups and to improve recruitment and retention.

"In the past, an employee who wanted to work in a different way might have made a personal deal with his or her boss," says Ellen Galinsky, president and co-founder of the Families and Work Institute in New York. "Today, employees and employers are working together to find new ways to restructure the workplace in unique ways to give people the flexibility they need and to improve bottom-line business measures like productivity and retention."

Take ARUP Laboratories in Salt Lake City, where employees suggested the unusual idea of a seven-days-on, seven-days-off scheme. Workdays are 10 hours each, so employees log 70 hours in all during any given two-week period. They're paid, however, for two 40-hour weeks.

This flexible scheduling, and other forms of flexibility, help the medical-testing company recruit employees in the face of a national health care talent shortage.

Each worker is paired with a counterpart handling the opposite schedule; the two cover for each other if they have conflicts.

"We've created a self-functioning, stable team in which employees essentially get 26 free weeks a year to do with what they choose or need—take time with children, take a class, do volunteer work or go skiing," says Von Madsen, assistant vice president, human resources manager. Along with its menu of equal and neutral employee benefits, the flexible-schedule policy has helped the 2,100-employee company reduce turnover from an industry average of 22 percent to about 14 percent, Madsen says.

The flexibility also has had a positive effect on perceived scheduling and time-off inequities among singles and families.

"It helped eliminate the rift between employees with children and those without, who sometimes felt they had to cover the workload for parents who took additional time off for their children's needs," Madsen says. "It's created a more even footing."

At accounting giant Deloitte & Touche USA LLP, a new approach to career planning will become a corporate mandate in the next year.

Called "mass career customization," the initiative encourages every employee to engage in upfront, open discussion and custom planning about the course of his or her career and life-balance needs, according to Cathleen Benko, vice chairman and managing principal of talent, and co-author of a book about the program, *Mass Career Customization: Aligning the Workforce with Today's Nontraditional Workforce* (Harvard Business School Press, September 2007).

Changing demographics played a part in the design.

"The family structure has fundamentally changed in this country—83 percent of U.S. households are now considered 'nontraditional,' and singles are certainly a part," Benko says. "There's little wonder why many executives are either sensing or already confronting mounting tensions."

Benko suspects these tensions are rooted in the misalignment between the traditional workplace and the largely nontraditional workforce, explaining, "The one-size-fits-all approach no longer works."

Her model divides work into four dimensions—pace, workload, location and schedule, and role—and then builds career objectives in each dimension that match employees' life circumstances along the way, allowing employees to "dial up and down," she says, and then revisiting these choices periodically as circumstances change.

Since 2005, the concept has been pilot tested and is now in the midst of a phased, 12-month rollout companywide, Benko says. Eventually, all 42,000 employees will be enrolled.

U.S. households in thousands

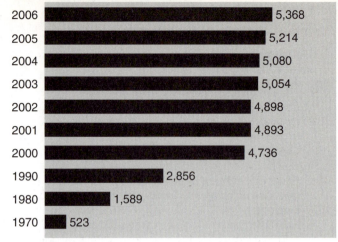

2006	5,368
2005	5,214
2004	5,080
2003	5,054
2002	4,898
2001	4,893
2000	4,736
1990	2,856
1980	1,589
1970	523

The Number of Unmarried-Couple Households Increases . . . , 1970–2006.

Sources: U.S. Census Bureau, Current Population Survey, 2006 Annual Social and Economic Supplement (released March 2007), and earlier reports.

Children under 18

2005	32.3%
2000	32.8%
1990	34.6%
1980	38.4%
1970	42.2%

. . . While the Percentage of Households with One or More Children Decreases, 1970–2006.

Source: U.S. Census Bureau, Statistical Abstract of the U.S., various years.

Interestingly, she notes, the pilots so far have found that "rather than dialing down on their careers, many employees were choosing to dial up," reflecting, in part, the fact that 65 percent of Deloitte's employees are under the age of 35. "Dialing up" refers to increasing one's professional commitment, perhaps by returning to full-time hours or adding hours, seeking the promotion fast-track, or going after opportunities for higher rewards and compensation.

During the pilots, Benko says, employee job satisfaction and retention also rose.

"This approach works because it takes a lattice, rather than ladder, approach to job moves," she says. "Work doesn't have to be an 'up or out' route, and we have a system here that's fluid and adaptable through all life and career stages."

Including All Perspectives

As Deloitte & Touche and other employers test employment customization, one thing is certain: Employment and work/life policies will continue to evolve, as different demographic groups force change and inclusion. And unlike the personal demographic characteristics that workers bring to their jobs, experts say that employers hold the power to create supportive workplace policies.

Demographics change in a clear direction, says DePaulo. Raising awareness and thinking in a broader perspective about the makeup of the workplace become more important. "A singles perspective should be acknowledged right along with the other perspectives. It's not the *only* perspective, but it should be one of them."

Critical Thinking

1. What impact does the nontraditional family structure have on the provision of benefits? Should the health insurance benefits, for example, accrue to the working single parent who has custody of a child or to the working single parent who does not have custody of a child? Why?

2. As an employer, what kind of benefit could be provided to employees who do not have childcare responsibilities to equalize the benefits package?

SUSAN J. WELLS, a business journalist in the Washington, D.C., area and a contributing editor of *HR Magazine,* has more than 20 years of experience covering business news and workforce issues.

High Rates of Misconduct at All Levels of Government

Curtis C. Verschoor, CMA

The results of the National Government Ethics Survey (NGES) show that the high incidence of ethical misconduct isn't limited to the public sector of business. The survey was completed by the not-for-profit Ethics Resource Center (ERC). It marks the first time that survey results for government employees have been reported separately from the overall national workplace. The NGES results lead to the conclusion that, "The next Enron could occur within government," says ERC President Patricia Harned.

Harned continues, "Almost one-quarter of public sector employees identify their work environments as conducive to misconduct—places where there is strong pressure to compromise standards, where situations invite wrongdoing, and/or employees' personal values conflict with the values espoused at work." As a consequence, public trust in government is at risk, and the problem of ethical misconduct is likely to get worse in the future.

The overall rate of observed misconduct across all levels of government is nearly 60%, higher than the results in earlier, unpublished biennial surveys—57% in 2005 and 52% in 2003. This year's results mirror the ethical experiences in the business sector. The highest observed levels of wrongdoing were at the local government level, with 62% of respondents having observed misconduct. The lowest amount was at the federal level, with 52% observing misconduct. Local government also had the poorest record of reporting misconduct, with 34% of respondents failing to report observed misconduct, compared to 25% of federal employees. Overall, 30% of current misconduct in government goes unreported to management. This is significantly better than the unreported rate in business (42%) and is likely due to the stronger whistleblower protection that is available to most government employees.

The most common types of misconduct observed by government employees include:

- Conflicts of interest—observed by 27% of those surveyed, up from 20% two years ago. This involves putting one's own interests ahead of those of the organization.
- Lying—observed by 28%, up from 25% two years ago. Lies are committed to employees, vendors, customers, and to the public at large.
- Abusive or intimidating behavior—observed by 25%, although overtly illegal acts are on the decline as they have been subject to increased scrutiny.
- Financial and other forms of fraud, which are at least as common in government as they are in business.

One of the most disturbing findings of the NGES study is the fact that nearly 25% of all government employees work in an environment that is conducive to or invites misconduct. This includes workplace environments where perceived pressures lead employees to feel they need to commit an ethics or compliance violation in order to do their jobs. These pressures have increased to 14% of all government employees from 10% in 2000. An astounding 98% of employees in environments conducive to misconduct report observing actual wrongdoing.

Very few of the government employees who observed misconduct utilized established whistle-blowing hotlines to report wrongdoing to the highest levels of the organization. Instead, government employees opted to report to their immediate supervisor or management of the local entity for which they work. The poor perception of management increases the likelihood that employees won't report wrongdoing to anyone. The two primary reasons for not reporting are fear of retaliation from management and a feeling of futility that nothing would be done.

Magnifying the lack of reporting is the poor perception that a surprisingly large proportion of government employees, about one quarter, have regarding the qualities of senior management:

- More than one in five (21%) think top leadership isn't held accountable for violations of ethical standards.

- 25% of government employees believe that top leadership tolerates retaliation against those who report misconduct. Many reporters of wrongdoing did experience retaliation.
- 30% of government employees don't believe top leadership keeps their promises and commitments.

An overarching factor perhaps explaining the continuing high levels of observed misconduct and failure to report it is the fact that government agencies aren't subject to the provisions of the Sarbanes-Oxley Act, as noted in this column in March 2008. The NGES reports that the overall number of government employees who say that their organization has a comprehensive ethics and compliance program has grown steadily over the years but still remains below half. The federal government has the most robust ethics and compliance programs in place (roughly 60%). Both state and local governments lag behind despite being subject to several federal mandates and provisions that encourage the implementation of such a program.

A comprehensive ethics and compliance program includes all of the following elements: a code of conduct, a way to report observed violations anonymously, a mechanism for employees to seek advice on ethical matters, training for all employees on code of conduct and ethics policies, a mechanism to discipline employees who violate the code or ethics policies, and evaluation of ethical behavior as a part of regular performance appraisals.

The NGES report indicates that government ethics and compliance programs, when they do exist, contain more legalistic and compliance oriented program resources that emphasize what employees must avoid rather than imparting the ethical framework of what employees should do. As a result, most government programs feature element mandated by law or regulation (code, hotline, and discipline). These elements only describe and punish inappropriate conduct and invite behavior that circumscribes the letter but not the intent of the law or regulation. Government agencies are also less likely to have implemented the more critical aspects of an effective ethical culture, such as ethics training, evaluation, advice lines that offer guidance and demonstrable actions that reinforce ethical conduct that does occur.

Because of the barriers to implementing an effective ethics and compliance program, less than 20% of government organizations have a well-implemented program that contains all of the required elements. Thus, an astounding 80% of government organizations are missing the benefits of having an ethical culture:

- Employees willing to seek ethics advice
- Employees receiving positive feedback for ethical conduct

- Employees who are prepared to handle situations that invite misconduct
- Employees who can question the decisions of management without fear of reprisal
- Employees being rewarded for following ethical standards
- Employees who achieve success through questionable means not getting rewarded
- Employees who feel positive about the organization's efforts to encourage ethical conduct, and
- Employees who feel their organization is an ethical workplace.

In fact, the NGES reports that only 8% of government workplaces have strong ethical cultures, and the trend since 2003 is unfavorable—half of government workplaces have weak or weak-leaning ethical cultures, a noticeable increase over 2003 (40%) and 2005 (47%). One of the largest factors contributing to this small percentage of organizations with ethical cultures is the absence of embedded ethical values in so many government workplaces. Only 8% of government employees indicated that their workplace was effective in living the values of the organization in daily decisions.

More than one-third of employees say their government organization doesn't put its values into practice by using socially responsible decision making. Additionally, 32% of government employees believe leaders don't consider the effects of their decisions on the environment, and 29% don't believe government leaders consider the effects their decisions will have on the future.

Mirroring previous findings in the public sector, NGES reports that well-implemented, comprehensive ethics and compliance programs have a very positive effect of reducing ethical misbehavior. Even more important is a strong agency-wide ethical culture that involves:

1. **Ethical leadership.** An appropriate tone at the top and belief that leaders can be trusted to do the right thing.
2. **Supervisor reinforcement.** Individuals directly above the employee in the organization's hierarchy set a good example and encourage ethical behavior.
3. **Peer commitment to ethics.** Ethical actions of peers support employees who "do the right thing."
4. **Embedded ethical values.** Values promoted through informal communications channels are complementary and consistent with a government's official values.

All citizens should encourage legislators at all levels of government to pass laws that extend the ethics-related requirements of Sarbanes-Oxley to government agencies. All of us should also demonstrate through the ballot box our unwillingness to accept anything less than a strong ethical climate at every government agency.

Critical Thinking

1. Which have been shown to be more effective in curbing ethical misconduct in the workplace—compliance programs or imparting ethical frameworks? Why?

2. What can be done to improve the record of ethical conduct in the public sector?

CURTIS C. VERSCHOOR is the Ledger & Quill Research Professor, School of Accountancy and MIS, and Wicklander Research Fellow in the Institute for Business and Professional Ethics, both at DePaul University, Chicago. He is also a Research Scholar in the Center for Business Ethics at Bentley College, Waltham, Mass. John Wiley & Sons has recently published his latest book, *Audit Committee Essentials*. His e-mail address is curtisverschoor@sbcglobal.net.

From *Strategic Finance*, July 2008, pp. 11–14. Copyright © 2008 by Institute of Management Accountants—IMA. Reprinted by permission via Copyright Clearance Center.

Under Pressure, Teachers Tamper with Test Scores

Trip Gabriel

The staff of Normandy Crossing Elementary School outside Houston eagerly awaited the results of state achievement tests this spring. For the principal and assistant principal, high scores could buoy their careers at a time when success is increasingly measured by such tests. For fifth-grade math and science teachers, the rewards were more tangible: a bonus of $2,850.

But when the results came back, some seemed too good to be true. Indeed, after an investigation by the Galena Park Independent School District, the principal, assistant principal and three teachers resigned May 24 in a scandal over test tampering.

The district said the educators had distributed a detailed study guide after stealing a look at the state science test by "tubing" it—squeezing a test booklet, without breaking its paper seal, to form an open tube so that questions inside could be seen and used in the guide. The district invalidated students' scores.

Of all the forms of academic cheating, none may be as startling as educators tampering with children's standardized tests. But investigations in Georgia, Indiana, Massachusetts, Nevada, Virginia and elsewhere this year have pointed to cheating by educators. Experts say the phenomenon is increasing as the stakes over standardized testing ratchet higher—including, most recently, taking student progress on tests into consideration in teachers' performance reviews.

Colorado passed a sweeping law last month making teachers' tenure dependent on test results, and nearly a dozen other states have introduced plans to evaluate teachers partly on scores. Many school districts already link teachers' bonuses to student improvement on state assessments. Houston decided this year to use the data to identify experienced teachers for dismissal, and New York City will use it to make tenure decisions on novice teachers.

The federal No Child Left Behind law is a further source of pressure. Like a high jump bar set intentionally low in the beginning, the law—which mandates that public schools bring all students up to grade level in reading and math by 2014—was easy to satisfy early on. But the bar is notched higher annually, and the penalties for schools that fail to get over it also rise: teachers and administrators can lose jobs and see their school taken over.

No national data is collected on educator cheating. Experts who consult with school systems estimated that 1 percent to 3 percent of teachers—thousands annually—cross the line between accepted ways of boosting scores, like using old tests to prep students, and actual cheating.

"Educators feel that their schools' reputation, their livelihoods, their psychic meaning in life is at stake," said Robert Schaeffer, public education director for FairTest, a nonprofit group critical of standardized testing. "That ends up pushing more and more of them over the line."

Others say that every profession has some bad apples, and that high-stakes testing is not to blame. Gregory J. Cizek, an education professor at the University of North Carolina who studies cheating, said infractions were often kept quiet. "One of the real problems is states have no incentive to pursue this kind of problem," he said.

Recent scandals illustrate the many ways, some subtle, that educators improperly boost scores:

At a charter school in Springfield, Mass., the principal told teachers to look over students' shoulders and point out wrong answers as they took the 2009 state tests, according to a state investigation. The state revoked the charter for the school, Robert M. Hughes Academy, in May.

In Norfolk, Va., an independent panel detailed in March how a principal—whose job evaluations had faulted the poor test results of special education students—pressured teachers to use an overhead projector to show those students answers for state reading assessments, according to The Virginian-Pilot, citing a leaked copy of the report.

In Georgia, the state school board ordered investigations of 191 schools in February after an analysis of 2009 reading and math tests suggested that educators had erased students' answers and penciled in correct responses. Computer scanners detected the erasures, and classrooms in which wrong-to-right erasures were far outside the statistical norm were flagged as suspicious.

The Georgia scandal is the most far-reaching in the country. It has already led to the referral of 11 teachers and administrators to a state agency with the power to revoke their licenses. More disciplinary referrals, including from a dozen Atlanta schools, are expected.

John Fremer, a specialist in data forensics who was hired by an independent panel to dig deeper into the Atlanta schools, and who investigated earlier scandals in Texas and elsewhere, said educator cheating was rising. "Every time you increase the stakes associated with any testing program, you get more cheating," he said.

That was also the conclusion of the economist Steven D. Levitt, of "Freakonomics" fame and a blogger for The New York Times, who with a colleague studied answer sheets from Chicago public schools after the introduction of high-stakes testing in the 1990s concluded that 4 percent to 5 percent of elementary school teachers cheat.

Not everyone agrees. Beverly L. Hall, who, as the superintendent of the Atlanta Public Schools has won national recognition for elevating test scores, said dishonesty was relatively low in education. "Teachers over all are principled people in terms of wanting to be sure what they teach is what students are learning," she said.

Educators ensnared in cheating scandals rarely admit to wrongdoing. But at one Georgia school last year, a principal and an assistant principal acknowledged their roles in a test-erasure scandal.

For seven years, their school, Atherton Elementary in suburban Atlanta, had met the standards known in federal law as Adequate Yearly Progress—A.Y.P. in educators' jargon—by demonstrating that a rising share of students performed at grade level.

Then, in 2008, the bar went up again and Atherton stumbled. In June, the school's assistant principal for instruction, reviewing student answer sheets from the state tests, told her principal, "We cannot make A.Y.P.," according to an affidavit the principal signed.

"We didn't discuss it any further," the principal, James L. Berry, told school district investigators. "We both understood what we meant."

Pulling a pencil from a cup on the desk of Doretha Alexander, the assistant principal, Dr. Berry said to her, "I want you to call the answers to me," according to an account Ms. Alexander gave to investigators.

The principal erased bubbles on the multiple-choice answer sheets and filled in the right answers.

Any celebrations over the results were short-lived. Suspicions were raised in December 2008 by The Atlanta Journal-Constitution, which noted that improvements on state tests at Atherton and a handful of other Georgia schools were so spectacular that they approached a statistical impossibility. The state conducted an analysis of the answer sheets and found "overwhelming evidence" of test tampering at Atherton.

Crawford Lewis, the district superintendent at the time, summoned Dr. Berry and Ms. Alexander to separate meetings. During four hours of questioning—"back and forth, back and forth, back and forth," Dr. Lewis said—principal and assistant principal admitted to cheating.

"They both broke down" in tears, Dr. Lewis said.

Dr. Lewis said that Dr. Berry, whom he had appointed in 2005, had buckled under the pressure of making yearly progress goals. Dr. Berry was a former music teacher and leader of celebrated marching bands who, Dr. Lewis said, had transferred some of that spirit to passing the state tests in a district where schools hold pep rallies to get ready.

Dr. Berry, who declined interview requests, resigned and was arrested in June 2009 on charges of falsifying a state document. In December, he pleaded guilty and was sentenced to probation. The state suspended him from education for two years and Ms. Alexander for one year.

Dr. Lewis, now retired as superintendent, called for refocusing education away from high-stakes testing because of the distorted incentives it introduces for teachers. "When you add in performance pay and your evaluation could possibly be predicated on how well your kids do testing-wise, it's just an emormous amount of pressure," he said.

"I don't say there's any excuse for doing what was done, but I believe this problem is going to intensify before it gets better."

Critical Thinking

1. What is the potential impact of tying student test scores to teacher tenure, compensation or benefits?
2. How do educational stakeholders (students, teachers, parents, individual schools, school systems) benefit or lose as a result of state, federal, and municipal achievement testing?

When You're Most Vulnerable to Fraud

In the best of times, entrepreneurs tend to take their eye off the ball.

Rob Johnson

Five years ago, Ed Couvrette was on top of the world. The manufacturing company he founded, E.F. Couvrette Co., was ringing up sales of $10 million a year and was negotiating contracts for triple that amount. On employees' birthdays, he routinely gave out bonus checks—a week's pay for every year they'd been at the company.

"Now I can hardly afford birthday cards," he laments.

His revenue is down more than half, customers have abandoned him in droves, and he has been forced to severely slash jobs. He can't line up credit, and some weeks there's not enough money in the bank to cover payroll at his Salem, Va., operation, which does business as Couvrette Building Systems.

Mr. Couvrette didn't get trapped by the collapsing economy or a shrinking industry. Instead, he says he was the victim of massive fraud by his chief operating officer—who, among other things, pocketed over $300,000 he was supposed to send to the Internal Revenue Service to cover payroll taxes. The former officer is now in prison; his attorney, Tony Anderson of Roanoke, Va., declined to comment on the case.

Mr. Couvrette's case offers a hard lesson for small businesses: When times are great—watch out. Because that's when you're most vulnerable to fraud. Sales are soaring, and the biggest problem seems to be where to fit all the new equipment and employees. But those heady days can be perilous, since success can distract the founder from such mundane financial duties as collecting payroll taxes and verifying the accuracy of bills.

"It's often when things are going well in a small business that betrayal strikes," says Walter Jones, a fraud examiner and retired IRS agent who's now a consultant to Mr. Couvrette. "In an atmosphere where sales and profits are increasing, the diversion of funds is masked by success."

'Small on Administration'

For some entrepreneurs, another factor makes them prime targets for fraud: Overseeing finances doesn't come naturally. That was the case with Mr. Couvrette, who has an engineering background. He was most comfortable on the factory floor at his company, which makes kiosks to house drive-up automated teller machines at banks; he enjoyed supervising everything from the welding of the steel housings to painting them with banks' logos.

"I was big on production, small on administration," says Mr. Couvrette, now 58.

Mr. Couvrette had also long taken his books for granted, thanks in large part to a series of dependable company controllers, including his father, a certified public accountant. Further, Mr. Couvrette says he couldn't imagine his company getting victimized—given that its mission involved *preventing* crime. "We got into the drive-up ATMs at a time when banks were becoming more security conscious about customers being robbed while walking up to the machines," Mr. Couvrette says. "More banks were interested in ATM facilities where the customers could stay in their cars and leave quickly if they felt threatened."

He admits his guard was down in 2001 when he hired Roy Dickinson, an accountant with a sound track record, as the growing company's chief operating officer.

After hiring Mr. Dickinson, Mr. Couvrette says he made a mistake in judgment that is common in small-business embezzlement cases: He put the same employee—Mr. Dickinson—in charge of both receipts and disbursements. While entrusting both ends of the money-moving chores to one employee may seem to streamline paperwork, it's just too risky, says Mr. Jones, the fraud expert. "I believe in what Reagan said about nuclear-missile treaties: Trust but verify."

In February 2005, Mr. Couvrette says he noticed that a high-profile new area of his business being run by Mr. Dickinson—making software and hardware adjustments on dozens of ATMs around the country—wasn't producing a profit. "I kept waiting for our cash flow and margins to get where they should be with expenses, and they didn't," says Mr. Couvrette.

In March 2005, Mr. Couvrette scheduled a meeting with his chief operating officer, calling him back to Salem from a

How to Steer Clear of Fraud? The Experts Weigh In

Small businesses are victimized by embezzlement far more often than bigger companies, according to a survey this year by the Association of Certified Fraud Examiners, a trade group based in Austin, Texas.

In fact, 31% of all business frauds nationally were in companies with fewer than 100 employees, according to the study, and an additional 23% were suffered by those with under 999 workers. Only 21% were committed in companies with more than 10,000 employees.

What's more, small businesses in the U.S. typically suffer larger losses than big companies do. The median loss for companies with fewer than 100 employees was about $150,000–compared with $84,000 in businesses with payrolls exceeding 10,000.

Andi McNeal, director of research at the ACFE, says small businesses are relatively easy targets for internal fraud "because there are usually less formal financial controls. There's usually a lot of trust put in one person, which may be necessary for these businesses to run, but it can come back to haunt."

So, how to protect your company from fraud? Here are some tips from the association.

- If you're delegating responsibility for accounts receivable and the company's disbursements, don't put the same person in charge of both, even if it means you have to hire an additional employee.
- Bring in an outside accountant at least once a year to review your business financial records. Typical fees are $100 to $150 an hour, depending on how organized your records are. Consider retaining different outside accountants occasionally to have a fresh eye involved in the review.
- Be aware of employees who are involved with your company's finances and never take time off. Embezzlers rarely take vacations for fear their theft will be discovered by someone filling in.

- Embezziers usually spend the money they steal very quickly. Tip-offs include changes in lifestyle such as spending on expensive cars and vacations.
- One common internal fraud is kickbacks involving vendors, so stay alert to unusually close relationships between employees responsible for finances and suppliers and customers.
- Be the first person to open your monthly business bank statements. Even if you don't have time to examine them closely, your attention sends a message to any potential fraudster.
- When perusing your bank statements, don't just look at the numbers; examine the actual images of canceled checks. Otherwise you can't confirm where the money really went.
- Remember that some internal theft doesn't leave an audit trail.

For example, skimming involves stealing a company's cash before the receipts are entered into the accounting ledger. In a sales skim, the fraudster collects a customer's payment at the point of sale and simply pockets the money without recording it. The loss may come to light only via clues such as inventory shortages or lower-than-expected cash flow.

- Look at receipts for deposits of both federal and state taxes.
- Remember that liabilities can double the amount of taxes due, including penalties and interest, within a year, so don't take more than a few months between your informal audits.
- Maintain an open-door policy that encourages employees who have suspicions about misappropriations or questionable spending to tell you in confidence.

—Rob Johnson

New York business trip. "He didn't show, so I fired him," says Mr. Couvrette.

That confrontation led to the hiring of an outside auditor, Mr. Jones. The examination revealed myriad financial problems, including payroll taxes that had been collected but not forwarded to the IRS, according to Mr. Jones. Mr. Couvrette was ultimately responsible for paying the IRS; the agency agreed to a settlement of about $320,000, according to Mr. Jones, who was Mr. Couvrette's intermediary with the government. "Stealing payroll taxes is a form of misappropriation that small-business owners don't catch because the money isn't going for company expenses anyway," says Mr. Jones.

In February of last year, meanwhile, Mr. Dickinson pleaded guilty in the U.S. District Court in Roanoke to

conspiracy to commit mail and wire fraud, and attempting to interfere with IRS laws. He was sentenced to three years in prison—a term he's currently serving—and ordered to pay restitution of more than $300,000.

Beyond pocketing the money intended for the IRS, Mr. Dickinson pleaded guilty to several acts of fraud. He used company money to cover remodeling costs for his home, for instance, and covered his tracks by altering company records, according to his plea. And he used his company American Express card to purchase items such as a $6,850 Rolex watch and altered the bills to show those transactions as business expenses, according to his plea.

In 2005, word that the IRS had issued tax liens against Couvrette Building Systems spread to the company's creditors and customers, according to Mr. Jones. Both categories consisted largely of banks, and "tax problems are the kiss of death when you're dealing with banks," says Mr. Jones. "So, Ed's credit quickly dried up and he lost millions of dollars in contracts."

Now Mr. Couvrette's annual revenue has been slashed by 60% and so has his production line—to about 30 workers, down from 150 five years ago. The hulking gray manufacturing plant on his company's 10-acre site contains pockets of workers, but most of the production line is quiet. Many of his former bank customers have found other suppliers. And Mr. Couvrette's credit is shot.

"I have zero elasticity of funds right now," he says. "I need loans to rebuild my delivery trucks and pay vendors," and of course meet payroll.

A Death in the Family

Sometimes it isn't just success that distracts entrepreneurs. Personal issues can also take owners' focus off the business and leave them vulnerable to fraud. Consider **Interactive Solutions** Inc. in Memphis, Tenn. In 2002, the videoconferencing company achieved its then-highest annual sales, about $6 million, and was recording double-digit profit margins.

"Things were going so well I bought a brand-new BMW 525 for my company car, and paid cash for it," says Jay Myers, the 53-year-old founder and chief executive.

Amid the success, Mr. Myers suffered a personal loss: His brother, John, died at age 50. The two had been close, and Mr. Myers started taking occasional days off while in mourning. His attention wandered from the company's finances, and he began relying more heavily on Linda Merritt, a bookkeeper who had come on board a month before John's death, to keep things straight.

"I wasn't paying the attention I should have to the business," says Mr. Myers, adding that his trust in Ms. Merritt was based on her solid job references, which he says included "a lawyer and someone who sang with her in the church choir."

"It was dumb luck," he says, that finally caused him to become suspicious in May 2003, after he read a magazine article detailing a case of internal fraud at a small machinery supplier in Illinois. "Something clicked as I read the story: That could happen to me."

Although he vowed to have his books checked by an outside auditor, Mr. Myers feared what might be found—a common reaction that fraud investigators say sometimes delays the uncovering of embezzlement. After all, says Mr. Myers, "this was humiliating—a potential disaster if my employees found out. It might sink the company. What about my clients and vendors?"

The thefts—in the form of bogus bonuses and commissions by the dozens, according to evidence later presented in court—weren't difficult to verify. When the outside auditor showed Mr. Myers some of the checks for such payments, he says, "Some of them were to a receptionist. I thought, 'A receptionist doesn't get commissions, she answers the phone.' I felt like such a fool for not knowing this was going on."

In November 2005, Ms. Merritt pleaded guilty to misappropriating funds in federal district court in Memphis, and is now serving an eight-year term in a Texas federal prison. According to the sentencing document in the case, she was ordered to repay more than $260,000, to Mr. Myers and an insurance company and bank involved in Interactive Solutions' finances.

Ms. Merritt's attorney, Stephen Shankman, a federal public defender in Memphis, declined to comment on the case.

New Vigilance

Mr. Myers was able to recover $80,000 via a "dishonest employee liability" rider on his insurance policy. Such clauses can be written to cover everything from credit-card fraud to embezzlement.

Today, Mr. Myers says, he's insured for about $240,000 in losses due to employee dishonesty. He also made an arrangement for partial restitution from an accounting firm that had failed to uncover the embezzlement in a routine examination of Interactive Solutions' books a few months before it was discovered.

Since the fraud episode, Interactive Solutions is riding high. Sales have more than doubled to about $14 million annually. In part, that's thanks to timing; the videoconferencing business is surging as companies look to cut travel costs during the recession. The company has also branched into new areas that are proving popular, such as telemedicine, in which doctors and patients can huddle over long distances.

Mr. Myers is being careful not to get taken unawares again. In fact, he credits part of his recent success to better hiring and employee-retention practices. He takes more time to get to know prospective workers and to check out their backgrounds. These days, Mr. Myers has separate employees who are responsible for handling accounts receivable and paying the company's bills. What's more, he says, he's much more vigilant personally. "When those monthly bank statements come in, nobody opens them now before me."

Mr. Myers now makes it a point to let employees know that if they betray his trust, they could risk jail time. In a recent meeting he warned his 40 workers: "I said if you steal a dollar or a thousand dollars, and I catch you, I will prosecute."

Meanwhile, at Couvrette Building Systems, the employees soldier on. Matt Musselman, a Couvrette design engineer, works at his computer screen on a recent afternoon with an eye to the future. Hoping innovation can win more orders, Mr. Musselman, a member of Couvrette's research-and-development team, diagrams a solar-powered ATM for one of the company's longtime bank customers that has remained loyal, Wells Fargo & Co.

"We're going into green technology," Mr. Musselman says.

Ross Campbell, a painter, sticks around even though he occasionally isn't paid for weeks at a time. He says, "Ed Couvrette is a good guy. I have a lot of faith in him."

Critical Thinking

1. Why are entrepreneurs vulnerable to fraud?
2. What can they do to protect themselves?

MR. JOHNSON is a writer in Roanoke County, Va. He can be reached at reports@wsj.com.

More Men Make Harassment Claims

DANA MATTIOLI

S ince the start of the recession, a growing number of sexual harassment complaints have come from men. Some 16.4% of all sexual harassment claims—or 2,094 claims—were filed by men in fiscal 2009, up from 15.4%, or 1,869 claims, in fiscal 2006, according to the U.S. Equal Employment Opportunity Commission.

While male victims sometimes experience behavior like groping and unwanted sexual advances, employment lawyers say increasingly "locker room" type behavior like vulgar talk and horseplay with sexual connotations have been the subject of claims.

Ron Chapman, an attorney with employment law firm Ogletree Deakins in Dallas, says in most cases the man suing is someone who has been fired or laid off.

Cintas Corp., a Cincinnati business services company that makes uniforms and other products, is involved in a case where two former male employees alleged a male co-worker at a Pennsylvania location sexually groped and made unwanted sexual advances. The two men who filed the complaint were laid off as part of a broader work-force reduction and filed the complaint several months later in October 2008, says a Cintas spokeswoman. The case, which was filed in the Eastern District of Pennsylvania in September 2009, is still pending.

The spike in male sexual harassment claims coincides with a recession that has hit men harder than women. From September 2008 to January 2010, 4.4 million men lost their jobs compared with 2.3 million women, according to Bureau of Labor Statistics figures. As the economic downturn took hold in 2008, sexual harassment filings by men and women jumped by 10.8% to 13,920 claims. Employment lawyers say that when jobs are harder to obtain, many forms of litigation, especially discrimination, increase.

In the past, victims of harassment—especially men—might have "voted with their feet," and found new jobs rather than turning to the legal system, says Greg Grant, an attorney with Shulman Rogers in Washington, D.C. "When they can't get other jobs and they still have to pay the bills and support families," they have to either live with the harassment or risk the potential stigma of speaking out, says Mr. Grant. And sexual harassment experts say the numbers are still under-reported because of the stigma associated with men who are sexually harassed.

The share of claims filed by men rose more in some states with higher than average unemployment rates. Although the numbers by state are sometimes too small to compare, in states that were hit hard by the recession, there is enough data to show the link. In Michigan, where unemployment stood at 14.6% in January 2009, the percentage of claims by men increased to 26.6% in 2009 from 16.6% in 2007. California saw a rise to 23.6% from 18.7% over the same period.

In states where unemployment didn't climb as much, claims actually dropped. Nebraska, which had a 4.7% unemployment rate in 2009, saw claims drop from 23.4% in 2007 to 12.7% in 2009.

Stephen Anderson, president of Anderson-davis Inc., a workplace training company in Denver, says filing a claim is often a no-win situation for a man. "If a woman is harassing you, people might think 'What is wrong with you? You should be flattered,'" he says. In cases where another man is the harasser, the victim might be afraid that he comes across as unmanly or homosexual, he says.

The EEOC doesn't track the sex of the alleged harasser, but Ms. Lisser says the EEOC has observed an increasing number of men alleging sexual harassment from other male co-workers—and not as many cases of men accusing female bosses or co-workers of sexual harassment. Employment attorneys have also seen an increase in man-on-man harassment complaints.

Recently Andria Lure Ryan, a partner with employment law firm Fisher & Phillips in Atlanta, handled three male-on-male

The Other Harassment Victims: Men

Sexual harassment claims filed by men make up a larger percentage of claims than ever before.

State	2009	2007
Utah	32.2%	21.7%
West Virginia	27.3	33.3
Michigan	26.6	16.6
Wyoming	24	9.5
Wisconsin	23	18.7

Source: The EEOC

sexual harassment cases, two in the construction industry and one for a trucking company, predominately male sectors. In two cases, the company settled and one case was resolved through an internal grievance process.

Stephen Drinnon, an attorney in Dallas has filed three male sexual harassment cases over the past two years—two in the oil and gas industry and one in the legal field. In all three instances, employers settled and the victims received one or two times their annual salaries, Mr. Drinnon says. He says it would have been no easy task to get a win had the cases gone to trial. While most juries are sympathetic to women being unable to defend themselves against men, many could find it hard to sympathize with a man in the same situation, he says.

Mr. Chapman agrees. When he explains male-on-male sexual harassment claims to most people, the overwhelming response is something like: "Why didn't the guy just hit him upside the head?" he says.

Male victims are often reluctant to draw attention to what is taking place in the office. Geraldo Reyes, a 23-year-old student in Albuquerque, N.M., was sexually harassed by a male manager when he was working at a local McDonald's franchise in 2003. He said the manager started by making sexually related comments, then escalated to touching his backside and attempting to grab his genitals. At that point, the then 17-year-old told his mother of the harassment. "I struggled emotionally and I felt weird about all the people around me looking at me differently," says Mr. Reyes.

He and three other co-workers at the McDonald's worked with the EEOC and in February 2006 settled with the restaurant chain for a total of $90,000. Says McDonald's spokeswoman, Danya Proud: "We work hard to provide a safe and respectful workplace for all our employees and have a strict policy prohibiting any form of harassment or discrimination in our restaurants."

The lawsuits often come with hefty price tags for companies. In November, the Cheesecake Factory restaurant chain paid six male employees at its Chandler, Ariz., location $345,000 in a settlement, according to EEOC senior attorney adviser Justine Lisser. In the lawsuit filed in July 2008, the EEOC alleged that the restaurant allowed abuse such as groping and sexual simulation by a group of male coworkers, Ms. Lisser says. A spokesman for the Cheesecake Factory declined to comment.

Companies have educated employees about sexual harassment for years, but some are making their messages more male-focused to safeguard themselves from potential litigation. Freada Klein, a workplace bias expert in San Francisco, has been advising companies to add examples of sexual harassment levied against men to their training and education programs. She encourages clients to bring up scenarios like public humiliation, bullying and inappropriate banter. "More types of behaviors are put in the sexual harassment bucket when men are the victims," she says.

Critical Thinking

1. What is the connection between sexual harassment claims by men and the unemployment rate?

2. Why are men's claims of sexual harassment taken less seriously than women's claims?

Older Workers: Running to the Courthouse?

Do greater numbers of aging baby boomers result in more age discrimination suits?

ROBERT J. GROSSMAN

In March, when the U.S. Equal Employment Opportunity Commission (EEOC) issued its annual report of private-sector discrimination charges, the data painted a disheartening picture. All told—with charges based on age, race, disability, sex and gender, religion, and retaliation—almost 83,000 claims were filed in 2007, representing the largest year-over-year increase since 1993. Age discrimination claims, with 19,103 charges, had the dubious distinction of increasing the fastest, with a caseload 15 percent greater than the prior year.

Reflecting on the numbers, EEOC Chair Naomi Earp voices sharp criticism of employers. Corporate America needs to do a better job of proactively preventing discrimination and addressing complaints promptly and effectively," she wrote in a press release earlier this year.

But a closer look at EEOC data raises an interesting question about age discrimination: In 2007, according to the U.S. Bureau of Labor Statistics (BLS), 76.9 million people in the workforce were age 40 and older. Last year, 99.98 percent of them did not complain to the EEOC about age discrimination. In contrast, people were more than six times more likely to allege race discrimination.

Tempest in a Teapot?

The relative scarcity of age discrimination cases is perplexing in light of the rationale the EEOC offers for last year's increase in complaints: "The jump in filings may be due to a combination of factors, including greater awareness of the law, changing economic conditions, and increased diversity and demographic shifts in the labor force."

True, age filings did inch up, but in context the overall number remains minuscule. By EEOC officials' own reasoning, if age discrimination exists, cases should be pouring in because:

- Older workers have AARP, one of the most vocal and influential lobbies in the country, in their corner educating and advocating for them.

- Workers age 40 and older—who are protected by the Age Discrimination in Employment Act (ADEA)—now account for more than 50 percent of the workforce, according to the BLS.

- The percentage of older workers will continue to trend up as baby boomers move through their work lives.

- The faltering economy is forcing people who had intended to retire to extend their time at work.

Still, last year only 0.02 percent of workers age 40 and older complained of age bias. So, when it comes to age discrimination, is the EEOC's criticism of employers over-the-top?

Brenda McChriston, SPHR, a principal at Spectrum HR Solutions in Baltimore, formerly an HR executive with an international hospitality company, says so: "Age discrimination is not as rampant as the EEOC suggests. The agency is just trying to beef up its case for what it does. In fact, employers have become increasingly savvy about how to keep their workplaces free from litigation—and the EEOC numbers show it."

On the other hand, is it really possible for there to be so little age bias and negative stereotyping? Or has the EEOC, the federal government's star player in the fight against discrimination, moved from center court to the sidelines? Belying the EEOC statistics, workers, job seekers and even employers say the scourge of age discrimination continues to be endemic. For example, in a survey of 5,000 workers age 50 and older conducted by Bob Skladany, vice president of research for RetirementJobs.com in Waltham, Mass., 77 percent said they have experienced or observed workplace age bias. In a companion survey of 165 employers, 78 percent indicated that age discrimination was "a fact of life".

These findings parallel a study prepared by RoperASW for AARP, finding that two-thirds of workers ages 45 to 74 had experienced or observed age bias on the job and that 80 percent of job seekers said they were facing age discrimination.

Why So Few?

Perceptions, of course, are not necessarily reality. But with so many people acknowledging and experiencing bias, why so few EEOC cases? Among the reasons:

- Older workers are less likely to complain, especially if they're still employed. "People don't want to be at war," says Robert Gordon, a partner at Ropes & Gray in Boston and author of *Dealing with Employee Lawsuits: Strategies for the Prevention & Defense of Workplace-Related Claims* (Aspatore Books, 2005). "They don't want to paint a bull's-eye on the back of their heads. Perhaps with some justification, they feel [if they make noise] it will place a taint on them. Instead, they suffer in silence."
- Employers, in the main, are practical and compassionate. They offer face-saving severance tied to counsel-approved releases that ease nonperforming workers out the door. "I find myself advising clients, 'If you want to get rid of Joe Doakes, isn't it better to pay him three months' severance than paying the money to your lawyer?'" Gordon says.
- "Most people are willing to sign the release if they get financial incentive," says Donna Ballman, an attorney in Fort Lauderdale, Fla., who represents claimants.
- High-powered executives and star performers trade in the right to sue when they're hired. Employers tie them to binding arbitration clauses in employment contracts, ensuring that discrimination claims will be handled quickly and quietly.
- The legal process is costly and creeps along. Though lawyers for plaintiffs still take cases on a contingency fee basis, many charge fees, requiring the complainant to pony up at least some money early on. Of course, employers could include arbitration clauses in employment contracts for everyone, but the speed, lower cost and easier access to a hearing might encourage more people to come forward.

Heart of the Storm

Despite the low number of age discrimination claims being filed, HR professionals know too well that quantity means little when you're in the heart of the storm. Even one case wears HR professionals and other managers down. And almost everyone has at least one. "It's a huge drain on an organization's resources; it eats away in terms of morale and productivity," says Michael Buda, SPHR, a consultant in Atlanta who served for seven years as executive vice president of HR and legal counsel at Jackson Healthcare Solutions in Alpharetta, Ga., a health care staffing and software company.

For HR managers, a charge filing from the EEOC marks the onset of a time-consuming, emotionally draining journey. Some insights into the agency will help you prepare—and endure.

A charge filing marks the onset of a time-consuming, emotionally draining journey.

America's Watchdog

EEOC officials have near-impossible jobs. Citizens ask them to serve as champions for workers who see themselves as victims of discrimination, but the agency has limited leverage and resources. For example, it has the power to investigate and conciliate claims, issue findings of "reasonable cause," and bring cases to court. But it lacks authority to render final judgments on the merits of cases or issue financial awards to aggrieved parties.

Hence, EEOC officials learn to cherry-pick from among the charges, looking for obvious winners, especially those that will have an impact beyond the complainant and, perhaps most important, generate publicity, serving as a deterrent.

As complaints flow in, they're assigned to three baskets: Basket A, which contains potentially high-profile claims and those where discrimination seems apparent; Basket B, which holds claims that could go either way; and Basket C, which contains claims that don't look promising. When employers receive a charge, they are not told what basket it falls in. For cases in baskets B and C, the EEOC generally offers parties a chance to settle through mediation.

The EEOC is not the only game in town. Most states and many municipalities have comparable agencies. Their powers vary depending on state laws. Most have work-sharing arrangements with EEOC officials, so claims can be handled interchangeably.

If the complainant has a lawyer, the lawyer often will try to select the forum that can generate the best payday. For example, under the ADEA, when discrimination is found and the employer has acted willfully, the victim may be awarded "liquidated damages" of double the salary he or she lost. In some state courts, such as California and Ohio, the plaintiff may be awarded more-lucrative "punitive" damages.

Toll Booth to a Big Payday

While the EEOC or a state or municipal agency investigates, mediates and conciliates, plaintiffs' lawyers wait in the wings. They can't move cases to court until the agency issues a right-to-sue letter giving them access to what plaintiffs yearn for: a jury of their peers. On occasion, the EEOC may issue a letter soon after the charge is filed. However, it does not have to provide one until the case has been in-house for at least 180 days while EEOC officials investigate "reasonable cause" to suspect the employer has violated the ADEA. In at least one state, Ohio, a complainant can bypass agency consideration and file directly in court, however.

When the EEOC finds reasonable cause, it may go on to federal court on behalf of the complainant, who may choose to also be represented by private counsel. But with only 200 attorneys for the whole country, the EEOC initiates relatively few cases. For example, in 2007, a year when EEOC investigators found reasonable cause in 625 age discrimination cases, the agency's general counsel filed 32 lawsuits, the majority alleging discriminatory discharge. Overall, in 2006, for all types of discrimination, the EEOC filed 383 suits. Of these, 339 ended in consent decrees or settlements and 11 were resolved by voluntary dismissal; of the 33 cases actually resolved by court orders, the EEOC prevailed nine times.

Questionable Victories

When the EEOC finds "no reasonable cause," as it did 10,002 times in 2007, employers feel vindicated. That number represents 62 percent of the age discrimination cases resolved that year. But plaintiffs' lawyers soldier on, undaunted. "Some employers think they're home free, but they're not," says Janet Hill of Hill & Associates in Atlanta, former president of the National Employment Lawyers Association of San Francisco. EEOC lawyers are "hugely overworked, and they don't have the personnel to do complete investigations. The fact that they don't find cause indicates little about the merits of the cases."

During an EEOC investigation, the employer's response to the charge is not shared with the complainant. Unless attorneys for both sides talk or unless a lawsuit is filed, the complainant's lawyer may not know the strength of the employer's defense. Usually, it's during the discovery phase of a suit that the complainant's lawyer knows for sure whether he has a case worth pursuing.

"If I gave up on every case where the EEOC or a state EEO agency didn't find reasonable cause, I wouldn't have a career in employment law," says Rik Siro, principal at Siro Law in Kansas City, Mo. Siro recently won a $2.7 million court verdict for a client who was denied a reasonable cause finding by the Missouri Commission on Human Rights. "Ninety-nine percent of the time when I take a case, there was no reasonable cause." In 2007, the EEOC found reasonable cause in 3.9 percent of the age discrimination cases investigated.

"Employers always try to make a big deal about reasonable cause findings, but judges usually refuse to admit the result into evidence because juries might think the EEOC [officials] investigate more than they actually do," says Dennis Egan, of The Popham Law Firm PC in Kansas City, Mo. Egan, who has been a lawyer for 30 years, has represented plaintiffs in 92 jurytrials, winning 72. He says the EEOC failed to find reasonable cause in all of those cases.

But winning a jury trial is one thing; surviving preliminary steps leading to the trial is another. More than 70 percent of federal cases, including those under the ADEA, never get to a jury; they're dismissed by judges granting motions in favor of the employer. "Most court cases settle," says Condon McGlothlen, a partner at Seyfarth Shaw in Chicago. "Of those that don't, employers usually prevail by winning a motion for a summary judgment. At that point in the process, the judge is presented extensive documentation from both sides and is required to apply it in the most favorable light from the plaintiff's perspective."

Winning a jury trail is one thing; surviving preliminary steps leading to the trial is another. More than 70 percent of federal cases . . . are dismissed by judges granting motions in favor of the employer.

In 2007, through settlements and conciliations, the EEOC collected $66.8 million, an average of $4,140 for every claim filed. In addition, the negative publicity that companies suffer after agreeing to high-priced settlements—rather than litigating—serve as not-so-subtle signals to employers of what happens when the EEOC puts them under its microscope.

Sources of Complaints

Complaints of age discrimination generally involve hiring, treatment at work, or termination and dismissal. Dismissal cases account for more than half the cases filed and represent the ones most likely to move beyond the agency to court.

"These cases account for 99 percent of the litigation because that's where the money is," Gordon says. "People who don't get hired usually don't bring lawsuits because in those cases all the employer has to show is a more qualified hire. And people who are still working tend to keep their problems to themselves."

Lisa Whitmore, SPHR, director of HR for Johnson Controls in Waukesha, Wis., an automotive products company with 140,000 employees, agrees. "Our cases almost always are termination cases," she says.

Predominantly, age discrimination cases are based on disparate treatment—requiring the complainant to demonstrate how the employer or its agents acted or failed to act because of age bias or stereotyping, says Dianna Johnston, an EEOC assistant legal counsel in Washington, D.C. The employer must show that reasons for the actions—right or wrong—were not tainted by discrimination. Typical termination cases might encompass scenarios such as the following:

- The person supported a mainframe computer that's being phased out and replaced with a system that he's unable to operate.
- The pace of work has increased, and the person is unable or unwilling to keep up.
- The person is not excited about her job; she has lost her spark and is not performing as well as in the past.

Disparate Impact

Beginning in 2005, the U.S. Supreme Court in *Smith v. City of Jackson* established that the ADEA included a right to sue under a theory of disparate impact. In such cases—and usually when reductions in force occur—if the complainant can demonstrate that a disproportionate number of older workers were laid off, the employer is required to demonstrate that the decisions were made for legitimate, nondiscriminatory business reasons.

So far, employers have been successful in defending all disparate impact cases that have gone to trial. "If your business reason is not outright discriminatory, you'll be OK," McGlothlen says. "Since the *City of Jackson* case, virtually every federal court has bought the defendant's story."

But court decisions don't tell the whole story. At least some cases—class actions involving hundreds of employees—have settled without employers admitting liability. One age discrimination case involving 1,697 former employees laid off by Sprint Nextel settled in 2005 for $57 million, with attorneys for the plaintiffs walking off with a cool $19.4 million in legal fees. "When companies are having trouble hewing to the nutty imperative of Wall Street, they have to slash and burn," says Egan, one of the plaintiffs' lawyers. "If you leave management undirected to decide who should stay or go, they'll drift into saying, 'I'm going to keep the person who is blessed with plenty of runway ahead of them.'"

The Economy's Effect

With the economy in turmoil, employment lawyers on both sides report that the EEOC's prophecy of an increase in age discrimination cases may still come true. "There's a lag between the start of an economic downturn and the legal consequences," McGlothlen says. "We're seeing a steady stream of EEOC charges and lawsuits alleging age discrimination and expect to see more."

The prospect of more claims—no matter the merit—discourages HR professionals. "The entire organization has to be engaged in pulling together documentation, meeting with counsel, interviewing witnesses, answering interrogatories; it's an enormous burden," McChriston says. "In the end, we win, but when you factor in the lost time and expense, what did we win?"

Critical Thinking

1. Why have age discrimination suits decreased in recent years?
2. What is the economic impact of age discrimination suits on the employer?
3. What is meant by "disparate impact"?

ROBERT J. GROSSMAN, a contributing editor of *HR Magazine,* is a lawyer and a professor of management studies at Marist College in Poughkeepsie, N.Y.

Cost Reductions, Downsizing-related Layoffs, and HR Practices

FRANCO GANDOLFI

Introduction

Organizational decimation, or downsizing, has been a pervasive managerial practice for the past three decades. If a firm finds itself in financial difficulties, the widely accepted corporate panacea has been to cut personnel. While strong empirical evidence suggests that reduction-inforce (RIF) activities rarely return the anticipated economic and organizational gains (Cascio. Young, and Morris, 1997), there is increased understanding and awareness that downsized companies are forced to deal with the human and societal after-effects, also known as secondary effects, in a post-downsizing phase (Gandolfi, 2007). Research shows that the human consequences of layoffs are costly and devastating for individuals, their families, and entire communities (Macky, 2004). While workforce reductions cannot always be completely avoided, downsizing-related layoffs must be a managerial tool of absolute last rather than first resort (Gandolfi, 2006).

During an economic downturn, a company must carefully consider its options and assess the feasibility and applicability of cost-reduction alternatives prior to adopting RIF-related layoffs. While a large body of research presenting and discussing the alternatives to downsizing has emerged (Littler, 1998; Mirabal and De Young, 2005), there is still a lack of conceptual understanding of downsizing-related layoffs as part of an organization's cost-reduction stages (Gandolfi, 2008). It is vital for a firm to factor in the concept of cost-reduction and recognize the specific cost-reduction stage that characterizes the firms' current business position and environment. Ideally, a company should be in a position to determine the expected duration and severity of the business downturn as accurately as possible. To perform that task successfully, the executives need to know the cost-cutting phase that the firm is currently in (Vernon. 2003). A firm's cost-reduction stage refers to the time-frame the organization requires to be able to reduce operational expenditures

(George, 2004). In reality, however, accurately forecasting a business downturn can be extremely difficult. Thus, firms have a natural tendency to react to rather than anticipate economic declines (Gandolfi. 2006).

The primary objective of this paper is to present a methodology enabling firms to minimize, defer, or avoid the adoption of RIF, layoffs, and downsizing-related activities. The research introduces and showcases a conceptual framework presenting the cost-reduction stages of a firm coupled with a brief introduction of contemporary human resources (HR) practices that some firms have adopted. Fundamentally, the paper builds upon Vernon's (2003), George's (2004), and Gandolfi's (2008) work of three cost-reduction stages: short-range, mid-range, and long-range phases. Technically speaking, the article constitutes a review and extension of previously published work. The underlying conceptual framework of the cost-reduction stages is depicted in Figure 1.

Cost-reduction Stages

The conceptual framework shown in Figure 1 encompasses three timeframe-related phases commanding several internal cost adjustments that have produced a variety of stage-related HR practices. It is important to note that the HR practices are cumulative. In other words, the practices in each stage are not unique to the actual phase, but applicable in subsequent phases in a cumulative fashion.

First Stage: Short-range Cost Adjustments

The first stage of the cost-reduction framework represents short-range cost adjustments in response to a short, temporary decline in business activities (Vernon, 2003). These business slowdowns are expected to last less than six months (Gandolfi, 2008). Most likely, the firm resorts to minor, moderate cost-reduction measures in this stage.

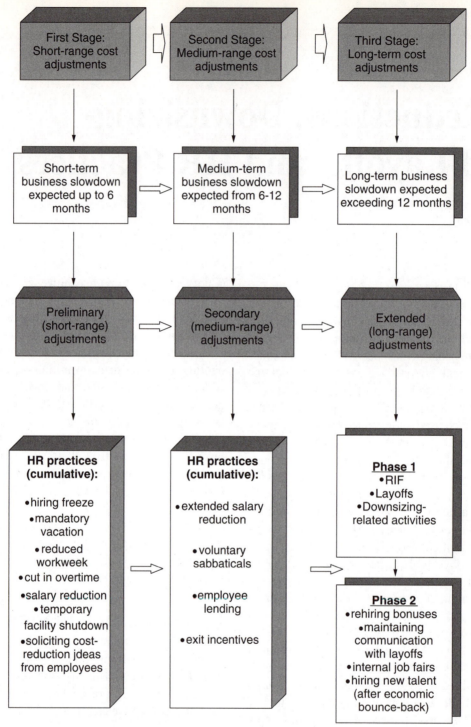

Figure 1   Conceptual framework of cost-reduction stages.

Source: Adapted from Vernon (2003), George (2004), and Gandolfi (2008).

These preliminary adjustments should enable the firm to shun RIF-related layoffs and involuntary cutbacks and return to normal business activity within four to six months (Gandolfi, 2008). Typically, this phase originates with an unexpected drop in sales or a decline in sales forecast. It is characterized by short-term expenditure adjustments to prevent a medium-range downturn or a more lasting, long-range decline. The immediate recognition of a temporary business slip and the resolute engagement in preliminary cost-reduction methods should allow the firm to focus its operations in a cost-sensitive mode for a quick recovery (Vernon, 2003).

The probability of success for the short-range cost adjustments hinges on a number of factors: First, senior management must be able to articulate the business necessity for the cost-adjustment measures effectively and stress the short timeframe of the strategy. A firm's ability to convey the message that preliminary cost-reduction measures at the present time will likely prevent RIF-related layoffs in the future is critical. Second, the HR's role is to communicate decisions made by the board of directors to the entire workforce promptly and to implement the cost-reduction methods swiftly. Third, the employees' flexibility in allowing the firm to modify cost structures increases the chance of success for the planned cost alterations. Therefore, a firm's capacity to overcome a business downturn in the first stage will depend to a large degree on its organization's ability to respond to the new environment by immediately and resolutely modifying expenditures (Vernon, 2003).

Suggested HR Practices for Short-range Cost Adjustments

A review of the literature and the popular press reveals several HR-related practices that firms have implemented for preliminary cost reductions. The following is a non-exhaustive overview and explanation of some of the approaches suggested by scholars and implemented by firms in the global corporate landscape.

• Hiring freeze

A hiring freeze is a mild form of downsizing that reduces labor costs in the short term (Littler, 1998). However, a hiring freeze does not imply that there is no hiring activity at all. Some firms hire new employees while cutting jobs at the same time (Vernon, 2003). While this practice may make sense in terms of supplying the firm with key personnel, it tends to send a confusing message to the workforce. As an example, in its latest attempt to fight rising jet fuel costs and a deteriorating U.S. economy, American Airlines imposed an immediate hiring freeze on all management and support staff (Maxon, 2008).

• Mandatory vacation

Mandatory vacation involves requiring employees to use their accrued vacation days or requiring them to take a number of unpaid vacation days during a certain time period. While employees might not want to be told when and how to use their entitlements, they will nonetheless appreciate the reaffirmed job security (Vernon, 2003). At the time of writing. Chrysler plans a corporate-wide shutdown of its U.S. operations during two weeks in July 2008 to improve the automaker's efficiency and boost productivity (Govreau, 2008).

• Reduced workweek

Firms sometimes resort to a reduced workweek. This may translate into a reduction from 40 to 35 or fewer hours, thereby reducing short-term payroll expenditures. While most employees appreciate being able to spend more time with their families, a reduced paycheck is not always welcomed. Also, employees may find that the same amount of work still needs to be performed while they spend less time on the job (Gandolfi, 2008). Nucor Steel Corporation in South Carolina has avoided layoffs for 35 years by resorting to two and three workdays for its employees during downturns (George, 2004). In a similar vein, in 2008, workers at a St. Thomas automotive parts plant in the U.K. voted a reduction in their workweek rather than see 200 employees leave permanently (De Bono, 2008).

• Cut in overtime pay

Minimizing or abolishing overtime pay for employees can be a powerful technique of reducing operational costs in the short term (Vernon, 2003). Firms may institute an across-the-board (i.e., all employees) abolition or confine the cut to selected categories, such as nonmanagerial, blue-collar, or salaried employees (Gandolfi, 2008). In 2004, GM and Ford and car-supplier Visteon Corporation slashed overtime pay for most employees indefinitely (Dybis and Garsten, 2004).

• Salary reduction

Salary reduction methods have been standard practice for firms experiencing unexpected financial pressure. Whereas salary reductions mitigate financial concerns in the short run, extended salary reductions can negatively affect employee morale and loyalty. Also, while companywide salary reductions prevent layoffs, there is a clear risk that top performers will be encouraged to leave for competitors that dangle superior compensation (Gandolfi, 2008). In 2006, White Electronics Designs introduced salary reductions of 5% for salaried employees and 10% for management, while the hourly workers remained unaffected. In 2006, a collation of Intel managers agreed to take a temporary 100% pay cut to avoid permanent layoffs. Prior to that, Intel announced that it had planned to cut 10,000 employees, including 1,000 managers (Paul, 2006).

• Temporary facility shutdown

Temporary facility shutdowns occur when a work site closes for a designated period of time, while some administrative functions still perform (Vernon, 2003). A shutdown allows employees to have time off without using their vacation days. While overall company production decreases, the firm can achieve considerable costs savings, thereby avoiding layoffs. In early 2008, Aleris International shut down its rolling mill production in Virginia to align production with demand. As a consequence, production for customers was phased out and transferred to other facilities within the U.S. (Aleris, 2008).

- **Soliciting cost-reduction ideas from employees**

Employees appreciate the opportunity to make a positive impact on their workplace and environment. Firms frequently solicit cost-reduction ideas from employees, who are often creative in producing such solutions. This HR practice has proven to be most effective when employees are able to make suggestions in the early stages of cost cutting (Vernon, 2003). At Martin Heyman Associates, all professional construction consultants are encouraged to contribute cost-reduction ideas. Unfortunately, many executives still do not realize that employees are the best source of such ideas because workers on the job are in a prime position to identify and recognize waste (Yorke, 2005).

This overview has shown that there are numerous HR tools at an executive's disposal to reduce short-term expenditures. While some firms have come up with innovative ideas, others have used layoffs as a very first resort. Again, it must be understood that the techniques introduced in this stage are cumulative and applicable in other stages. Moreover, the utilization of each HR practice is unique in that each selected tool will have certain consequences that need to be carefully considered by management prior to adoption.

Second Stage: Medium-range Cost Adjustments

The second stage of the cost-reduction framework comprises medium-term cost adjustments in response to a medium-range business downturn exceeding six months (Vernon, 2003) and up to 12 months (Gandolfi, 2008). These secondary cost-reduction adjustments are frequently signaled through extended company-wide or industry-wide forecasts of diminished sales activity. If properly recognized and executed, the firm may be able to transition to mid-range cost adjustments and thus prevent long-term, RIF-related layoffs and forced downsizing. In this phase constituencies need to recognize that deeper cost-reduction strategies may be required to avert downsizing-related layoffs. Senior management must be able to present the purpose and objectives of the expenditure adjustments convincingly to the entire workforce. This should ensure employee buy-in and commitment. Adopting HR practices in this stage could potentially alter employees' work environment. Therefore, the HR department will play an essential role in the conduct and transition of these practices (Gandolfi, 2008).

Suggested HR Practices for Medium-range Cost Adjustments

A review of the literature and the popular press reveals several HR-related practices that corporations have used trying to obtain secondary cost reductions. The following is a non-exhaustive summary of practices recommended by scholars and introduced in the corporate landscape.

- **Extended salary reductions**

Extending salary reductions can be a method of choice if an economic downturn exceeds six months (Vernon, 2003). While the extension of salary reductions can negatively affect employee commitment and morale, advocates stress that employees would prefer a smaller income temporarily than a permanent loss of their jobs. As with short-term salary reductions, there is a risk that high-performing individuals are encouraged to pursue external employment opportunities (Gandolfi. 2008). Firms have generally been innovative regarding altering variable pay options. Specifically, while some firms balance the reduced salaries by distributing once-a-year payments over 12 months, others substitute stock awards for variable cash payment. For example, U.S. firm 415 Production offered an overall 5% pay cut or a four-day work week reflecting the appropriate decrease in pay to its employees (Morss, 2008).

- **Voluntary sabbaticals**

Voluntary sabbaticals, also called furloughs, allow salaried employees to take voluntary leaves for a designated period of time. Companies may offer sabbaticals with considerably reduced or no pay. Most firms continue to provide benefits during sabbaticals. Sabbaticals enable firms to reduce their medium-term expenditure and can be effective in avoiding downsizing-related layoffs (Gandolfi, 2008). While employees may feel motivated and re-energized upon their return, HR professionals point out that medium-and long-term sabbaticals may cause employees to lose their leading edge and to return with outdated skills. Interestingly, evidence suggests that firms offer generous sabbaticals during times of economic growth but refrain from this HR practice during tough financial periods (Vernon, 2003). Practical examples abound. For example, in 2001, consulting firm Accenture announced that 800 employees qualified for a special voluntary sabbatical program, while 600 employees were going to be laid off permanently (Taub, 2001). In 2001, Information and Communication Mobile, a Siemens division, offered its employees a one- year time-out at reduced pay without losing their jobs permanently (Perera, 2001). Siemens was thus able to reduce costs without losing high- performing employees during difficult economic times.

- **Employee lending**

With this HR practice, the current employer lends an employee to another employer firm for a set period of time while continuing to pay salary and providing benefits

(Vernon, 2003). The borrowing firm, which can be a competitor, in return, reimburses the lending company for part or all of the salary. While employee lending can dramatically decrease medium-range expenditure of the lending firm, some employees may not wish to work for a third party. There is also the risk that the borrowing firm decides to hire the employee permanently once the contracted period is lapsed. As a consequence, the lending firm would loose a critical knowledge base (Gandolfi, 2008). Texas Instruments engaged in lending HR staffers to vendors for up to eight months with the intention of bringing them back to their original jobs at the end of that period. The supplier reimbursed Texas Instruments for their staffers' salaries during the loan period and agreed not to offer them permanent jobs (Morss, 2008).

- **Exit incentives**

Exit incentive options give employees the option of leaving the firm and collecting severance pay or taking early retirement (Vernon, 2003). This strategy enables firms to target jobs while recognizing employees for their service and helps the firm retain the remaining employees (Gandolfi, 2008). Exit incentives can be costly and may create an entitlement mentality for the remaining workforce in the future (George, 2004). In 2007, technology-outsourcing firm EDS (Electronic Data Systems) offered extra retirement benefits to its 12,000 U.S. employees in an offer to accept early retirement (EDS, 2007).

Corporate leaders need to be innovative about reducing medium-term expenditures. As with the previous stage, some firms have demonstrated creativity and resourcefulness regarding the design and implementation of medium-range cost-reduction practices. Anecdotal evidence indicates a natural tendency for firms to resort to layoffs hastily by default without considering legitimate alternatives (Gandolfi, 2008).

Third Stage: Long-range Cost Adjustments

The third stage of the cost-reduction framework represents long-term adjustments that are necessary if a firm experiences a prolonged business downturn exceeding 12 months. This stage may be recognized through an extended decline of current and projected customer demand or extremely volatile economic conditions (Vernon, 2003). The third stage generally requires extended expenditure adjustments by the firm (Gandolfi, 2008). In this timeframe RIF, layoffs, and downsizing-related activities are frequently inevitable. The third stage has two phases (see Figure 1). Phase 1 contains workforce reduction strategies that firms commonly adopt after a prolonged business downturn. While RIF and downsizing activities should always be seen as a last resort, firms should avoid mass layoffs at all costs (Macky 2004; Gandolfi, 2007). Companies who find themselves engaged in deep workforce cuts must adopt HR practices that instill loyalty and commitment in the remaining and exiting workforces (Vernon, 2003). In contrast. Phase 2 encompasses HR activities that aim to re-attract formerly laid off individuals and hire new employees in a post-downsizing period. This presupposes that the RIF have been implemented, that the business downturn has ended and reversed, and that the firm is able and willing to re-hire.

Suggested HR Practices for Long-range Cost Adjustments

Firms forced to embrace permanent RIF and layoffs have reported mixed results. While the execution of downsizing promises immediate financial relief, considerable empirical evidence demonstrates that downsizing-related strategies do not automatically translate into improved organizational performance (Littler, 1998; Macky, 2004). Such strategies have significant secondary consequences for the firm and its stakeholders (Gandolfi, 2006). While downsizing and RIF-related layoffs should always be a strategy of absolute last resort (Gandolfi, 2007), it is clear that layoffs are at times warranted, desirable, or unavoidable. Once the firm has conducted RIF-related activities, the firm will need to re-position itself to be able to re-attract those laid off or hire new employees. Again, this presumes that the economy has bounced back sufficiently and that the firm is in a position to hire again. Some firms re-hire formerly laid off employees, whereas others opt to return to the labor market and seek out new talent. How does the firm attract previous employees? The following constitutes a brief summary of three commonly-used practices.

- **Rehiring bonuses**

While some firms provide a monetary rehiring bonus for veterans to return within a specified period, others hire laid-off employees as external consultants. In some cases, firms realize that they cut too many or the wrong employees, while in other cases management decides to hire back after the economic downturn (Vernon, 2003). Evidence suggests that employees and consultants return to the downsized firm with improved monetary rewards (Gandolfi, 2006). For instance, in 2001 and after two rounds of deep layoffs, Charles Schwab Corp. offered a $7,500 hiring bonus for any previously downsized employee rehired by the firm within 18 months following the layoffs (Morss, 2008).

- **Maintaining communication with laid-off employees**

Firms frequently make a concerted effort to maintain friendly relations with laid-off employees (Vernon, 2003). Modem-day technology, including Internet forums, 24-7 hotlines, and e-mail, provides effective ways to foster and sustain positive employer-employee relationships (Lublin, 2007). This is particularly important if firms intend to rehire the former employees when the economic climate has improved.

- **Internal job fairs**

Firms should make every possible attempt to retain high-performing employees (Gandolfi, 2008). A powerful method is an internal job fair, where firms host events to help place and redeploy downsized employees within the company. For example, the Ford Motor Company is currently putting on internal job fairs in its U.S. plants to entice employees to find new careers beyond the assembly-line (Vlasic, 2008).

Concluding Comments

This paper has presented a methodology of cost-reduction stages enabling firms to minimize, delay, or circumvent reductions-in-force, layoffs, and downsizing-related activities. The depicted conceptual framework is an extension of Vernon's (2003), George's (2004), and Gandolfi's (2008) original work on cost-reduction stages, including an expansion of the third stage incorporating two distinct phases. The research has shown that the key to responsible cost reduction and the selection of appropriate cost reduction methods can be found in the alignment of a firm's cost reduction practices with its current cost-reduction stage. The paper has further established that it is difficult for a firm to accurately forecast the duration and magnitude of a business downturn. Consequently, firms have a natural tendency to respond reactively rather than to anticipate economic declines.

References

Aleris. (2008). Aleris announces temporary shutdown of its Richmond, Virginia, rolling mill facility. Retrieved from www.prnewswire.com/cgi-bin/stories,pl? ACCT =]09&STORY=/www/story/Ü2-22-2008/ 00047 60651&EDATE=

Cascio. W. F.. Young. C., and Morris, J. (1997). Financial consequences of employment-change decisions in major U.S. corporations. *Academy of Management Journal, 40(5),* 1175-1189.

DeBono. N. (2008, March 18). Presstran workers vote for reduced work week. *Sun Media.* Retrieved from http://Ifpress.ca/cgi-bin/ publish.cgi?p=2281OO&s=wheels

Dybis, K., and Garsten, E. (2004, March 18). Michigan firms cut overtime. *The Detroit News.* Retrieved from www .detnews,com/2004/specialreport/0403/18/a0196041,htm

EDS. (2007, September 13). EDS offers exit incentives lo 12,000 workers. *The New York Times.* Retrieved from www.nytimes.com/2007/09/13/technology/13data. html?partner=rssnyt&emc=rss

Gandolfi, F. (2006). *Corporate downsizing demystified: A scholarly analysis of a business phenomenon,* Hyderabad. India: ICFAI University Press.

Gandolfi, F. (2007). How do large Australian and Swiss banks implement downsizing? *Journal of Management & Organization, 13*(2), 145–159.

Gandolfi, F. (2008, July/August). HR strategies that can take the sting out of downsizing-related layoffs. *Ivey Business Journal.*

George, J. (2004). Cutting costs: should personnel be the first to go? *Employment Practices Solution.* Retrieved from www.epexperts. com/modules.php?op=modload&name=News&file=article& sid=1409

Govreau, J. (2008, March 14). Chrysler announces mandatory two-week shutdown of all plans in July 2008. *Market Watch from Dow Jones.* Retrieved from www.marketwatch.com/news/ story/chrysler-announces-mandatory-two-week-shutdown/ siory.aspx?guid=%7BD7228E3E-9177-4EC7-A0EB- 3946EAA50A66%7D

Littler, C.R. (1998). Downsizing organisations: The dilemmas of change. *Human Resources Management Bulletin.* CCH Australia Limited, Sydney.

Lublin, J. (2007, September 24). Employers see value in helping those laid off. *The Watt Street Journal Online.* Retrieved from http://online.wsj.com/public/article/SB119058596757936693 .html

Macky, K. (2004). Organizational downsizing and redundancies: The New Zealand workers' experience. *New Zealand Journal of Employment Relations, 29*(1), 63-87,

Maxon, T. (2008, April 4). American Airlines imposes hiring freeze on management and support staff. *The Dallas Morning News.* Retrieved from www.dallasnews.com/shared content/dws/bus/ stories/040508dnbusaafreeze. 368d67e.html

Mendels, P. (2001, April 18). Downsizing pay, not people. *BusinessWeek.* Retrieved from www.businessweek.com/ careers/content/apr2001/ca20010418_060,htm

Mirabal, N., and De Young, R. (2005). Downsizing as a strategic intervention. *Journal of American Academy of Business, 6(1).* 39—5.

Morss, R. (2008). Creative layoff policy and alternatives to layoffs, *Salary.com.* Retrieved from www.salary.com/personal/ layoutscripts/psnl_articles.asp?tab=psn&cat=cat011&ser= ser032&part=par276

Paul. (2006), 100 % pay reduction for all Intel employees. Retrieved from www.starkedsf.com/archives/100-pay-reduction-for-all- intel-employees-a-tnt-special-report/

Perera, R. (2001, August 31). Siemens offers workers 'lime outs ' to save cash. *IDG News Service.* Retrieved from www.thestandard .com/article/0,1902,28858.00.html

Taub, P. (2001, June 7). Accenture to cut 600 jobs, *CFO.com.* Retrieved from www.cfo.com/article.cfm/2996624?f=search

Vernon, L. (2003, March). The downsizing dilemma; a manager's toolkit for avoiding layoffs. *Society for Human Resources Management (SHRM),* White Paper.

Vlasic, B. (2008. February 26), Ford is pushing buyouts lo workers. *The New York Times.* Retrieved from www.nytimes.com/2008/02/26/business/26ford.html?_r=1&oref=slogin

Yorke, C. (2005). Why employees are the best source of cost-cutting ideas. Ezine Articles. Retrieved from http://ezinearticles.com/?Why-Employees-Are-the-Best-Source-of-Cost-cutting-Ideas&id=66695

Critical Thinking

1. As an employee, what is your opinion of reduced salaries, voluntary sabbaticals or furloughs, or reduced workweek to help avoid layoffs?

2. As an employer, what must you do to maintain satisfactory morale in the face of solutions such as those listed in this article?

3. Is implementing solutions such as these ethically preferable to layoffs even when they affect all employees instead of just a percentage of employees?

DR. GANDOLFI, currently director of the MBA/EMBA programs at Regent University, specializes in human resource management and change management and regularly advises corporations in Australia and Switzerland. His published books include *Corporate Downsizing Demystified: A Scholarly Analysis of a Business Phenomenon.*

The Factory That Refused to Die

In an Ohio town with rampant unemployment, the mayor, a worker, and 12 local families fought to save Norwalk Furniture.

NANETTE BYRNES

The Norwalk Custom Order Furniture factory in Norwalk, Ohio, is 430,000 square feet, enough to encompass four football fields. On a rainy June afternoon, though, the facility is quiet—except for the sounds of a radio playing 1970s rock classics and the occasional hum of a sewing machine or pop of a staple gun. This time last year more than 300 people worked on the floor, producing hundreds of pieces of furniture a day. Now the headcount is 59.

That Norwalk is still producing furniture at all, however, is a business miracle. The 107-year-old manufacturer has been buffeted by the housing bust, Chinese competition, its own poor judgment, and the credit crunch—a toxic brew if there ever was one. Last year Norwalk's owners, the fourth generation of the founding Gerken family, gave up the fight and closed the factory's doors, unable to meet the demands of lenders. Dozens of retailers who relied on the company stood to go out of business themselves.

But instead of becoming one more piece of bad news floating on a sea of economic disasters, Norwalk has emerged as a survivor of sorts. An unlikely coalition of investors, factory workers, and politicians have joined together to reopen the factory. Now the business is above water, if just barely.

These people and thousands of fighters like them are the difference between 9.5% national unemployment and something even worse. Companies big and small are struggling to deal with the double whammy of slowing sales and restricted credit. U.S. bankruptcy filings surged to 7,874 in May, a 55% rise from a year earlier, according to bankruptcy tracker AACER. With loan delinquencies soaring too, banks—along with CIT Group and other other commercial lenders—are raising their credit standards: Federal Reserve figures show that banks have tightened up on small business lending for 10 consecutive quarters. "It's very difficult for banks to embrace lending to smaller businesses," says Robert Coleman, editor of the La Canada (Calif.)-based *Coleman Report,* which tracks small business loans.

Against that grim backdrop Norwalk has somehow managed to survive. The company was founded in 1902, when upholsterer Charles Edward Gerken first crafted a chair for his son, Raymond. Over the decades, Norwalk came to own all or part

of 13 different companies, from wood exporters to low-end furniture makers. None, however, was as profitable as the core custom-order furniture business, which produced its upscale wares in the Norwalk factory in Ohio and sold them through 57 franchises around the country and through independent dealers that carried multiple brands.

Earlier this decade foreign competition in the furniture industry intensified, particularly at the low end. Imports from China rose 154% from 2001 to 2005, to more than $12 billion. But because the strong housing market was fueling demand for high-end furniture, Norwalk kept production steady.

When the real estate market crashed, the company's fortunes quickly changed. Sales plunged from $163 million at the peak in 2005 to $137 million in 2007, according to investment bank Beacon Associates. In the first four months of 2008, the company had revenues of just $40 million and was on track to lose $4.9 million for the year.

Making matters worse, Jim and Bill Gerken, the fourth-generation cousins running the company, were slow to cut costs and pare the losses. Instead they tapped their $13 million credit line to keep the business afloat. "Most of what happened to Norwalk was our own mismanagement," admits Bill Gerken. "I'd love to blame someone else, but we screwed up."

In early 2008 the Gerkens grew concerned about Norwalk's performance. They persuaded factory workers to take a cut in benefits, hired restructuring firm Morris Anderson, and in April submitted a turnaround plan to their bank of 12 years, Dallas-based Comerica. But the bankers were reluctant to give the Gerkens all the money they asked for and demanded a personal guarantee as collateral, says Bill Gerken. The cousins balked. "Why would we sign those personal guarantees?" asks Gerken. "That would have been insane."

Banks, of course, were dealing with their own nightmare in 2008: the credit crunch. Comerica, which was headquartered in Detroit for 158 years before moving to Texas in 2007, held a worrisome number of loans made to hard-hit manufacturers in the upper Midwest and was heavily exposed to the California real estate meltdown. In July 2008, Comerica announced that its quarterly net income had dropped 71% from a year earlier (though its capital position remained strong). One day later it pulled Norwalk's credit line. "They were doing what other banks were doing at the time," says Norwalk's controller, Peg Whitehurst. A spokesman for Comerica says the bank was trying to find a solution for Norwalk outside of bankruptcy, even though the company was in default on its loan, and says Norwalk management's decisions led to its problems.

Without the credit line, the Gerkens could no longer meet payroll, and on July 18, 2008, they shut the factory doors, seemingly for good.

That's when Norwalk's mayor, Sue Lesch, sprang into action. Lesch grew up on a farm in nearby Peru, Ohio, and was the owner of a construction company and served as a fund-raiser for the Catholic Church before taking office in 2004. Since then she has spent much of her time on economic matters. With a population of 16,000, Norwalk is the biggest town in a county whose unemployment rate sits at 15.4%, among the worst in the country. "We've just been hit and hit and hit," says Lesch. Although she attends a prayer group and tries to walk every day to relieve stress, "I don't sleep well," she says.

Lesch focused much of her attention last summer on trying to save Norwalk Furniture. "This company not only was the largest factory in town—theirs were the best jobs in town," she says. Lesch repeatedly called the bank to badger it into reconsidering its credit decision. She drove to Columbus to lobby state officials for an emergency loan and to hunt up potential buyers. She assigned her business development team to canvass local investors as well. The team found several groups of potential investors, but Comerica wasn't negotiating.

When factory worker Kim Gross heard that Comerica was refusing to talk with potential buyers, she decided to organize a protest. The mother of three has deep connections to Norwalk Furniture. She has been sewing cushion backs and pillows there for 20 years. Her grandmother worked there before her. And Norwalk is where she met her husband, Jeff, a plant manager. Gross persuaded 40 fellow employees to take three pickup trucks filled with armchairs and sofas to Comerica's Detroit offices, two hours away. When they got there they put the furniture on the sidewalk, carrying signs and marching in hopes of attracting media coverage. "We thought, 'This is crazy. Why not let these investors make an offer?'" TV stations and newspapers sent reporters, and by that afternoon the bank had agreed to talk to potential investors.

More than 1,000 miles away, near Denver, retailer Jodi Zippo's once-thriving business was crashing. Zippo, a former telecom executive, and her husband, Rob, a sales manager for an electronics manufacturer, had put their life's savings into a Norwalk furniture store in an upscale Colorado mall. Jodi had left the telecom field in 2001 to spend more time with her two young daughters. But she'd always wanted to build a business of her own, and she had a knack for interior design. In March 2007 she bought the Norwalk store—and quickly tripled the average sale amount, pushing the outlet from the 46th most productive of Norwalk's 57 franchise stores to No. 3. Business was so good that Zippo paid down $125,000 of her $415,000 small business loan, also held by Comerica, in just 12 months. But when Norwalk lost its credit line and closed, her business ground to a halt.

Zippo thought of shutting the store but was distraught at the idea of running into people who'd given her money for furniture and then gotten stiffed. Her husband told her it was O.K. to fail, but that only panicked her more. "I said back to him, 'Don't talk to me that way. It's not going to fail. I don't fail,'" Zippo recalls. "Deep down I thought, 'Oh my god. We're going to fail.'"

The agitating in Ohio was paying off, though. On July 28, Comerica agreed to meet with potential buyers. Over the course of a day, in a conference room at Cleveland's airport, the bankers talked with a series of private equity firms and individual investors. Comerica was there at the request of Ohio Lieutenant Governor Lee Fisher, who on Lesch's urging had put a $1.8 million loan offer on the table. Eventually one group of private equity investors made an acceptable bid, and while they did due diligence through the month of August, Norwalk reopened its doors and resumed operations.

But by Labor Day the deal was in trouble. The investors have since filed suit in Huron County Common Pleas Court accusing Comerica of demanding they complete their due diligence faster than was possible, among other things. On Sept. 16, after the two sides couldn't come to terms, Norwalk closed its doors for the second time, almost certainly for good.

Then something extraordinary happened. A group of 12 local families called the company and said they were interested in making a bid for just the Ohio factory. Both Comerica and the Gerkens liked the idea. After just a few days of due diligence, the investors bought the plant for $4 million. The next week the investors started taking applications to rehire workers.

The new company is called Norwalk Custom Order Furniture and is run by Daniel J. White, one of the 12 investors. White has long ties to the town of Norwalk—his family has lived there for more than 100 years—and he says concern for the community is what drove him to step in. Before taking the reins at Norwalk, White, a retiree, had founded Geotrac of America, a company specializing in the flood zone research required by mortgage lenders, which he sold in 2004.

For the 12 families that invested in Norwalk, reviving the factory meant a stronger local economy and higher property values.

For most of the other 11 Norwalk investors, the desire to save well-paying jobs wasn't purely humanitarian. Doing so would mean a stronger local economy, higher property values, and better business in general, says Tom Bleile, one of the investors and co-owner of the Saw Mill Creek Resort on the shore of Lake Erie, a half hour to the north. "If our community benefits, then we benefit," says Bleile.

In his first two weeks as CEO, White visited 28 of Norwalk's retailers. They had been without product for 30 to 60 days, and many were on the verge of bankruptcy. They'd been caught off guard by Norwalk's problems and "felt betrayed," White says. He quickly took steps to win them back. First he started work on the $4.5 million in orders that had gone unfulfilled. Next he changed the company's production cycle to make sure retailers wouldn't have to wait months before they could start selling Norwalk's newest line.

White insists the new Norwalk is built to last. The company has no significant debt aside from the $1.8 million loan from the state of Ohio and a $225,000 equipment loan from the town of Norwalk. White expects the Norwalk plant to generate more than $25 million in sales by 2011, less than half the level it once enjoyed but far more sustainable.

Jodi Zippo's outlook is brighter these days, too. When Norwalk closed last year, she was on the hook for $280,000 worth of orders. Sitting at her husband's desk in their Littleton (Colo.) home one night, she called one customer after another to beg them for a chance to find another vendor. By the end of the night all but four agreed, and she had to refund only $25,000. Still, she's out some $150,000 worth of floor models and samples she sold for a fraction of their value last fall because she thought Norwalk would no longer be making them. All 31 lenders she has approached to refinance her Comerica loan have declined.

But now that Norwalk is back producing furniture, Zippo is selling it again, along with several other lines. Sales are improving, and she's current on her loan payments. The panic attacks she suffered last summer have eased. "We're past the scary part," she says.

For Kim Gross, survivor guilt may be creeping in. She and her husband, Jeff, were among the 94 workers who successfully reapplied for their jobs at the factory. Most of the 800 who applied were turned away, including many with decades' worth of experience. Gross has run into some of them at the grocery store, and the encounters have been awkward. Now Gross shops at odd hours to avoid her former factory mates.

Rightly or wrongly, much of the anger around town is directed toward the former owners. Bill and Jim Gerken may have mismanaged Norwalk, but they also fought desperately to save it. Now they're financially devastated. Bill says 90% of his net worth was tied up in the company, and all of it is gone. "No one lost more than I did," he says. Mayor Lesch says the Gerkens "were wonderful" through the process, talking to her every day. "It's so easy to point fingers from the outside," she says. "It's always more complicated than that."

While the Norwalk saga created rifts in this small Ohio town, it will be remembered more for bringing people together. Whenever a prominent company is about to close, "the temptation for too many people is to throw up their hands and say it's inevitable," says Lesch. "We said, 'Wait a minute, this is really, really important. We're going to stand up and fight.'"

Critical Thinking

1. What specific management decisions led to Norwalk Furniture's near-closure?
2. Discuss the stakeholder participation in saving Norwalk Furniture. Which stakeholders were the most influential/successful in saving the company?

Protecting the Whistleblower

Companies should fine-tune internal probes to make investigation more asset than liability.

R. Scott Oswald and Jason Zuckerman

In litigating whistleblower retaliation claims, we have found that poorly conducted internal investigations can be extraordinarily helpful to plaintiffs and harmful to employers. In particular, investigations that are intended to discredit the concerned employee or cover up wrongdoing to protect the accused will, at a minimum, deprive the employer of an affirmative defense and can also provide circumstantial evidence of retaliatory intent.

Employers, however, can take fairly simple measures to prevent an investigation from becoming more of a liability than an asset. Following are five tips for conducting an effective internal investigation.

- **Keep the Concerned Employee Apprised of the Investigation.** For any employees, disclosing wrongdoing is a daunting experience. Therefore, a concerned employee likely will be anxious about potential retaliation and focused on achieving a prompt resolution to the problem or wrongdoing that the employee disclosed.

If the concerned employee believes that the company is not taking the employee's concerns seriously or is failing to take necessary corrective actions, the employee likely will pursue other avenues to remedy the problem, such as contacting the media or a regulatory agency. Accordingly, it is essential for the investigator to keep the concerned employee apprised of the status of the investigation. The investigator should periodically update the concerned employee regarding the investigator's findings and give the concerned employee a chance to respond and provide additional information, documents or corroborating witnesses.

At the conclusion of the investigation, the concerned employee should be informed of corrective actions, such as strengthened internal controls to prevent the type of accounting fraud that the concerned employee brought to light.

- **Focus on the Concerned Employee's Allegation Rather than the Employee's Motive.** The surest sign that an investigation is pretextual is when the investigation focuses on the concerned employee's motive for disclosing wrongdoing. As a matter of law, a whistleblower's motive is irrelevant. Accordingly, the investigation should focus on uncovering the veracity of the concerned employee's allegations, not on discrediting the source of the allegations.

- **Protect the Concerned Employee and Witnesses from Retaliation.** Not surprisingly, an employee accused of misconduct can be prone to resent the accuser and employees who assisted in an investigation. Accordingly, the employer should stay attuned to any retaliation resulting from an investigation, and should promptly respond to any retaliation.

If the concerned employee is harassed or subjected to pretextual discipline, co-workers would be chilled from disclosing wrongdoing. A chilled work environment is harmful to any organization because it will undermine management's ability to learn early on of future wrongdoing or misconduct. Moreover, a retaliatory investigation can result in liability for the employer.

For example, retaliating against a whistleblower by conducting a sham investigation and intentionally spreading false allegations of misconduct by the whistleblower gives rise to a claim of intentional infliction of emotional distress and other tort and employment actions.

Moreover, the Supreme Court recently clarified that a retaliation claim does not require proof of a tangible adverse job detriment, such as a termination or a demotion. Instead, the standard for retaliation is whether the conduct in question would dissuade an objective, reasonable person from making or supporting a charge of discrimination, or engaging in other forms of protected conduct.

Therefore, investigations must be conducted in a manner that will not discourage employees from reporting additional misconduct or wrongdoing.

- **Pay Heed to the Rights of the Accused.** Investigative findings based on uncorroborated allegations or dubious evidence can expose an employer to liability for a negligent investigation claim. Before taking any corrective actions based on the investigation's finding, such as terminating a manager accused of harassment, the investigative findings should be carefully scrutinized by at least one company official who was not involved in the investigation and has no stake in the outcome.

Factors to assess include whether the investigator failed to pursue leads, such as failing to interview a key witness; whether the investigator gave undue weight to hearsay; and whether the documentary evidence is consistent with the investigator's conclusions. Moreover, it is critical throughout an investigation to avoid defaming the accused.

- **Steer Clear of Unlawful Investigation Techniques and Preserve the Authenticity of Electronic Documents.** The Hewlett-Packard "pretexting" scandal, which resulted in a $14.5 million settlement and other sanctions, is a stark reminder of the importance of complying with state and federal privacy laws.

Throughout the investigation, consider whether any particular technique might run afoul of state wiretapping laws, the Electronic Communications Privacy Act, the Fair Credit Reporting Act or the Health Insurance Portability and Accountability Act.

Investigators should also take steps to avoid inadvertent corruption of electronic documents. As most documents are now created and transmitted electronically, an investigation will likely entail the gathering and review of various types of electronic documents. Merely opening or reading an electronic file, such as an email or a spreadsheet, alters the metadata of the file.

The metadata itself could contain critical evidence that might resolve conflicting accounts, such as when a document was transmitted, received or opened. To ensure that evidence uncovered in an investigation will retain its authenticity and be deemed reliable in potential litigation, create a "mirror image" or bit-by-bit copy of the source drive or database.

Critical Thinking

1. What steps should a company take to protect both the whistleblower and its own corporate interests?
2. What sort of values-based changes would have to occur in order to make whistleblowing a corporate asset?

R. SCOTT OSWALD and **JASON ZUCKERMAN** are Principals at The Employment Law Group. They represent employees in whistleblower retaliation claims brought under the Sarbanes-Oxley Act and other protection provisions.

Whistleblowers Get a Raise

The SEC will offer up to 30 percent of the money from fines.
The Volume of leads "is going to go up exponentially."

JESSE WESTBROOK

In the 21 years since the Securities & Exchange Commission introduced rewards for insider-trading tipsters, the agency has disbursed just $1.16 million to six claimants, including a $1 million payout earlier this month to a woman who blew the whistle on the founder of the hedge fund **Pequot Capital Management.** With the financial-regulation overhaul signed into law by President Barack Obama on July 21, that stately pace is expected to accelerate dramatically.

Stung by accusations that it ignored reports of Bernard Madoff's misdeeds, the commission asked Congress to increase bounties and expand the SEC's authority to reward tipsters for leads on other types of misconduct, including Ponzi schemes and accounting frauds. Those wishes were answered: The financial overhaul says the agency can make whistleblower awards in any case that triggers a sanction exceeding $1 million. And tipsters are now entitled to as much as 30 percent of all the money the SEC collects, including fines and ill-gotten profits. In the past, claimants were eligible for only a 10 percent share of any fine. "The whistleblower provision will substantially benefit our enforcement program by encouraging those with evidence of fraud to come forward," says SEC spokesman John Nester.

What it won't ensure is that the SEC has the resources or expertise to uncover frauds better than it has in the past, particularly as the regulator braces for a flood of whistleblowers attracted by more lucrative bounties. To prepare, the SEC has hired consultants and is studying successful tipster programs at the IRS and Justice Dept. The agency also is using increased funding from Congress to acquire technology that will make it easier for investigators to sort through reams of information on companies accused of wrongdoing. The SEC says its computer system will be upgraded by the end of the year. "They already get a lot of tips, and the number is going to go up exponentially," says Daniel J. Hurson, a former SEC attorney now in private practice in Washington. "They are going to have to have a good system in place to separate the wheat from the chaff."

The goal is to avoid a repeat of past enforcement failures. In 2005, whistleblower Harry Markopolos gave investigators a 21-page report about Madoff titled "The World's Largest Hedge Fund Is a Fraud." Even with that road map, the SEC fumbled the investigation. The $65 billion Ponzi scheme wasn't exposed until December 2008, when Madoff couldn't meet his investors' withdrawal requests.

Some critics warn that the additional powers granted by Congress may create a new set of problems for the agency. One unintended consequence, says former SEC Commissioner Paul S. Atkins, is that disgruntled corporate employees now have more incentive to lodge complaints, which will lead to higher legal fees for companies that have to respond to investigations. The flood of tips may also divert the SEC's limited resources away from legitimate cases, Atkins says.

Critical Thinking

1. Are increased payoffs to whistleblowers likely to allow the SEC to do a better job of catching miscreants?

2. What are some unintended consequences of the increased whistleblowing bounties?

The Parable of the Sadhu

After encountering a dying pilgrim on a climbing trip in the Himalayas, a businessman ponders the differences between individual and corporate ethics.

BOWEN H. MCCOY

Last year, as the first participant in the new six-month sabbatical program that Morgan Stanley has adopted, I enjoyed a rare opportunity to collect my thoughts as well as do some traveling. I spent the first three months in Nepal, walking 600 miles through 200 villages in the Himalayas and climbing some 120,000 vertical feet. My sole Western companion on the trip was an anthropologist who shed light on the cultural patterns of the villages that we passed through.

During the Nepal hike, something occurred that has had a powerful impact on my thinking about corporate ethics. Although some might argue that the experience has no relevance to business, it was a situation in which a basic ethical dilemma suddenly intruded into the lives of a group of individuals. How the group responded holds a lesson for all organizations, no matter how defined.

The Sadhu

The Nepal experience was more rugged than I had anticipated. Most commercial treks last two or three weeks and cover a quarter of the distance we traveled.

My friend Stephen, the anthropologist, and I were halfway through the 60-day Himalayan part of the trip when we reached the high point, an 18,000-foot pass over a crest that we'd have to traverse to reach the village of Muklinath, an ancient holy place for pilgrims.

Six years earlier, I had suffered pulmonary edema, an acute form of altitude sickness, at 16,500 feet in the vicinity of Everest base camp—so we were understandably concerned about what would happen at 18,000 feet. Moreover, the Himalayas were having their wettest spring in 20 years; hip-deep powder and ice had already driven us off one ridge. If we failed to cross the pass, I feared that the last half of our once-in-a-lifetime trip would be ruined.

The night before we would try the pass, we camped in a hut at 14,500 feet. In the photos taken at that camp, my face appears wan. The last village we'd passed through was a sturdy two-day walk below us, and I was tired.

During the late afternoon, four backpackers from New Zealand joined us, and we spent most of the night awake, anticipating the climb. Below, we could see the fires of two other parties, which turned out to be two Swiss couples and a Japanese hiking club.

To get over the steep part of the climb before the sun melted the steps cut in the ice, we departed at 3:30 A.M. The New Zealanders left first, followed by Stephen and myself, our porters and Sherpas, and then the Swiss. The Japanese lingered in their camp. The sky was clear, and we were confident that no spring storm would erupt that day to close the pass.

At 15,500 feet, it looked to me as if Stephen were shuffling and staggering a bit, which are symptoms of altitude sickness. (The initial stage of altitude sickness brings a headache and nausea. As the condition worsens, a climber may encounter difficult breathing, disorientation, aphasia, and paralysis.) I felt strong—my adrenaline was flowing—but I was very concerned about my ultimate ability to get across. A couple of our porters were also suffering from the height, and Pasang, our Sherpa sirdar (leader), was worried.

Just after daybreak, while we rested at 15,500 feet, one of the New Zealanders, who had gone ahead, came staggering down toward us with a body slung across his shoulders. He dumped the almost naked, barefoot body of an Indian holy man—a sadhu—at my feet. He had found the pilgrim lying on the ice, shivering and suffering from hypothermia. I cradled the sadhu's head and laid him out on the rocks. The New Zealander was angry. He wanted to get across the pass before the bright sun melted the snow. He said, "Look, I've done what I can. You have porters and Sherpa guides. You care for him. We're going on!" He turned and went back up the mountain to join his friends.

I took a carotid pulse and found that the sadhu was still alive. We figured he had probably visited the holy shrines at Muklinath and was on his way home. It was fruitless to question why he had chosen this desperately high route instead of the safe, heavily traveled caravan route through the Kali Gandaki gorge. Or why he was shoeless and almost naked, or how long he had been lying in the pass. The answers weren't going to solve our problem.

Stephen and the four Swiss began stripping off their outer clothing and opening their packs. The sadhu was soon clothed from head to foot. He was not able to walk, but he was very much alive. I looked down the mountain and spotted the Japanese climbers, marching up with a horse.

When I reached them, Stephen glared at me and said, "How do you feel about contributing to the death of a fellow man?"

Without a great deal of thought, I told Stephen and Pasang that I was concerned about withstanding the heights to come and wanted to get over the pass. I took off after several of our porters who had gone ahead.

On the steep part of the ascent where, if the ice steps had given way, I would have slid down about 3,000 feet, I felt vertigo. I stopped for a breather, allowing the Swiss to catch up with me. I inquired about the sadhu and Stephen. They said that the sadhu was fine and that Stephen was just behind them. I set off again for the summit.

Stephen arrived at the summit an hour after I did. Still exhilarated by victory, I ran down the slope to congratulate him. He was suffering from altitude sickness—walking 15 steps, then stopping, walking 15 steps, then stopping. Pasang accompanied him all the way up. When I reached them, Stephen glared at me and said: "How do you feel about contributing to the death of a fellow man?"

I did not completely comprehend what he meant. "Is the sadhu dead?" I inquired.

"No," replied Stephen, "but he surely will be!"

After I had gone, followed not long after by the Swiss, Stephen had remained with the sadhu. When the Japanese had arrived, Stephen had asked to use their horse to transport the sadhu down to the hut. They had refused. He had then asked Pasang to have a group of our porters carry the sadhu. Pasang had resisted the idea, saying that the porters would have to exert all their energy to get them-

selves over the pass. He believed they could not carry a man down 1,000 feet to the hut, reclimb the slope, and get across safely before the snow melted. Pasang had pressed Stephen not to delay any longer.

The Sherpas had carried the sadhu down to a rock in the sun at about 15,000 feet and pointed out the hut another 500 feet below. The Japanese had given him food and drink. When they had last seen him, he was listlessly throwing rocks at the Japanese party's dog, which had frightened him.

We do not know if the sadhu lived or died.

For many of the following days and evenings, Stephen and I discussed and debated our behavior toward the sadhu. Stephen is a committed Quaker with deep moral vision. He said, "I feel that what happened with the sadhu is a good example of the breakdown between the individual ethic and the corporate ethic. No one person was willing to assume ultimate responsibility for the sadhu. Each was willing to do his bit just so long as it was not too inconvenient. When it got to be a bother, everyone just passed the buck to someone else and took off. Jesus was relevant to a more individualistic stage of society, but how do we interpret his teaching today in a world filled with large, impersonal organizations and groups?"

I defended the larger group, saying, "Look, we all cared. We all gave aid and comfort. Everyone did his bit. The New Zealander carried him down below the snow line. I took his pulse and suggested we treat him for hypothermia. You and the Swiss gave him clothing and got him warmed up. The Japanese gave him food and water. The Sherpas carried him down to the sun and pointed out the easy trail toward the hut. He was well enough to throw rocks at a dog. What more could we do?"

"You have just described the typical affluent Westerner's response to a problem. Throwing money—in this case, food and sweaters—at it, but not solving the fundamentals!" Stephen retorted.

I asked, "Where is the limit of our responsibility in a situation like this?"

"What would satisfy you?" I said. "Here we are, a group of New Zealanders, Swiss, Americans, and Japanese who have never met before and who are at the apex of one of the most powerful experiences of our lives. Some years the pass is so bad no one gets over it. What right does an almost naked pilgrim who chooses the wrong trail have to disrupt our lives? Even the Sherpas had no interest in risking the trip to help him beyond a certain point."

Stephen calmly rebutted, "I wonder what the Sherpas would have done if the sadhu had been a well-dressed Nepali, or what the Japanese would have done if the sadhu had been a well-dressed Asian, or what you would have done, Buzz, if the sadhu had been a well-dressed Western woman?"

"Where, in your opinion," I asked, "is the limit of our responsibility in a situation like this? We had our own well-being to worry about. Our Sherpa guides were unwilling to jeopardize us or the porters for the sadhu. No one else on the mountain was willing to commit himself beyond certain self-imposed limits."

Stephen said, "As individual Christians or people with a Western ethical tradition, we can fulfill our obligations in such a situation only if one, the sadhu dies in our care; two, the sadhu demonstrates to us that he can undertake the two-day walk down to the village; or three, we carry the sadhu for two days down to the village and persuade someone there to care for him."

"Leaving the sadhu in the sun with food and clothing—where he demonstrated hand-eye coordination by throwing a rock at a dog—comes close to fulfilling items one and two," I answered. "And it wouldn't have made sense to take him to the village where the people appeared to be far less caring than the Sherpas, so the third condition is impractical. Are you really saying that, no matter what the implications, we should, at the drop of a hat, have changed our entire plan?"

The Individual versus the Group Ethic

Despite my arguments, I felt and continue to feel guilt about the sadhu. I had literally walked through a classic moral dilemma without fully thinking through the consequences. My excuses for my actions include a high adrenaline flow, a superordinate goal, and a once-in-a-lifetime opportunity—common factors in corporate situations, especially stressful ones.

Real moral dilemmas are ambiguous, and many of us hike right through them, unaware that they exist. When, usually after the fact, someone makes an issue of one, we tend to resent his or her bringing it up. Often, when the full import of what we have done (or not done) hits us, we dig into a defensive position from which it is very difficult to emerge. In rare circumstances, we may contemplate what we have done from inside a prison.

Had we mountaineers been free of stress caused by the effort and the high altitude, we might have treated the sadhu differently. Yet isn't stress the real test of personal and corporate values? The instant decisions that executives make under pressure reveal the most about personal and corporate character.

As a group, we had no process for developing a consensus. We had no sense of purpose or plan.

Among the many questions that occur to me when I ponder my experience with the sadhu are: What are the practical limits of moral imagination and vision? Is there a collective or institutional ethic that differs from the ethics of the individual? At what level of effort or commitment can one discharge one's ethical responsibilities?

Not every ethical dilemma has a right solution. Reasonable people often disagree; otherwise there would be no dilemma. In a business context, however, it is essential that managers agree on a process for dealing with dilemmas.

Our experience with the sadhu offers an interesting parallel to business situations. An immediate response was mandatory. Failure to act was a decision in itself. Up on the mountain we could not resign and submit our résumés to a headhunter. In contrast to philosophy, business involves action and implementation—getting things done. Managers must come up with answers based on what they see and what they allow to influence their decision-making processes. On the mountain, none of us but Stephen realized the true dimensions of the situation we were facing.

One of our problems was that as a group we had no process for developing a consensus. We had no sense of purpose or plan. The difficulties of dealing with the sadhu were so complex that no one person could handle them. Because the group did not have a set of preconditions that could guide its action to an acceptable resolution, we reacted instinctively as individuals. The cross-cultural nature of the group added a further layer of complexity. We had no leader with whom we could all identify and in whose purpose we believed. Only Stephen was willing to take charge, but he could not gain adequate support from the group to care for the sadhu.

Some organizations do have values that transcend the personal values of their managers. Such values, which go beyond profitability, are usually revealed when the organization is under stress. People throughout the organization generally accept its values, which, because they are not presented as a rigid list of commandments, may be somewhat ambiguous. The stories people tell, rather than printed materials, transmit the organization's conceptions of what is proper behavior.

For 20 years, I have been exposed at senior levels to a variety of corporations and organizations. It is amazing how quickly an outsider can sense the tone and style of an organization and, with that, the degree of tolerated openness and freedom to challenge management.

When Do We Take a Stand?

I wrote about my experiences purposely to present an ambiguous situation. I never found out if the sadhu lived or died. I can attest, though, that the sadhu lives on in his story. He lives in the ethics classes I teach each year at business schools and churches. He lives in the classrooms of numerous business schools, where professors have taught the case to tens of thousands of students. He lives in several casebooks on ethics and on an educational video. And he lives in organizations such as the American Red Cross and AT&T, which use his story in their ethics training.

As I reflect on the sadhu now, 15 years after the fact, I first have to wonder, What actually happened on that Himalayan slope? When I first wrote about the event, I reported the experience in as much detail as I could remember, but I shaped it to the needs of a good classroom discussion. After years of reading my story, viewing it on video, and hearing others discuss it, I'm not sure I myself know what actually occurred on the mountainside that day!

I've also heard a wide variety of responses to the story. The sadhu, for example, may not have wanted our help at all—he may have been intentionally bringing on his own death as a way to holiness. Why had he taken the dangerous way over the pass instead of the caravan route through the gorge? Hindu businesspeople have told me that in trying to assist the sadhu, we were being typically arrogant Westerners imposing our cultural values on the world.

I've learned that each year along the pass, a few Nepali porters are left to freeze to death outside the tents of the unthinking tourists who hired them. A few years ago, a French group even left one of their own, a young French woman, to die there. The difficult pass seems to demonstrate a perverse version of Gresham's law of currency: The bad practices of previous travelers have driven out the values that new travelers might have followed if they were at home. Perhaps that helps to explain why our porters behaved as they did and why it was so difficult for Stephen or anyone else to establish a different approach on the spot.

Our Sherpa sirdar, Pasang, was focused on his responsibility for bringing us up the mountain safe and sound. (His livelihood and status in the Sherpa ethnic group depended on our safe return.) We were weak, our party was split, the porters were well on their way to the top with all our gear and food, and a storm would have separated us irrevocably from our logistical base.

The fact was, we had no plan for dealing with the contingency of the sadhu. There was nothing we could do to unite our multicultural group in the little time we had. An ethical dilemma had come upon us unexpectedly, an element of drama that may explain why the sadhu's story has continued to attract students.

I am often asked for help in teaching the story. I usually advise keeping the details as ambiguous as possible. A true ethical dilemma requires a decision between two hard choices. In the case of the sadhu, we had to decide how much to sacrifice ourselves to take care of a stranger. And given the constraints of our trek, we had to make a group decision, not an individual one. If a large majority of students in a class ends up thinking I'm a bad person because of my decision on the mountain, the instructor may not have given the case its due. The same is true if the majority sees no problem with the choices we made.

Any class's response depends on its setting, whether it's a business school, a church, or a corporation. I've found that younger students are more likely to see the issue as black-and-white, whereas older ones tend to see shades of gray. Some have seen a conflict between the different ethical approaches that we followed at the time. Stephen felt he had to do everything he could to save the sadhu's life, in accordance with his Christian ethic of compassion. I had a utilitarian response: do the greatest good for the greatest number. Give a burst of aid to minimize the sadhu's exposure, then continue on our way.

The basic question of the case remains, When do we take a stand? When do we allow a "sadhu" to intrude into our daily lives? Few of us can afford the time or effort to take care of every needy person we encounter. How much must we give of ourselves? And how do we prepare our organizations and institutions so they will respond appropriately in a crisis? How do we influence them if we do not agree with their points of view?

We cannot quit our jobs over every ethical dilemma, but if we continually ignore our sense of values, who do we become? As a journalist asked at a recent conference on ethics, "Which ditch are we willing to die in?" For each of us, the answer is a bit different. How we act in response to that question defines better than anything else who we are, just as, in a collective sense, our acts define our institutions. In effect, the sadhu is always there, ready to remind us of the tensions between our own goals and the claims of strangers.

Organizations that do not have a heritage of mutually accepted, shared values tend to become unhinged during stress, with each individual bailing out for himself or herself. In the great takeover battles we have witnessed during past years, companies that had strong cultures drew the wagons around them and fought it out, while other companies saw executives—supported by golden parachutes—bail out of the struggles.

Because corporations and their members are interdependent, for the corporation to be strong the members need to share a preconceived notion of correct behavior, a "business ethic," and think of it as a positive force, not a constraint.

As an investment banker, I am continually warned by well-meaning lawyers, clients, and associates to be wary of conflicts of interest. Yet if I were to run away from every difficult situation, I wouldn't be an effective investment banker. I have to feel my way through conflicts. An effective manager can't run from risk either; he or she has to confront risk. To feel "safe" in doing that, managers need the guidelines of an agreed-upon process and set of values within the organization.

After my three months in Nepal, I spent three months as an executive-in-residence at both the Stanford Business School and the University of California at Berkeley's Center for Ethics and Social Policy of the Graduate Theological Union. Those six months away from my job gave me time to assimilate 20 years of business experience. My thoughts turned often to the meaning of the leadership role in any large organization. Students at the seminary thought of themselves as antibusiness. But when I questioned them, they agreed that they distrusted all large organizations, including the church. They perceived all large organizations as impersonal and opposed to individual values and needs. Yet we all know of organizations in which people's values and beliefs are respected and their expressions encouraged. What makes the difference? Can we identify the difference and, as a result, manage more effectively?

The word *ethics* turns off many and confuses more. Yet the notions of shared values and an agreed-upon process for dealing with adversity and change—what many people mean when they talk about corporate culture—seem to be at the heart of the ethical issue. People who are in touch with their own core beliefs and the beliefs of others and who are sustained by them can be more comfortable living on the cutting edge. At times, taking a tough line or a decisive stand in a muddle of ambiguity is the only ethical thing to do. If a manager is indecisive about a problem and spends time trying to figure out the "good" thing to do, the enterprise may be lost.

Business ethics, then, has to do with the authenticity and integrity of the enterprise. To be ethical is to follow the business as well as the cultural goals of the corporation, its owners, its employees, and its customers. Those who cannot serve the corporate vision are not authentic businesspeople and, therefore, are not ethical in the business sense.

At this stage of my own business experience, I have a strong interest in organizational behavior. Sociologists are keenly studying what they call corporate stories, legends, and heroes as a way organizations have of transmitting value systems. Corporations such as Arco have even hired consultants to perform an audit of their corporate culture. In a company, a leader is a person who understands, interprets, and manages the corporate value system. Effective managers, therefore, are action-oriented people who resolve conflict, are tolerant of ambiguity, stress, and change, and have a strong sense of purpose for themselves and their organizations.

If all this is true, I wonder about the role of the professional manager who moves from company to company. How can he or she quickly absorb the values and culture of different organizations? Or is there, indeed, an art of management that is totally transportable? Assuming that such fungible managers do exist, is it proper for them to manipulate the values of others?

What would have happened had Stephen and I carried the sadhu for two days back to the village and become involved with the villagers in his care? In four trips to Nepal, my most interesting experience occurred in 1975 when I lived in a Sherpa home in the Khumbu for five days while recovering from altitude sickness. The high point of Stephen's trip was an invitation to participate in a family funeral ceremony in Manang. Neither experience had to do with climbing the high passes of the Himalayas. Why were we so reluctant to try the lower path, the ambiguous trail? Perhaps because we did not have a leader who could reveal the greater purpose of the trip to us.

Why didn't Stephen, with his moral vision, opt to take the sadhu under his personal care? The answer is partly because Stephen was hard-stressed physically himself and partly because, without some support system that encompassed our involuntary and episodic community on the mountain, it was beyond his individual capacity to do so.

I see the current interest in corporate culture and corporate value systems as a positive response to pessimism such as Stephen's about the decline of the role of the individual in large organizations. Individuals who operate from a thoughtful set of personal values provide the foundation for a corporate culture. A corporate tradition that encourages freedom of inquiry, supports personal values, and reinforces a focused sense of direction can fulfill the need to combine individuality with the prosperity and success of the group. Without such corporate support, the individual is lost.

That is the lesson of the sadhu. In a complex corporate situation, the individual requires and deserves the support of the group. When people cannot find such support in their organizations, they don't know how to act. If such support is forthcoming, a person has a stake in the success of the group and can add much to the process of establishing and maintaining a corporate culture. Management's challenge is to be sensitive to individual needs, to shape them, and to direct and focus them for the benefit of the group as a whole.

For each of us the sadhu lives. Should we stop what we are doing and comfort him; or should we keep trudging up toward the high pass? Should I pause to help the derelict I pass on the street each night as I walk by the Yale Club en route to Grand Central Station? Am I his brother? What is the nature of our responsibility if we consider ourselves to be ethical persons? Perhaps it is to change the values of the group so that it can, with all its resources, take the other road.

Critical Thinking

1. If you were Bowen McCoy, what would you have done? Refer to ethical theories to support your answer.

2. How do your personal values express themselves in your business life?

Bowen H. McCoy retired from Morgan Stanley in 1990 after 28 years of service. He is now a real estate and business counselor, a teacher and a philanthropist.

Editor's Note—This article was originally published in the September/October 1983 issue of *HBR*. For its republication as an HBR Classic, Bowen H. McCoy has written the commentary "When Do We Take a Stand?" to update his observations.

From *Harvard Business Review,* May/June 1997, pp. 54–56, 58–60, 62, 64. Copyright © 1997 by Harvard Business School Publishing. Reprinted by permission.

At Work, a Drug Dilemma

STEPHANIE SIMON

An employee recently approached Josh Ward, an executive at a Denver plumbing company, with a question he never thought he'd hear.

Her husband, the employee said, is a state-registered medical marijuana patient. Could she buy his marijuana with her company-provided flexible spending account?

"We were like, 'Whoa!'" Mr. Ward said.

Mr. Ward did a bit of research and quickly told the employee no. Her account, funded with pretax dollars, is regulated by the Internal Revenue Service and cannot be used to purchase a drug that's illegal under federal statutes, even if Colorado treats it as a legitimate medication.

The employee, whom the firm would not make available for comment, didn't press it, Mr. Ward said. Still, the issue made him uneasy. "It's a big can of worms," said Mr. Ward, vice president of Applewood Plumbing, Heating & Electric.

Employers from coast to coast are facing similar dilemmas. Many are closely watching a pending lawsuit against Wal-Mart Stores Inc. in Michigan. An employee who used medical marijuana was fired by the retailer after a positive drug test on the job.

Fourteen states and the District of Columbia have laws or constitutional amendments that allow patients with certain medical conditions such as cancer, glaucoma or chronic pain, to use marijuana without fear of prosecution. The Obama administration has directed federal prosecutors not to bring criminal charges against marijuana users who follow their states' laws.

But that can put employers in a difficult position, trying to accommodate state laws on medical marijuana use while at times having to enforce federal rules or company drug-use policies that are based on federal law.

"It's certainly an issue that's coming up regularly," said Danielle Urban, an attorney with Fisher & Phillips, a national labor and employment law firm. "Employers are between a rock and a hard place."

The federal government lists marijuana as a Schedule I drug on par with LSD or synthetic heroin. Employers can fire, or refuse to hire, employees for using the drug without running afoul of the Americans with Disabilities Act or any other federal anti-discrimination statute, said Christopher Kuczynski, assistant legal counsel with the U.S. Equal Employment Opportunity Commission.

State laws vary considerably. The state Supreme Courts in Oregon, California and Montana and the Washington Court of Appeals have all ruled that employers have a right to fire medical-marijuana patients for using the drug. The medical-marijuana laws in Rhode Island and Maine state that most employers may not penalize individuals solely because of their status as marijuana patients.

In Michigan, the law states that registered patients shall not be "denied any right or privilege" or face disciplinary action at work because they use pot. The only exception: Employers do have the right to terminate workers who use marijuana on site or come to work high.

But determining if a worker is impaired on the job can be difficult.

Sean Short, a 25-year-old college student, was injured last fall while taking pictures of skiers in Breckenridge, Colo., for his employer, an event photographer. Mr. Short says that, at the time, he was using marijuana in compliance with Colorado law to ease pain from a back injury.

He says he was not high when a skier smashed into him on the job, fracturing his shoulder. Mr. Short says he was required by his employer to take a urine drug screen after the accident. He flunked. He then gave managers his medical-marijuana card. "They said, 'Sorry, we're terminating you,'" Mr. Short said.

His employer did not return calls seeking comment.

Mr. Short says he's now reluctant to apply for any job requiring a drug test. "I can have a college degree. I can be well-spoken and intelligent," he said. "But as long as I'm a 'druggie,' I'm going to be discriminated against."

Sophisticated tests can measure the amount of THC, the active ingredient in marijuana, in blood samples taken within four to six hours of ingestion. Users are generally considered high at a level of five nanograms of THC per milliliter of blood, said Robert Lantz, director of Rocky Mountain Instrumental Laboratories, a drug-testing facility in Fort Collins, Colo.

Such precise tests require expensive instruments. Dr. Lantz's lab charges $450 for a single blood test; his bulk discount rate is $200 per test. Many employers use far cheaper, less sensitive urine screens. At OnSite Medical Testing, a lab in Greenwood Village, Colo., a basic urine test costs $35, or $25 for bulk clients.

The typical urine screen can detect the presence of metabolized THC compounds, but can't determine when the marijuana was ingested or in what quantities, Dr. Lantz said.

Advocates of legalized marijuana say they would never insist that workers be allowed to use the drug on duty. "No one thinks you should be able to get stoned and go to work, obviously," said Keith Stroup, legal counsel for the national advocacy group NORML. Still, Mr. Stroup argues that, absent clear signs of impairment, employers should trust workers who have valid medical-marijuana-registration cards to take the drug responsibly.

Too dangerous, some employers say. At Hoffman Construction Co. in Portland, Ore., cannabis has been implicated more than any other drug in workplace accidents resulting in injury or property damage, said Dan Harmon, a vice president.

Any move to permit off-duty drug use raises "real safety concerns," Mr. Harmon said. His firm doesn't accept medical-marijuana cards, he said. To do so would be "disastrous."

Employers and medical-marijuana patients are hoping the Michigan lawsuit can bring some clarity to the situation.

Joseph Casias, who says he uses medical marijuana to ease pain from an inoperable brain tumor, sued Wal-Mart in a state court in June, saying the retailer was wrong to fire him from his job as an inventory manager in Battle Creek, Mich., after he tested positive for marijuana.

Mr. Casias, who is represented by the American Civil Liberties Union, says he uses cannabis on his oncologist's advice and in compliance with Michigan law. The 30-year-old father of two says he takes the drug at night and has never come to work high. But last November, he failed a drug test that was administered as a matter of company policy after he twisted his knee on the job.

A Wal-Mart spokesman called the case "unfortunate" and the decision to fire Mr. Casias "difficult." But, he said: "As more states allow this treatment, employers are left without any guidelines except the federal standard. In these cases, until further guidance is available, we will always default to what we believe is the safest environment for our associates and customers."

Critical Thinking

1. Why is the use of medical marijuana at work a problem for employers?
2. Dilemmas are normally decisions between two equally undesirable alternatives. How can employers decide between two "goods"—workplace safety and personal rights?

From *The Wall Street Journal,* August 3, 2010, pp. D1, D4. Copyright © 2010 by Dow Jones & Company, Inc. Reprinted by permission via Rightslink.

His Most Trusted Employee Was a Thief

Jane had taken $20,000 to pay for a child's medical care.

SHEL HOROWITZ

Jane had worked for Edward faithfully for four years, and he trusted her with all the intimate details of his business. She was the one he relied on to solve any problem, to handle his paper-work, to be his personal confidante. She didn't have an accounting background, but she exercised day-to-day oversight over his company's finances, including depositing all the checks and cash that came in. Edward considered Jane a close personal friend. And while she was well-compensated, he paid out-of-pocket for special medical treatment for one of her children, when it fell outside the employee health plan that covered her, but not her family.

Jane had earned Edward's complete trust—until the day he discovered that, over the course of years, she had embezzled $20,000. When Edward confronted her, Jane immediately admitted the theft. She apologized and explained it was to pay for her child's high medical expenses. She agreed to begin a repayment plan, but Edward knew she didn't have the financial resources to pay back the entire $20,000.

Logic would dictate that Edward immediately terminate Jane and begin the process of criminal prosecution—but this was a close friend. Cold logic wasn't the only thing working here; there was a history of so many years working side by side. If only Jane had asked him, Edward would have contributed further toward the child's treatment. Now, what would sending Jane to jail accomplish? It wouldn't repair his trust, and it would not bring back the lost dollars. And how could he leave those children with no parent to take care of them, to say nothing of the medical problems? At the same time, if he allowed Jane to escape responsibility for her actions, who is to say she wouldn't do it again?

Archie Carroll
Robert W. Scherer Chair of Management Terry College of Business, University of Georgia

Carroll presented this case to the Social Issues in Management on-line faculty discussion group, asking for advice on behalf of the business owner, who is a friend of his (names have been changed). Comments below reflect both Carroll's own thoughts, as well as input from 15 of his colleagues.

When I asked my faculty colleagues about this, their advice ranged the gamut. Some said keep Jane as an employee, since she'd feel enough guilt and shame that she would not repeat the bad behavior (and thus Edward could avoid the high cost of training a replacement). At the other extreme, some said Edward should consider criminal prosecution.

As much as a consensus existed, it was that criminal prosecution would not help the situation, especially as the business owner wanted to put the episode behind him. There was recognition that the employee had worked "above and beyond," and that it would not help her family to put them through the trial and possible imprisonment. There was, of course, strong agreement that the embezzlement was wrong and that the business should institute accounting controls to prevent a similar theft in the future.

Some of the more innovative suggestions included:

- Fire Jane, but have her demonstrate how she was able to circumvent his fraud controls so that a future employee couldn't repeat the theft.
- Show generosity and forgive the money, out of respect for Jane's difficult financial situation.
- Hire Jane back on a probationary basis, and either forgive the debt or have her pay it back in small increments.
- Have her sign a promissory note, treating the theft as a loan.

What Actually Happened

Edward fired Jane. He forgave half of the $20,000 taken, in recognition of the extra effort she had gone to on his behalf for four years. For the other $10,000, he had her execute a promissory note to repay $100 per month (eight years and four months to repay in full). He felt, however, that this money was tainted. Instead of keeping it, he plans to donate it to charity. Edward will also upgrade his accounting controls (which already involve five people), but also take a much more active role in monitoring his company's financial situation.

Critical Thinking

1. What advice would you give to Edward?
2. What is your opinion of Edward's decision? Which laws of morality does it illustrate?

Shel Horowitz, (shel@principledprofits.com) author of *Principled Profit*: *Marketing That Puts People First,* initiated the Business Ethics Pledge movement at www.principledprofits.com/25000influencers.html.

UNIT 3

Business and Society: Contemporary Ethical, Social, and Environmental Issues

Unit Selections

Learning Outcomes

- How well are organizations responding to issues of work and family schedules, daycare, and telecommuting?

- Should corporations and executives face criminal charges for unsafe products, dangerous working conditions, or industrial pollution? Why or why not?

- What ethical dilemmas is management likely to face when conducting business in foreign environments?

Student Website
www.mhhe.com/cls

Internet References

National Immigrant Forum
www.immigrationforum.org
Workopolis.com
http://sympatico.workopolis.com
United Nations Environment Programme (UNEP)
www.unep.ch
United States Trade Representative (USTR)
www.ustr.

Both at home and abroad, there are social and environmental issues that have potential ethical consequences for management. Incidents of insider trading, deaths resulting from unsafe products or work environments, AIDS in the workplace, and the adoption of policies for involvement in the global market are a few of the issues that need to be seriously addressed by management.

This unit investigates the nature and ramifications of prominent ethical, social, and environmental issues facing management today. The unit articles are grouped into three sections. The first article scrutinizes the importance of companies' gaining and maintaining trust in the marketplace.

The first article in the second subsection reflects how Facebook and Google are facing a backlash from users and regulators alike over the way they have handled sensitive data. The second article in this subsection probes deeply into rising attacks on America's most sensitive computer networks.

The subsection *Global Ethics* concludes this unit with readings that provide helpful insight on ethical issues and dilemmas inherent in multinational operations. It describes adapting ethical decisions to a global marketplace and offers guidelines for helping management deal with product quality and ethical issues in international markets.

© Keith Brofsky/Getty Images

Trust in the Marketplace

JOHN E. RICHARDSON AND LINNEA BERNARD MCCORD

Traditionally, ethics is defined as a set of moral values or principles or a code of conduct.

. . . Ethics, as an expression of reality, is predicated upon the assumption that there are right and wrong motives, attitudes, traits of character, and actions that are exhibited in interpersonal relationships. Respectful social interaction is considered a norm by almost everyone.

. . . the overwhelming majority of people perceive others to be ethical when they observe what is considered to be their genuine kindness, consideration, politeness, empathy, and fairness in their interpersonal relationships. When these are absent, and unkindness, inconsideration, rudeness, hardness, and injustice are present, the people exhibiting such conduct are considered unethical. A genuine consideration of others is essential to an ethical life. (Chewning, pp. 175–176).

An essential concomitant of ethics is of trust. Webster's Dictionary defines trust as "assured reliance on the character, ability, strength or truth of someone or something." Businesses are built on a foundation of trust in our free-enterprise system. When there are violations of this trust between competitors, between employer and employees, or between businesses and consumers, our economic system ceases to run smoothly. From a moral viewpoint, ethical behavior should not exist because of economic pragmatism, governmental edict, or contemporary fashionability—it should exist because it is morally appropriate and right. From an economic point of view, ethical behavior should exist because it just makes good business sense to be ethical and operate in a manner that demonstrates trustworthiness.

Robert Bruce Shaw, in *Trust in the Balance*, makes some thoughtful observations about trust within an organization. Paraphrasing his observations and applying his ideas to the marketplace as a whole:

1. Trust requires consumers have confidence in organizational promises or claims made to them. This means that a consumer should be able to believe that a commitment made will be met.
2. Trust requires integrity and consistency in following a known set of values, beliefs, and practices.
3. Trust requires concern for the well-being of others. This does not mean that organizational needs are not given

appropriate emphasis—but it suggests the importance of understanding the impact of decisions and actions on others—i.e. consumers. (Shaw, pp. 39–40)

Companies can lose the trust of their customers by portraying their products in a deceptive or inaccurate manner. In one recent example, a Nike advertisement exhorted golfers to buy the same golf balls used by Tiger Woods. However, since Tiger Woods was using custom-made Nike golf balls not yet available to the general golfing public, the ad was, in fact, deceptive. In one of its ads, Volvo represented that Volvo cars could withstand a physical impact that, in fact, was not possible. Once a company is "caught" giving inaccurate information, even if done innocently, trust in that company is eroded.

Companies can also lose the trust of their customers when they fail to act promptly and notify their customers of problems that the company has discovered, especially where deaths may be involved. This occurred when Chrysler dragged its feet in replacing a safety latch on its Minivan (Geyelin, pp. A1, A10). More recently, Firestone and Ford had been publicly brought to task for failing to expeditiously notify American consumers of tire defects in SUVs even though the problem had occurred years earlier in other countries. In cases like these, trust might not just be eroded, it might be destroyed. It could take years of painstaking effort to rebuild trust under these circumstances, and some companies might not have the economic ability to withstand such a rebuilding process with their consumers.

A *20/20* and *New York Times* investigation on a recent *ABC 20/20* program, entitled "The Car Dealer's Secret" revealed a sad example of the violation of trust in the marketplace. The investigation divulged that many unsuspecting consumers have had hidden charges tacked on by some car dealers when purchasing a new car. According to consumer attorney Gary Klein, "It's a dirty little secret that the auto lending industry has not owned up to." (*ABC News 20/20*)

The scheme worked in the following manner. Car dealers would send a prospective buyer's application to a number of lenders, who would report to the car dealer what interest rate the lender would give to the buyer for his or her car loan. This interest rate is referred to as the "buy rate." Legally a car dealer is not required to tell the buyer what the "buy rate" is or how much the dealer is marking up the loan. If dealers did most of the loans at the buy rate, they only get a small fee. However, if they were able to convince the buyer to pay a higher rate, they made considerably more money. Lenders encouraged car dealers to charge the buyer a higher rate than the "buy rate" by agreeing to split the extra income with the dealer.

David Robertson, head of the Association of Finance and Insurance Professionals—a trade group representing finance managers—defended the practice, reflecting that it was akin to a retail markup on loans. "The dealership provides a valuable service on behalf of the customer in negotiating these loans," he said. "Because of that, the dealership should be compensated for that work." (*ABC News 20/20*)

Careful examination of the entire report, however, makes one seriously question this apologetic. Even if this practice is deemed to be legal, the critical issue is what happens to trust when the buyers discover that they have been charged an additional 1–3% of the loan without their knowledge? In some cases, consumers were led to believe that they were getting the dealer's bank rate, and in other cases, they were told that the dealer had shopped around at several banks to secure the best loan rate they could get for the buyer. While this practice may be questionable from a legal standpoint, it is clearly in ethical breach of trust with the consumer. Once discovered, the companies doing this will have the same credibility and trustworthiness problems as the other examples mentioned above.

The untrustworthiness problems of the car companies was compounded by the fact that the investigation appeared to reveal statistics showing that black customers were twice as likely as whites to have their rate marked up—and at a higher level. That evidence—included in thousands of pages of confidential documents which *20/20* and *The New York Times* obtained from a Tennessee court—revealed that some Nissan and GM dealers in Tennessee routinely marked up rates for blacks, forcing them to pay between $300 and $400 more than whites. (*ABC News 20/20*)

This is a tragic example for everyone who was affected by this markup and was the victim of this secret policy. Not only is trust destroyed, there is a huge economic cost to the general public. It is estimated that in the last four years or so, Texas car dealers have received approximately $9 billion of kickbacks from lenders, affecting 5.2 million consumers. (*ABC News 20/20*)

Let's compare these unfortunate examples of untrustworthy corporate behavior with the landmark example of Johnson & Johnson which ultimately increased its trustworthiness with consumers by the way it handled the Tylenol incident. After seven individuals who had consumed Tylenol capsules contaminated by a third party died, Johnson & Johnson instituted a total product recall within a week costing an estimated $50 million after taxes. The company did this, not because it was responsible for causing the problem, but because it was the right thing to do. In addition, Johnson & Johnson spearheaded the development of more effective tamper-proof containers for their industry. Because of the company's swift response, consumers once again were able to trust in the Johnson & Johnson name. Although Johnson & Johnson suffered a decrease in market share at the time because of the scare, over the long term it has maintained its profitability in a highly competitive market.

Certainly part of this profit success is attributable to consumers believing that Johnson & Johnson is a trustworthy company. (Robin and Reidenbach)

The e-commerce arena presents another example of the importance of marketers building a mutually valuable relationship with customers through a trust-based collaboration process. Recent research with 50 e-businesses reflects that companies which create and nurture trust find customers return to their sites repeatedly. (Dayal . . . . p. 64)

In the e-commerce world, six components of trust were found to be critical in developing trusting, satisfied customers:

- State-of-art reliable security measures on one's site
- Merchant legitimacy (e.g., ally one's product or service with an established brand)
- Order fulfillment (i.e. placing orders and getting merchandise efficiently and with minimal hassles)
- Tone and ambiance—handling consumers' personal information with sensitivity and iron-clad confidentiality
- Customers feeling that they are in control of the buying process
- Consumer collaboration—e.g., having chat groups to let consumers query each other about their purchases and experiences (Dayal . . . , pp. 64–67)

Additionally, one author noted recently that in the e-commerce world we've moved beyond brands and trademarks to "trustmarks." This author defined a trustmark as a

. . . (D)istinctive name or symbol that emotionally binds a company with the desires and aspirations of its customers. It's an emotional connection—and it's much bigger and more powerful than the uses that we traditionally associate with a trademark. . . . (Webber, p. 214)

Certainly if this is the case, trust—being an emotional link—is of supreme importance for a company that wants to succeed in doing business on the Internet.

It's unfortunate that while a plethora of examples of violation of trust easily come to mind, a paucity of examples "pop up" as noteworthy paradigms of organizational courage and trust in their relationship with consumers.

In conclusion, some key areas for companies to scrutinize and practice with regard to decisions that may affect trustworthiness in the marketplace might include:

- Does a company practice the Golden Rule with its customers? As a company insider, knowing what you know about the product, how willing would you be to purchase it for yourself or for a family member?
- How proud would you be if your marketing practices were made public . . . shared with your friends . . . or family? (Blanchard and Peale, p. 27)
- Are bottom-line concerns the sole component of your organizational decision-making process? What about human rights, the ecological/environmental impact, and other areas of social responsibility?
- Can a firm which engages in unethical business practices with customers be trusted to deal with its

employees any differently? Unfortunately, frequently a willingness to violate standards of ethics is not an isolated phenomenon but permeates the culture. The result is erosion of integrity throughout a company. In such cases, trust is elusive at best. (Shaw, p. 75)

- Is your organization not only market driven, but also value-oriented? (Peters and Levering, Moskowitz, and Katz)
- Is there a strong commitment to a positive corporate culture and a clearly defined mission which is frequently and unambiguously voiced by upper-management?
- Does your organization exemplify trust by practicing a genuine relationship partnership with your customers—*before, during, and after* the initial purchase? (Strout, p. 69)

Companies which exemplify treating customers ethically are founded on a covenant of trust. There is a shared belief, confidence, and faith that the company and its people will be fair, reliable, and ethical in all its dealings. ***Total trust is the belief that a company and its people will never take opportunistic advantage of customer vulnerabilities***. (Hart and Johnson, pp. 11–13)

References

ABC News 20/20, "The Car Dealer's Secret," October 27, 2000.

Blanchard, Kenneth, and Norman Vincent Peale, *The Power of Ethical Management*, New York: William Morrow and Company, Inc., 1988.

Chewning, Richard C., *Business Ethics in a Changing Culture* (Reston, Virginia: Reston Publishing, 1984).

Dayal, Sandeep, Landesberg, Helen, and Michael Zeissner, "How to Build Trust Online," *Marketing Management*, Fall 1999, pp. 64–69.

Geyelin, Milo, "Why One Jury Dealt a Big Blow to Chrysler in Minivan-Latch Case," *Wall Street Journal*, November 19, 1997, pp. A1, A10.

Hart, Christopher W. and Michael D. Johnson, "Growing the Trust Relationship," *Marketing Management*, Spring 1999, pp. 9–19.

Hosmer, La Rue Tone, *The Ethics of Management*, second edition (Homewood, Illinois: Irwin, 1991).

Kaydo, Chad, "A Position of Power," *Sales & Marketing Management*, June 2000, pp. 104–106, 108ff.

Levering, Robert; Moskowitz, Milton; and Michael Katz, *The 100 Best Companies to Work for in America* (Reading, Mass.: Addison-Wesley, 1984).

Magnet, Myron, "Meet the New Revolutionaries," *Fortune*, February 24, 1992, pp. 94–101.

Muoio, Anna, "The Experienced Customer," *Net Company*, Fall 1999, pp. 25–27.

Peters, Thomas J. and Robert H. Waterman Jr., *In Search of Excellence* (New York: Harper & Row, 1982).

Richardson, John (ed.), *Annual Editions: Business Ethics 00/01* (Guilford, CT: McGraw-Hill/Dushkin, 2000).

_____, *Annual Editions: Marketing 00/01* (Guilford, CT: McGraw-Hill/Dushkin, 2000).

Robin, Donald P., and Erich Reidenbach, "Social Responsibility, Ethics, and Marketing Strategy: Closing the Gap Between Concept and Application," *Journal of Marketing*, vol. 51 (January 1987), pp. 44–58.

Shaw, Robert Bruce, *Trust in the Balance*, (San Francisco: Jossey-Bass Publishers, 1997).

Strout, Erin, "Tough Customers," *Sales Marketing Management*, January 2000, pp. 63–69.

Webber, Alan M., "Trust in the Future," *Fast Company*, September 2000, pp. 209–212ff.

Critical Thinking

1. What is the role of trust in the marketplace?
2. Describe an incident of a violation of trust in the marketplace that you yourself have experienced. When you discovered this violation, what was your response?

DR. JOHN E. RICHARDSON is Professor of Marketing in the Graziadio School of Business and Management at Pepperdine University, Malibu, California. **DR. LINNEA BERNARD MCCORD** is Associate Professor of Business Law in the Graziadio School of Business and Management at Pepperdine University, Malibu, California.

Privacy and the Internet
Lives of Others

Facebook and Google face a backlash, from users and regulators alike, over the way they have handled sensitive data.

THE ECONOMIST

Jennifer Stoddart, Canada's privacy commissioner, is furious with Facebook. In August 2009 the social-networking site struck a deal, agreeing to change its policies within a year to comply with the country's privacy law. Now, says Ms Stoddart, the company appears to be reneging on an important part of that deal, which involved giving users a clear and easy-to-implement choice over whether to share private data with third parties. "It doesn't seem to me that Facebook is going in the right direction on this issue," she says, hinting that, without a change of course, the firm could soon become the subject of another formal investigation by her organisation.

Facebook is not the only internet giant to provoke the ire of data watchdogs. Google endured withering criticism this week following news that it had recorded some personal communications sent over unsecured Wi-Fi data networks in homes and offices in some 30 countries. On May 17th Peter Schaar, Germany's federal commissioner for data protection, called for an independent investigation into Google's behaviour, claiming that it had "simply disobeyed normal rules in the development and usage of software."

The cases highlight rising tension between guardians of privacy and internet firms. And they reflect concern among web users about how private data are made public. Several prominent internet types such as Cory Doctorow, a science-fiction author, and Leo Laporte, a podcaster, have abandoned Facebook. Sites such as QuitFacebookDay.com are urging others to do so, nominating May 31st for a mass Facebook "suicide."

This is unlikely to stop the meteoric rise of Facebook, which is poised to claim half a billion members and which draws even more visitors as a whole to its site. But nerves have been rattled at the company's headquarters in Silicon Valley, where bosses are mulling over how to respond. Several senior folk are now hinting that Facebook will soon roll out simpler privacy controls to make it easier to keep more data hidden. MySpace, a rival, is already making its controls simpler in an effort to woo disaffected Facebookers to its service.

A revolt over Facebook's handling of privacy has been brewing for some time. In December the social network changed the default settings on its privacy controls so that individuals' personal information would be shared with "everyone" rather than selected friends. Facebook argued this reflected a shift in society towards greater openness and noted that users could still adjust privacy settings back again. But incensed privacy activists lobbied for it to be reversed.

The switch should not have come as a surprise. Early on, many social networks impose fairly tough privacy policies in order to attract and reassure users. But as more join, controls are gradually loosened to encourage more sharing. As people share more, Facebook can increase the traffic against which it sells advertising. And the more it learns about users' likes and dislikes, the better it can target ads that generate hundreds of millions of dollars.

Protests grew louder still following a developers' conference last month at which Mark Zuckerberg, Facebook's boss, announced yet another series of policy changes. One that caused irritation was an "instant personalisation" feature that lets certain third-party websites access Facebook data when people visit. Critics say that Facebook has made it tricky to disable this feature, which may explain why Ms Stoddart dislikes it so much.

European officials are grumbling about Facebook too. This month a group of data-protection experts who advise the European Commission wrote to the social network, calling its decision to loosen the default settings "unacceptable." And in the United States, the Electronic Privacy Information Centre, a non-profit group, has asked America's Federal Trade Commission to see if Facebook's approach to privacy violates consumer-protection laws.

Privacy watchdogs are also seeing if Google has broken any laws by capturing Wi-Fi data without permission. The search firm says that an experimental software project designed to gather data from unencrypted Wi-Fi networks was accidentally rolled out along with its Street View initiative, which uses cameras mounted on cars to film streets and buildings. As a result snippets of sensitive private data were collected and stored for years, without the Street View leaders' knowledge.

Street Unwise

Google apologised and stressed that the unauthorised sampling collected only enough data to fill a single computer hard disk. It added that the information had not been used in any products nor shared outside Google. And it said it would appoint an independent body to review the fiasco in addition to conducting an internal review of its privacy practices. "We screwed up," admitted Sergey Brin, a Google cofounder, on May 19th.

Yet Google's reputation has been damaged. The episode shows that it needs to get a better grip on what its staff are up to. Initial denials that it had collected sensitive data, reversed when Germany's privacy watchdog demanded a more detailed review, also look like a public-relations blunder. And doubts have been raised about the quality of some managers. A spokesman for the firm blamed "a failure of communication between teams and within teams." That is a worrying admission, given the vast amounts of sensitive data in Google's digital coffers.

It had already suffered this year during the launch of Buzz, its own social-networking service. Users complained that the search giant had dipped into their Gmail accounts to find "followers" for them without clearly explaining what was happening—a practice that the firm quickly scrapped. Last month ten privacy commissioners from countries such as Britain, Canada and France urged the company not to sideline privacy in a rush to launch new technology.

At Google's European Zeitgeist conference this week, Eric Schmidt claimed that the firm has the most consumer-centric privacy policy of any online service. Google's chief executive added that no harm had been done by the Wi-Fi debacle. Others may reach a similar conclusion. But tussles over privacy issues will persist. "Nobody has a clear view of where to draw the line on privacy matters online," says Jonathan Zittrain, a professor at Harvard Law School. Privacy commissioners will be busy for a while yet.

Critical Thinking

1. What electronic data do you expect to remain private when you post it on Facebook or other social media? How private is "private" on the Internet?

2. How is consumer privacy protected?

The New E-spionage Threat

A *BusinessWeek* probe of rising attacks on America's most sensitive computer networks uncovers startling security gaps.

BRIAN GROW, KEITH EPSTEIN, AND CHI-CHU TSCHANG

The e-mail message addressed to a Booz Allen Hamilton executive was mundane—a shopping list sent over by the Pentagon of weaponry India wanted to buy. But the missive turned out to be a brilliant fake. Lurking beneath the description of aircraft, engines, and radar equipment was an insidious piece of computer code known as "Poison Ivy" designed to suck sensitive data out of the $4 billion consulting firm's computer network.

The Pentagon hadn't sent the e-mail at all. Its origin is unknown, but the message traveled through Korea on its way to Booz Allen. Its authors knew enough about the "sender" and "recipient" to craft a message unlikely to arouse suspicion. Had the Booz Allen executive clicked on the attachment, his every keystroke would have been reported back to a mysterious master at the Internet address cybersyndrome.3322.org, which is registered through an obscure company headquartered on the banks of China's Yangtze River.

The U.S. government, and its sprawl of defense contractors, have been the victims of an unprecedented rash of similar cyber attacks over the last two years, say current and former U.S. government officials. "It's espionage on a massive scale," says Paul B. Kurtz, a former high-ranking national security official. Government agencies reported 12,986 cyber security incidents to the U.S. Homeland Security Dept. last fiscal year, triple the number from two years earlier. Incursions on the military's networks were up 55% last year, says Lieutenant General Charles E. Croom, head of the Pentagon's Joint Task Force for Global Network Operations. Private targets like Booz Allen are just as vulnerable and pose just as much potential security risk. "They have our information on their networks. They're building our weapon systems. You wouldn't want that in enemy hands," Croom says. Cyber attackers "are not denying, disrupting, or destroying operations—yet. But that doesn't mean they don't have the capability."

A Monster

When the deluge began in 2006, officials scurried to come up with software "patches," "wraps," and other bits of triage. The effort got serious last summer when top military brass discreetly summoned the chief executives or their representatives from the 20 largest U.S. defense contractors to the Pentagon for a "threat briefing." *BusinessWeek* has learned the U.S. government has launched a classified operation called Byzantine Foothold to detect, track, and disarm intrusions on the government's most critical networks. And President George W. Bush on Jan. 8 quietly signed an order known as the Cyber Initiative to overhaul U.S. cyber defenses, at an eventual cost in the tens of billions of dollars, and establishing 12 distinct goals, according to people briefed on its contents. One goal in particular illustrates the urgency and scope of the problem: By June all government agencies must cut the number of communication channels, or ports, through which their networks connect to the Internet from more than 4,000 to fewer than 100. On Apr. 8, Homeland Security Dept. Secretary Michael Chertoff called the President's order a cyber security "Manhattan Project."

But many security experts worry the Internet has become too unwieldy to be tamed. New exploits appear every day, each seemingly more sophisticated than the previous one. The Defense Dept., whose Advanced Research Projects Agency (DARPA) developed the Internet in the 1960s, is beginning to think it created a monster. "You don't need an Army, a Navy, an Air Force to beat the U.S.," says General William T. Lord, commander of the Air Force Cyber Command, a unit formed in November, 2006, to upgrade Air Force computer defenses. "You can be a peer force for the price of the PC on my desk." Military officials have long believed that "it's cheaper, and we kill stuff faster, when we use the Internet to enable high-tech warfare,"

An Evolving Crisis

Major attacks on the U.S. government and defense industry—and their code names.

Solar Sunrise

February, 1998. Air Force and Navy computers are hit by malicious code that sniffed out a hole in a popular enterprise software operating system, patched its own entry point—then did nothing. Some attacks are routed through the United Arab Emirates while the U.S. is preparing for military action in Iraq. Turns out the attacks were launched by two teenagers in Cloverdale, Calif., and an Israeli accomplice who called himself the "Analyzer."

Moonlight Maze

March, 1998, through 1999. Attackers use special code to gain access to websites at the Defense Dept., NASA, the Energy Dept., and weapons labs across the country. Large packets of unclassified data are stolen. "At times, the end point [for the data] was inside Russia," says a source familiar with the investigation. The sponsor of the attack has never been identified. The Russian government denied any involvement.

Titan Rain

2004. Hackers believed to be in China access classified data stored on computer networks of defense contractor Lockheed Martin, Sandia National Labs, and NASA. The intrusions are identified by Shawn Carpenter, a cyber security analyst at Sandia Labs. After he reports the breaches to the U.S. Army and FBI, Sandia fires him. Carpenter later sues Sandia for wrongful termination. In February, 2007, a jury awards him $4.7 million.

Byzantine Foothold

2007. A new form of attack, using sophisticated technology, deluges outfits from the State Dept. to Boeing. Military cyber security specialists find the "resources of a nation-state behind it" and call the type of attack an "advanced persistent threat." The breaches are detailed in a classified document known as an Intelligence Community Assessment. The source of many of the attacks, allege U.S. officials, is China. China denies the charge.

---

says a top adviser to the U.S. military on the overhaul of its computer security strategy. "Now they're saying, Oh, shit."

Adding to Washington's anxiety, current and former U.S. government officials say many of the new attackers are trained professionals backed by foreign governments. "The new breed of threat that has evolved is nation-state-sponsored stuff," says Amit Yoran, a former director of Homeland Security's National Cyber Security Div. Adds one of the nation's most senior military officers: "We've got to figure out how to get at it before our regrets exceed our ability to react."

The military and intelligence communities have alleged that the People's Republic of China is the U.S.'s biggest cyber menace. "In the past year, numerous computer networks around the world, including those owned by the U.S. government, were subject to intrusions that appear to have originated within the PRC," reads the Pentagon's annual report to Congress on Chinese military power, released on Mar. 3. The preamble of Bush's Cyber Initiative focuses attention on China as well.

Wang Baodong, a spokesman for the Chinese government at its embassy in Washington, says "anti-China forces" are behind the allegations. Assertions by U.S. officials and others of cyber intrusions sponsored or encouraged by China are unwarranted, he wrote in an Apr. 9 e-mail response to questions from *BusinessWeek*. "The Chinese government always opposes and forbids any cyber crimes including 'hacking' that undermine the security of computer networks," says Wang. China itself, he adds, is a victim, "frequently intruded and attacked by hackers from certain countries."

Because the Web allows digital spies and thieves to mask their identities, conceal their physical locations, and bounce malicious code to and fro, it's frequently impossible to pinpoint specific attackers. Network security professionals call this digital masquerade ball "the attribution problem."

A Credible Message

In written responses to questions from *BusinessWeek*, officials in the office of National Intelligence Director J. Michael McConnell, a leading proponent of boosting government cyber security, would not comment "on specific code-word programs" such as Byzantine Foothold, nor on "specific intrusions or possible victims." But the department says that "computer intrusions have been successful against a wide range of government and corporate networks across the critical infrastructure and defense industrial base." The White House declined to address the contents of the Cyber Initiative, citing its classified nature.

The e-mail aimed at Booz Allen, obtained by *BusinessWeek* and traced back to an Internet address in China, paints a vivid picture of the alarming new capabilities of America's cyber enemies. On Sept. 5, 2007, at 08:22:21 Eastern time, an e-mail message appeared to be sent to John F. "Jack" Mulhern, vice-president for international military assistance programs at Booz Allen. In the high-tech world of weapons sales, Mulhern's specialty, the e-mail looked authentic enough. "Integrate U.S., Russian, and Indian weapons and avionics," the e-mail noted, describing the Indian government's expectations for its fighter jets. "Source code given to India for indigenous computer upgrade capability." Such lingo could easily be understood by Mulhern. The 62-year-old former U.S. Naval officer and 33-year veteran of Booz Allen's military consulting business is an expert in helping to sell U.S. weapons to foreign governments.

The e-mail was more convincing because of its apparent sender: Stephen J. Moree, a civilian who works for a group that reports to the office of Air Force Secretary Michael W. Wynne. Among its duties, Moree's unit evaluates the security of selling U.S. military aircraft to other countries. There would be little reason to suspect anything seriously amiss in Moree's passing along the highly technical document with "India MRCA Request for Proposal" in the subject line. The Indian government had just released the request a week earlier, on Aug. 28, and the language in the e-mail closely tracked the request. Making the message appear more credible still: It referred to upcoming Air Force communiqués and a "Teaming Meeting" to discuss the deal.

But the missive from Moree to Jack Mulhern was a fake. An analysis of the e-mail's path and attachment, conducted for *BusinessWeek* by three cyber security specialists, shows it was sent by an unknown attacker, bounced through an Internet address in South Korea, was relayed through a Yahoo! server in New York, and finally made its way toward Mulhern's Booz Allen in-box. The analysis also shows the code—known as "malware," for malicious software—tracks keystrokes on the computers of people who open it. A separate program disables security measures such as password protection on Microsoft Access database files, a program often used by large organizations such as the U.S. defense industry to manage big batches of data.

An E-mail's Journey

While hardly the most sophisticated technique used by electronic thieves these days, "if you have any kind of sensitive documents on Access databases, this [code] is getting in there and getting them out," says a senior executive at a leading cyber security firm that analyzed the e-mail. (The person requested anonymity because his firm provides security consulting to U.S. military departments, defense contractors, and financial institutions.) Commercial computer security firms have dubbed the malicious code "Poison Ivy."

But the malware attached to the fake Air Force e-mail has a more devious—and worrisome—capability. Known as a remote administration tool, or RAT, it gives the attacker control over the "host" PC, capturing screen shots and perusing files. It lurks in the background of Microsoft Internet Explorer browsers while users surf the Web. Then it phones home to its "master" at an Internet address currently registered under the name cybersyndrome.3322.org.

The digital trail to cybersyndrome.3322.org, followed by analysts at *BusinessWeek*'s request, leads to one of China's largest free domain-name-registration and e-mail services. Called 3322.org, it is registered to a company called Bentium in the city of Changzhou, an industry hub outside Shanghai. A range of security experts say that 3322.org provides names for computers and servers that act as the command and control centers for more than 10,000 pieces of malicious code launched at government and corporate networks in recent years. Many of those PCs are in China; the rest could be anywhere.

The founder of 3322.org, a 37-year-old technology entrepreneur named Peng Yong, says his company merely allows users to register domain names. "As for what our users do, we cannot completely control it," says Peng. The bottom line: If Poison Ivy infected Jack Mulhern's computer at Booz Allen, any secrets inside could be seen in China. And if it spread to other computers, as malware often does, the infection opens windows on potentially sensitive information there, too.

It's not clear whether Mulhern received the e-mail, but the address was accurate. Informed by *BusinessWeek* on Mar. 20 of the fake message, Booz Allen spokesman George Farrar says the company launched a search to find it. As of Apr. 9, says Farrar, the company had not discovered the e-mail or Poison Ivy in Booz Allen's networks. Farrar says Booz Allen computer security executives examined the PCs of Mulhern and an assistant who received his e-mail. "We take this very seriously," says Farrar. (Mulhern, who retired in March, did not respond to e-mailed requests for comment and declined a request, through Booz Allen, for an interview.)

Air Force officials referred requests for comment to U.S. Defense Secretary Robert M. Gates' office. In an e-mailed response to *BusinessWeek,* Gates' office acknowledges being the target of cyber attacks from "a variety of state and non-state-sponsored organizations to gain unauthorized access to, or otherwise degrade, [Defense Dept.] information systems." But the Pentagon declined to discuss the attempted Booz Allen break-in. The Air Force, meanwhile, would not make Stephen Moree available for comment.

The bogus e-mail, however, seemed to cause a stir inside the Air Force, correspondence reviewed by *BusinessWeek* shows. On Sept. 4, defense analyst James Mulvenon also received the message with Moree and Mulhern's names on it. Security experts believe Mulvenon's e-mail address was secretly included in the "blind copy" line of a version of the message. Mulvenon is director of the Center for Intelligence Research & Analysis and a leading consultant to U.S. defense and intelligence agencies on China's military and cyber strategy. He maintains an Excel spreadsheet of suspect e-mails, malicious code, and hacker groups and passes them along to the authorities. Suspicious of the

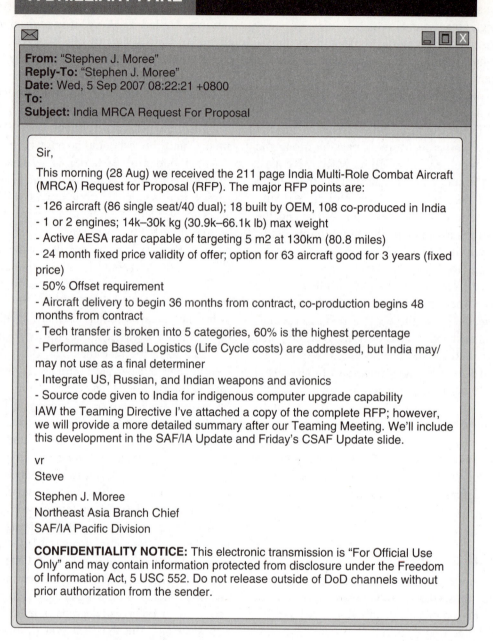

A BRILLIANT FAKE
The bogus e-mail aimed at Booz Allen Hamilton

From: "Stephen J. Moree"
Reply-To: "Stephen J. Moree"
Date: Wed, 5 Sep 2007 08:22:21 +0800
To:
Subject: India MRCA Request For Proposal

Sir,

This morning (28 Aug) we received the 211 page India Multi-Role Combat Aircraft (MRCA) Request for Proposal (RFP). The major RFP points are:

- 126 aircraft (86 single seat/40 dual); 18 built by OEM, 108 co-produced in India
- 1 or 2 engines; 14k–30k kg (30.9k–66.1k lb) max weight
- Active AESA radar capable of targeting 5 m2 at 130km (80.8 miles)
- 24 month fixed price validity of offer; option for 63 aircraft good for 3 years (fixed price)
- 50% Offset requirement
- Aircraft delivery to begin 36 months from contract, co-production begins 48 months from contract
- Tech transfer is broken into 5 categories, 60% is the highest percentage
- Performance Based Logistics (Life Cycle costs) are addressed, but India may/ may not use as a final determiner
- Integrate US, Russian, and Indian weapons and avionics
- Source code given to India for indigenous computer upgrade capability

IAW the Teaming Directive I've attached a copy of the complete RFP; however, we will provide a more detailed summary after our Teaming Meeting. We'll include this development in the SAF/IA Update and Friday's CSAF Update slide.

vr
Steve

Stephen J. Moree
Northeast Asia Branch Chief
SAF/IA Pacific Division

CONFIDENTIALITY NOTICE: This electronic transmission is "For Official Use Only" and may contain information protected from disclosure under the Freedom of Information Act, 5 USC 552. Do not release outside of DoD channels without prior authorization from the sender.

note when he received it, Mulvenon replied to Moree the next day. Was the e-mail "India spam?" Mulvenon asked.

"I apologize—this e-mail was sent in error—please delete," Moree responded a few hours later.

"No worries," typed Mulvenon. "I have been getting a lot of trojaned Access databases from China lately and just wanted to make sure."

"Interesting—our network folks are looking into some kind of malicious intent behind this e-mail snafu," wrote Moree. Neither the Air Force nor the Defense Dept. would confirm to *BusinessWeek* whether an investigation was conducted. A Pentagon spokesman says that its procedure

is to refer attacks to law enforcement or counterintelligence agencies. He would not disclose which, if any, is investigating the Air Force e-mail.

Digital Intruders

By itself, the bid to steal digital secrets from Booz Allen might not be deeply troubling. But Poison Ivy is part of a new type of digital intruder rendering traditional defenses—firewalls and updated antivirus software—virtually useless. Sophisticated hackers, say Pentagon officials, are developing new ways to creep into computer networks sometimes before those vulnerabilities are known. "The offense has a big advantage over the defense right now," says Colonel Ward E. Heinke, director of the Air Force Network Operations Center at Barksdale Air Force Base. Only 11 of the top 34 antivirus software programs identified Poison Ivy when it was first tested on behalf of *BusinessWeek* in February. Malware-sniffing software from several top security firms found "no virus" in the India fighter-jet e-mail, the analysis showed.

"Poison ivy" is part of a new type of digital intruder rendering traditional perimeter defenses like firewalls virtually useless.

Over the past two years thousands of highly customized e-mails akin to Stephen Moree's have landed in the laptops and PCs of U.S. government workers and defense contracting executives. According to sources familiar with the matter, the attacks targeted sensitive information on the networks of at least seven agencies—the Defense, State, Energy, Commerce, Health & Human Services, Agriculture, and Treasury departments—and also defense contractors Boeing, Lockheed Martin, General Electric, Raytheon, and General Dynamics, say current and former government network security experts. Laura Keehner, a spokeswoman for the Homeland Security Dept., which coordinates protection of government computers, declined to comment on specific intrusions. In written responses to questions from *BusinessWeek,* Keehner says: "We are aware of and have defended against malicious cyber activity directed at the U.S. Government over the past few years. We take these threats seriously and continue to remain concerned that this activity is growing more sophisticated, more targeted, and more prevalent." Spokesmen for Lockheed Martin, Boeing, Raytheon, General Dynamics, and General Electric declined to comment. Several cited policies of not discussing security-related matters.

The rash of computer infections is the subject of Byzantine Foothold, the classified operation designed to root out the perpetrators and protect systems in the future, according to three people familiar with the matter. In some cases, the government's own cyber security experts are engaged in "hack-backs"—following the malicious code to peer into the hackers' own computer systems. *BusinessWeek* has learned that a classified document called an intelligence community assessment, or ICA, details the Byzantine intrusions and assigns each a unique Byzantine-related name. The ICA has circulated in recent months among selected officials at U.S. intelligence agencies, the Pentagon, and cyber security consultants acting as outside reviewers. Until December, details of the ICA's

---

Anatomy of a Spear-Phish

The three stages of a successful spear-phishing attack.

Net Reconnaissance

Online cunning need not start with insiders or illegally obtained information. Attackers can scour the Web—studying public documents, chat rooms, and blogs—to build digital dossiers about the jobs, responsibilities, and personal networks of targets.

Constructing the "Spear-Phish"

Attackers build an e-mail with a web link or attachment on a subject likely to trick the victim into clicking on it. Common spear-phish topics include news events, earnings results, and Word and PowerPoint documents containing real info. The e-mail address is made to look like it comes from a logical sender.

Harvesting the Data

When the victim opens the attachment or clicks on the web link, malicious code hidden inside combs document files, steals passwords, and sends the data to a "command and control" server, often in a foreign country, which collects the data for study.

---

contents had not even been shared with congressional intelligence committees.

Now, Senate Intelligence Committee Chairman John D. Rockefeller (D-W. Va.) is said to be discreetly informing fellow senators of the Byzantine operation, in part to win their support for needed appropriations, many of which are part of classified "black" budgets kept off official government books. Rockefeller declined to comment. In January a Senate Intelligence Committee staffer urged his boss, Missouri Republican Christopher "Kit" Bond, the committee's vice-chairman, to supplement closed-door testimony and classified documents with a viewing of the movie *Die Hard 4* on a flight the senator made to New Zealand. In the film, cyber terrorists breach FBI networks, purloin financial data, and bring car traffic to a halt in Washington. Hollywood, says Bond, doesn't exaggerate as much as people might think. "I can't discuss classified matters," he cautions. "But the movie illustrates the potential impact of a cyber conflict. Except for a few things, let me just tell you: It's credible."

"Phishing," one technique used in many attacks, allows cyber spies to steal information by posing as a trustworthy entity in an online communication. The term was coined in the mid-1990s when hackers began "fishing" for information (and tweaked the spelling). The e-mail attacks on government agencies and defense contractors, called "spear-phish" because they target specific individuals, are the Web version of laser-guided missiles. Spear-phish creators gather information about people's jobs and social networks, often from publicly available information and data stolen from other infected computers, and then trick them into opening an e-mail.

Devious Script

Spear-phish tap into a cyber espionage tactic that security experts call "Net reconnaissance." In the attempted attack on Booz Allen, attackers had plenty of information about Moree: his full name, title (Northeast Asia Branch Chief), job responsibilities, and e-mail address. Net reconnaissance can be surprisingly simple, often starting with a Google search. (A lookup of the Air Force's Pentagon e-mail address on Apr. 9, for instance, retrieved 8,680 e-mail addresses for current or former Air Force personnel and departments.) The information is woven into a fake e-mail with a link to an infected website or containing an attached document. All attackers have to do is hit their send button. Once the e-mail is opened, intruders are automatically ushered inside the walled perimeter of computer networks—and malicious code such as Poison Ivy can take over.

By mid-2007 analysts at the National Security Agency began to discern a pattern: personalized e-mails with corrupted attachments such as PowerPoint presentations, Word documents, and Access database files had been turning up on computers connected to the networks of numerous agencies and defense contractors.

A previously undisclosed breach in the autumn of 2005 at the American Enterprise Institute—a conservative think tank whose former officials and corporate executive board members are closely connected to the Bush Administration—proved so nettlesome that the White House shut off aides' access to the website for more than six months, says a cyber security specialist familiar with the incident. The Defense Dept. shut the door for even longer. Computer security investigators, one of whom spoke with *BusinessWeek,* identified the culprit: a few lines of Java script buried in AEI's home page, www.aei.org, that activated as soon as someone visited the site. The script secretly redirected the user's computer to another server that attempted to load malware. The malware, in turn, sent information from the visitor's hard drive to a server in China. But the security specialist says cyber sleuths couldn't get rid of the intruder. After each deletion, the furtive code would reappear. AEI says otherwise—except for a brief accidental recurrence caused by its own network personnel in August, 2007, the devious Java script did not return and was not difficult to eradicate.

The breach of a highly sensitive State Dept. Bureau posed a risk to CIA operatives in embassies around the globe.

The government has yet to disclose the breaches related to Byzantine Foothold. *BusinessWeek* has learned that intruders managed to worm into the State Dept.'s highly sensitive Bureau of Intelligence & Research, a key channel between the work of intelligence agencies and the rest of the government. The breach posed a risk to CIA operatives in embassies around the globe, say several network security specialists familiar with the effort to cope with what became seen as an internal crisis. Teams worked around-the-clock in search of malware, they say, calling the White House regularly with updates.

The attack began in May, 2006, when an unwitting employee in the State Dept.'s East Asia Pacific region clicked on an attachment in a seemingly authentic e-mail. Malicious code was embedded in the Word document, a congressional speech, and opened a Trojan "back door" for the code's creators to peer inside the State Dept.'s innermost networks. Soon, cyber security engineers began spotting more intrusions in State Dept. computers across the globe. The malware took advantage of previously unknown vulnerabilities in the Microsoft operating system. Unable to develop a patch quickly enough, engineers watched helplessly as streams of State Dept. data slipped through the back door and into the Internet ether. Although they were unable to fix the vulnerability, specialists came up with a temporary scheme to block further infections. They also yanked connections to the Internet.

One member of the emergency team summoned to the scene recalls that each time cyber security professionals thought they had eliminated the source of a "beacon" reporting back to its master, another popped up. He compared the effort to the arcade game Whack-A-Mole. The State Dept. says it eradicated the infection, but only after sanitizing scores of infected computers and servers and changing passwords. Microsoft's own patch, meanwhile, was not deployed until August, 2006, three months after the infection. A Microsoft spokeswoman declined to comment on the episode, but said: "Microsoft has, for several years, taken a comprehensive approach to help protect people online."

There is little doubt among senior U.S. officials about where the trail of the recent wave of attacks leads. "The Byzantine series tracks back to China," says Air Force Colonel Heinke. More than a dozen current and former U.S. military, cyber security, and intelligence officials interviewed by *BusinessWeek* say China is the biggest emerging adversary—and not just clubs of rogue or enterprising hackers who happen to be Chinese. O. Sami Saydjari, a former National Security Agency executive and now president of computer security firm Cyber Defense Agency, says the Chinese People's Liberation Army, one of the world's largest military forces, with an annual budget of $57 billion, has "tens of thousands" of trainees launching attacks on U.S. computer networks. Those figures could not be independently confirmed by *BusinessWeek*. Other experts provide lower estimates and note that even one hacker can do a lot of damage. Says Saydjari: "We have to look at this as equivalent to the launch of a Chinese Sputnik." China vigorously disputes the spying allegation and says its military posture is purely defensive.

Hints of the perils perceived within America's corridors of power have been slipping out in recent months. In Feb. 27 testimony before the U.S. Senate Armed Services Committee, National Intelligence Director McConnell echoed the view that the threat comes from China. He told Congress he worries less about people capturing information than altering it. "If someone has the ability to enter information in systems, they can destroy data. And the destroyed data could be something like money supply, electric-power distribution, transportation sequencing, and that sort of thing." His conclusion: "The federal government is not well-protected and the private sector is not well-protected."

Worries about China-sponsored Internet attacks spread last year to Germany, France, and Britain. British domestic intelligence agency MI5 had seen enough evidence of intrusion and theft of corporate secrets by allegedly state-sponsored Chinese hackers by November, 2007, that the agency's director general, Jonathan Evans, sent an unusual letter of warning to 300 corporations, accounting firms, and law firms—and a list of network security specialists to help block computer intrusions. Some recipients of the MI5 letter hired Peter Yapp, a leading security consultant with London-based Control Risks. "People treat this like it's just another hacker story, and it is almost unbelievable," says Yapp. "There's a James Bond element to it. Too many people think, 'It's not going to happen to me.' But it has."

Identifying the thieves slipping their malware through the digital gates can be tricky. Some computer security specialists doubt China's government is involved in cyber attacks on U.S. defense targets. Peter Sommer, an information systems security specialist at the London School of Economics who helps companies secure networks, says: "I suspect if it's an official part of the Chinese government, you wouldn't be spotting it."

A range of attacks in the past two years on U.S. and foreign government entities, defense contractors, and corporate networks have been traced to Internet addresses registered through Chinese domain name services such as

The Government's Response

Key elements of the U.S. "Cyber Initiative," signed on Jan. 8.

Cut Connections

Aims to cut the number of portals between government networks and the Internet from more than 4,000 to fewer than 100.

Passive Intrusion Prevention

Requires a plan to identify when unauthorized entities have gained access to computer networks.

Active Intrusion Prevention

Requires a program to trace cyber intrusions back to their source, both countries and people.

Counterintelligence Strategy

Requires a plan to deter and prevent future computer network breaches.

Counterintelligence Tools

Launches a program to develop the technology for cyber forensic analysis.

Education

Creates training programs to develop technical skills to improve cyber security.

Fusing Operations

Combines the computer command posts known as "network operations centers" of an unknown number of agencies.

Cyber R&D

Launches a plan to develop offensive and defensive cyber capabilities, including those developed by contractors.

Leap-Ahead Technologies

Aims to invent "killer apps" to win the cyber arms race.

Critical Infrastructure Protection

Calls for a plan to work with the private sector, which owns and operates most of the Internet.

Revisit Project Solarium

Like the Eisenhower project to deter nuclear war, aims to prevent a cyber war.

Improve Federal Acquisitions

Starts program to ensure government IT products and services are secure.

3322.org, run by Peng Yong. In late March, *BusinessWeek* interviewed Peng in an apartment on the 14th floor of the gray-tiled residential building that houses the five-person office for 3322.org in Changzhou. Peng says he started

3322.org in 2001 with $14,000 of his own money so the growing ranks of China's Net surfers could register websites and distribute data. "We felt that this business would be very popular, especially as broadband, fiber-optic cables, [data transmission technology] ADSL, these ways of getting on the Internet took off," says Peng (translated by *BusinessWeek* from Mandarin), who drives a black Lexus IS300 bought last year.

His 3322.org has indeed become a hit. Peng says the service has registered more than 1 million domain names, charging $14 per year for "top-level" names ending in .com, .org, or .net. But cyber security experts and the Homeland Security Dept.'s U.S. Computer Emergency Readiness Team (CERT) say that 3322.org is a hit with another group: hackers. That's because 3322.org and five sister sites controlled by Peng are dynamic DNS providers. Like an Internet phone book, dynamic DNS assigns names for the digits that mark a computer's location on the Web. For example, 3322.org is the registrar for the name cybersyndrome.3322.org at Internet address 61.234.4.28, the China-based computer that was contacted by the malicious code in the attempted Booz Allen attack, according to analyses reviewed by *BusinessWeek*. "Hackers started using sites like 3322.org so that the malware phones home to the specific name. The reason? It is relatively difficult to have [Internet addresses] taken down in China," says Maarten van Horenbeeck, a Belgium-based intrusion analyst for the SANS Internet Storm Center, a cyber threat monitoring group.

Target: Private Sector

Peng's 3322.org and sister sites have become a source of concern to the U.S. government and private firms. Cyber security firm Team Cymru sent a confidential report, reviewed by *BusinessWeek*, to clients on Mar. 7 that illustrates how 3322.org has enabled many recent attacks. In early March, the report says, Team Cymru received "a spoofed e-mail message from a U.S. military entity, and the PowerPoint attachment had a malware widget embedded in it." The e-mail was a spear-phish. The computer that controlled the malicious code in the PowerPoint? Cybersyndrome.3322.org—the same China-registered computer in the attempted attack on Booz Allen. Although the cybersyndrome Internet address may not be located in China, the top five computers communicating directly with it were—and four were registered with a large state-owned Internet service provider, according to the report.

A person familiar with Team Cymru's research says the company has 10,710 distinct malware samples that communicate to masters registered through 3322.org. Other groups reporting attacks from computers hosted by 3322.org

include activist group Students for a Free Tibet, the European Parliament, and U.S. Bancorp according to security reports. Team Cymru declined to comment. The U.S. government has pinpointed Peng's services as a problem, too. In a Nov. 28, 2007, confidential report from Homeland Security's U.S. CERT obtained by *BusinessWeek*, "Cyber Incidents Suspected of Impacting Private Sector Networks," the federal cyber watchdog warned U.S. corporate information technology staff to update security software to block Internet traffic from a dozen Web addresses after spear-phishing attacks. "The level of sophistication and scope of these cyber security incidents indicates they are coordinated and targeted at private-sector systems," says the report. Among the sites named: Peng's 3322.org, as well as his 8800.org, 9966.org, and 8866.org. Homeland Security and U.S. CERT declined to discuss the report.

Peng says he has no idea hackers are using his service to send and control malicious code. "Are there a lot?" he says when asked why so many hackers use 3322.org. He says his business is not responsible for cyber attacks on U.S. computers. "It's like we have paved a road and what sort of car [users] drive on it is their own business," says Peng, who adds that he spends most of his time these days developing Internet telephony for his new software firm, Bitcomm Software Tech Co. Peng says he was not aware that several of his websites and Internet addresses registered through them were named in the U.S. CERT report. On Apr. 7, he said he planned to shut the sites down and contact the U.S. agency. Asked by *BusinessWeek* to check his database for the person who registered the computer at the domain name cybersyndrome.3322.org, Peng says it is registered to Gansu Railway Communications, a regional telecom subsidiary of China's Railways Ministry. Peng declined to provide the name of the registrant, citing a confidentiality agreement. "You can go through the police to find out the user information," says Peng.

U.S. cyber security experts say it's doubtful that the Chinese government would allow the high volume of attacks on U.S. entities from China-based computers if it didn't want them to happen. "China has one of the best-controlled Internets in the world. Anything that happens on their Internet requires permission," says Cyber Defense Group's Saydjari. The Chinese government spokesman declined to answer specific questions from *BusinessWeek* about 3322.org.

Britain's MI5 intelligence agency sent a warning in 2007 to 300 companies about thefts of corporate secrets by Chinese hackers.

But Peng says he can do little if hackers exploit his goodwill—and there hasn't been much incentive from the Chinese government for him to get tough. "Normally, we take care of these problems by shutting them down," says Peng. "Because our laws do not have an extremely clear method to handle this problem, sometimes we are helpless to stop their services." And so, it seems thus far, is the U.S. government.

Critical Thinking

1. What is the responsibility of registration domains such as cybersyndrome.3322.org vis-à-vis the activities of the domains they provide?

2. How can an e-mail recipient confirm that an e-mail received is from a reliable source?

Emerging Lessons

For multinational companies, understanding the needs of poorer consumers can be profitable and socially responsible.

Madhubalan Viswanathan, José Antonio Rosa, and Julie A. Ruth

Businesses, take note: An underserved and poorly understood consumer group is poised to become a driving force in economic and business development, by virtue of sheer numbers and rising globalization.

They are subsistence consumers—people in developing nations like India who earn just a few dollars a day and lack access to basics such as education, health care and sanitation.

As these consumers gain access to income and information over the next decade, their combined purchasing power, already in the trillions of dollars, likely will grow at higher rates than that of consumers in industrialized nations. The lesson for multinational companies: Understanding and addressing the needs of the world's poorest consumers is likely to become a profitable, as well as a socially responsible, strategy.

A characteristic associated with low-income consumers, and one that has major implications for doing business with them, is that many struggle with reading and math. Like the 14% of Americans estimated to be functionally illiterate in a U.S. government survey, subsistence consumers have difficulty reading package labels, store signs or product-use instructions, or subtracting the purchase price of an item from cash on hand—all of which hampers their ability to put their limited incomes to best use.

Our research shows that low-literacy consumers process market information and approach purchasing decisions differently than other groups of shoppers. As a result, companies may have to alter marketing practices such as packaging, advertising, pricing, store signage and the training of retail-store employees in order to communicate with them more effectively and win their business.

Here is what we learned from our studies on low-literacy, low-income consumers in the U.S. and subsistence consumers in developing markets, and our recommendations on how marketers can improve the value these groups get from product purchase and use.

Concrete Thinking

One of the key observations we made is that low-literacy consumers have difficulty with abstract thinking. These individuals tend to group objects by visualizing concrete and practical situations they have experienced.

They exhibited what science would call a low grasp of abstract categories—tools, cooking utensils or protein-rich foods, for example—which suggests low-literacy consumers may have difficulty understanding advertising and store signs that position products that way. Their natural inclination is to organize merchandise according to the ingredients needed to make a particular dish or the products needed to complete a specific task, such as doing laundry or cleaning the bathroom, and that is often what they are envisioning as they navigate store aisles, deciding what to buy.

This is reminiscent of research on low-literacy peasants in Central Asia in the early 20th century, who, when presented with a set of objects such as hammer-saw-log-hatchet and asked to select the three that could be placed in one group or be described by one word, didn't derive abstract categories such as "tools" even when prompted. Instead, they grouped the objects primarily around envisioned tasks such as chopping firewood.

Being anchored in the perceptual "here and now" also interferes with the ability of low-literacy consumers to perform mathematical computations, especially those

For Further Reading

See these related articles from MIT Sloan Management Review.

Strategic Innovation at the Base of the Pyramid

By Jamie Anderson and Costas Markides (Fall 2007)
   Strategic innovation in developing markets is fundamentally different from what occurs in developed economies. http://sloanreview.mit.edu/smr/issue/2007/fall/16/

The Great Leap: Driving Innovation from the Base of the Pyramid

By Stuart L. Hart and Clayton M. Christensen (Fall 2002)
   Companies can generate growth and satisfy social and environmental stakeholders through a "great leap" to the base of the economic pyramid. http://sloanreview.mit .edu/smr/issue/2002/fall/5/

Has Strategy Changed?

By Kathleen M. Eisenhardt (Winter 2002)
   Globalization has quietly transformed the economic playing field. http://sloanreview.mit.edu/smr/issue/2002/winter/10/

The Need for a Corporate Global Mind-Set

By Thomas M. Begley and David P. Boyd (Winter 2003)
   Many international business leaders consider a global mind-set desirable, but few know how to embed it companywide. http://sloanreview.mit.edu/smr/issue/2003/winter/3/

The Dynamic Synchronization of Strategy and Information Technology

By C.K. Prahalad and M.S. Krishnan (Summer 2002)
   The authors' work with 500 executives revealed that few managers believed their information infrastructure was able to handle the pressures from deregulation, globalization, ubiquitous connectivity and the convergence of industries and technologies. http://sloanreview.mit .edu/smr/issue/2002/summer/2/

framed in abstract terms. For example, when we asked low-literacy shoppers in the U.S. to estimate whether they had enough cash to pay for the groceries in their cart, many needed to physically handle cash and envision additional piles of currency or coins to accurately estimate the cost of goods in their cart; when the sensorial experience of counting cash was taken away, they often were at a loss.

Because handling cash while walking store aisles isn't advisable, many low-literacy consumers arrive at checkout counters not knowing whether they have enough money to cover their purchases. All too often, they hand all of their cash to the register attendant and hope for an honest transaction.

One of the most potentially detrimental results of concrete thinking, however, is the difficulty that low-literacy consumers have with performing price/volume calculations. They tend to choose products based solely on the lowest posted price or smallest package size, even when they have sufficient resources for a larger purchase, because they have difficulty estimating the longevity and savings that come from buying in larger volumes. Some base purchase decisions on physical package size, instead of reported volume content, or on the quantity of a particular ingredient—such as fat, sodium or sugar—but without allowing for the fact that acceptable levels of an ingredient can vary across product categories or package size.

Misspent Energy

We found that low-literacy consumers spend so much time and mental energy on what many of us can do quickly and with little thought that they have little time to base purchase decisions on anything other than surface attributes such as size, color or weight.

They tend to think in pictures, so any change in visual cues such as sign fonts, brand logos or store layouts can leave them struggling to locate a desired product category or brand. Price displays can cause confusion because of the many numbers presented, such as original prices, discounted percentages and discounted prices. Even estimating the price of two gallons of milk if the price of one is known may require a pencil-and-paper calculation unless the price is set in whole or half-unit increments, such as $3 or $3.50.

Because so much shopping time is devoted to deciphering product labels and locating products, we found that low-literacy consumers are less able than other groups to assess the value of products based on subsurface attributes—this computer has more memory and will do what I need more effectively, for example.

When shopping in unfamiliar stores, some low-literacy consumers will choose products at random, buying the first brand they see once they locate a desired product category or aisle. Others simply walk through the store, choosing items that look attractive based on factors such as packaging colors or label illustrations, without regard to whether they even need the product.

When shopping in familiar stores, many low-literacy consumers buy only the brands they recognize by appearance or have purchased previously. While this approach reduces the incidence of product purchases for which the consumer has no use, it precludes the adoption of new and improved products as a category evolves and improves over time.

The pitfalls and uncertainty that come from choosing products at random, based on surface attributes or out of habit provoke anxiety in many low-literacy consumers, leading us to another finding: Shopping takes a heavy emotional toll on this group.

Buying the wrong items, running short of cash at the register or having to ask for help in the aisle to locate products are recurring worries, even cause for despair. The anticipation of such stressful experiences prompts some low-literacy consumers to avoid new, large or what they perceive to be threatening shopping venues or to delay shopping until family or friends can assist, even if waiting means doing without essentials. Although low-literacy consumers tend to be passive in public settings, they will remember episodes of poor treatment by service personnel and won't patronize stores or brands they associate with disrespectful treatment.

Despite the significant constraints that low-literacy consumers face, their ingenuity in coping and positive outlook are a testament to human adaptiveness. For instance, subsistence consumers overcome many of the challenges that come from not being able to read or do math problems by relying on their interpersonal networks—family and friends who may have complementary skills and knowledge. In many situations, the network includes the owners of neighborhood stores who offer very limited product assortments and high prices, but who can answer questions and offer advice to consumers unable to read the labels and determine the value of products on their own.

Subsistence consumers are resource-poor but likely to be relationship-rich, and this must be taken into account by businesses seeking to serve them.

Drawing them in

To win and enhance customer loyalty in developing markets, manufacturers and retailers need to understand the difficulties faced by low-literacy consumers and create shopping environments that make them feel less vulnerable. Here are a few ways that companies can help customers make better purchases and avoid embarrassment:

- Display prices and price reductions graphically—a half-circle to indicate a 50% markdown, for example, or a picture of three one-dollar bills to indicate a purchase price of $3. Price products in whole and half numbers to make it easier for low-literacy consumers to calculate the price of, say, two bags of rice. These pricing practices are critically important in marketplaces where general stores and kiosks are being replaced by self-service stores, where there is less interaction between customer and store owner.

- Clearly post unit prices in common formats across stores, brands and product categories to make it easier for low-literacy consumers to perform price/volume calculations.

- Include illustrations of product categories on store signs to make it easier for low-literacy consumers to navigate new or refurbished stores. Similarly, use graphical representations of sizes, ingredients, instructions and other information to communicate product information more effectively in shelf and other in-store displays.

- Put the ingredients required for the preparation of popular local dishes in the same section of the store. This would be helpful to low-literacy consumers who often envision the sequence of activities involved in fixing specific dishes to identify the ingredients and quantities they need to purchase. The same can be done for other domestic tasks.

- Incorporate familiar visual elements—such as color schemes or font types—into new store concepts or redesigned brand logos to minimize confusion and anxiety among low-literacy shoppers and increase the likelihood that they will try new products and stores.

- Create a friendly store environment by training store personnel to be sensitive to the needs of low-literacy shoppers and by verbally disclosing and consistently applying store policies. In addition, allow employees to form relationships with consumers by learning their names and offering small amounts of individualized assistance. This is particularly important for global brands and companies entering markets where foreigners are mistrusted or have accrued a history of mistreating people.

As subsistence markets become more attractive, additional opportunities to serve low-literacy consumers will probably become available. Because literacy deficiencies are likely to be addressed at a slower pace than the pace at which poor consumers gain discretionary income and the ability to spend it on products and services, the companies that respond to this group's needs early on will have an advantage. Low-literacy consumers can be a profitable and loyal customer group if treated properly.

Critical Thinking

1. Identify some common challenges faced by subsistence consumers. What impact do these have on purchasing decisions?

2. What are some adaptations companies will need to undertake to attract subsistence consumers?

DR. VISWANATHAN is an associate professor of marketing at the University of Illinois at Urbana-Champaign in Champaign, Ill. **DR. ROSA** is a professor of marketing and sustainable business practices at the University of Wyoming in Laramie, Wyo. **DR. RUTH** is an associate professor of marketing at Rutgers University in Camden, N.J. They can be reached at reports@wsj.com.

UNIT 4

Ethics and Social Responsibility in the Marketplace

Unit Selections

Learning Outcomes

- What responsibility does an organization have to reveal product defects to consumers?

- Given the competitiveness of the business arena, is it possible for marketing personnel to behave ethically and both survive and prosper? Explain. Give suggestions that could be incorporated into the marketing strategy for firms that want to be both ethical and successful.

- Name some organizations that make you feel genuinely valued as a customer. What are the characteristics of these organizations which distinguish them from their competitors? Explain.

- Which area of marketing strategy is most subject to public scrutiny in regard to ethics—product, pricing, place, or promotion? Why? Give some examples of unethical techniques or strategies involving each of these four areas.

- Explain how philanthropic giving fits into a corporation's business model.

Student Website
www.mhhe.com/cls

Internet References

Business for Social Responsibility (BSR)
    www.bsr.org/
Total Quality Management Sites
    www.nku.edu/~lindsay/qualhttp.html
U.S. Navy
    www.navy.mil

From a consumer viewpoint, the marketplace is the "proof of the pudding" or the place where the "rubber meets the road" for business ethics. In other words, what the company has promulgated about the virtues of its product or service has little meaning if the company's actual marketing practices and its treatment of the consumer contradict its claims.

At its core, marketing has a very noble and moral purpose: to satisfy human needs and wants and to help people through the exchange process. Marketing involves the coordination of the variables of product, price, place, and promotion to effectively and efficiently address the needs of consumers. Unfortunately, at times, the unethical marketing practices of some firms have cast a shadow of suspicion over marketing in general. Since marketing is the aspect of business that is most visible to the public, it has perhaps taken a disproportionate share of the criticism directed toward the free-enterprise system.

This unit takes a careful look at the strategic process and practice of incorporating ethics into the marketplace. The first subsection, **Marketing Strategy and Ethics,** contains articles describing how marketing strategy and ethics can be integrated in the marketplace. The first article wrestles with how ethical issues in new product development could be affecting innovation growth. The last two articles in this subsection

© Jack Hollingsworth/Corbis

reveal how rude and blatantly unjust customers should be treated and the culpability of the participants in the mortgage market meltdown.

The first article in the last subsection describes how TOMS shoes practices "philanthropic capitalism."

Honest Innovation

Ethics issues in new product development could be stalling innovation growth.

CALVIN L. HODOCK

Product innovation is the fuel for America's growth. Two Harvard economists described its importance as follows: "Innovation is no mere vanity plate on the nation's economic engine. It trumps capital accumulation and allocation of resources as the most important contributor to growth."

Innovative initiatives are a high risk game; failures widely outnumber successes. While enthusiasm, conviction and creativity should flourish in the hearts and minds of the innovation team, judgments must remain totally, even brutally, objective. But unconscious and conscious marketing dishonesty may make this easier said than done.

Unconscious Marketing Dishonesty

People fall in love with what they create, including movies, television pilots, novels, art and new products. And all too often that love is blind: As objectivity eludes the creator, normally rational people become evangelical rather than practical, rational marketing executives.

The Coca-Cola executive suite was convinced that New Coke was the right thing to do. Procter & Gamble's research and development (R&D) believed that Citrus Hill was a better-tasting orange juice than Tropicana and Minute Maid. The spirited Pepsi Blue team overlooked the obvious knowledge that colas should be brown. Ford's MBA crowd believed in a "cheap Jag" strategy. And Motorola's engineers were misguided in their devotion to the Iridium satellite telephone system.

Crest Rejuvenating Effects was fake innovation: It basically was just regular Crest with a great cinnamon vanilla flavor and feminine packaging, positioned for the "nip and tuck" generation of women aged 30 to 45. Similar to Rice Krispies' famous "snap, crackle, and pop" campaign, it encountered a tepid reception, but the brand's custodians believed that America was ready for "his and hers" tubes of toothpaste in their medicine cabinets.

These were well-meaning people who wandered off course because they became enamored with what they created. But let's face it, optimism has limits. The marketplace disagreed, and that's the only vote that counts in any innovation effort.

Conscious Marketing Dishonesty

Conscious marketing dishonesty is more insidious. Blinded passion may still be part of the equation, but in this case the innovation team consciously pushes the envelope across the line of propriety. Before long, there are disquieting signs or signals that all is not well with the new product.

Unfavorable data or information might be ignored, perhaps even suppressed. There might be the blithe assumption that some miracle will surface, and make it all right. Successful innovation initiatives are not products of miracles, but simply take a good idea and execute all the basic steps that are part of the discovery process. The reward goes to those who excel in executing the thousands of details associated with the dirt of doing.

Either way, conscious or unconscious, marketing dishonesty means resources are wasted, valuable time and energy are lost forever and shareholder value may be diminished (depending on the magnitude of the mistake). Often, nobody takes the blame—and many get promoted, because activity gets rewarded over achievement.

There's often no accountability, even though the new product blueprint is peppered with the fingerprints of many. New product assignments are similar to a NASCAR pit stop. The players are constantly moved around the chess board. The brand manager working on a new product for six to nine months moves to mouthwash. The mouthwash brand manager moves to shampoos. And what we have is a game of musical chairs, with no accountability. It is understandable why innovation teams are willing to "run bad ideas up the flag pole" in lassiez-faire-type innovation environments.

While there are supposed to be security checkpoints in the development process, the marketing "id" finds ways to maneuver around them. When important marketing research findings are ignored or rationalized away, because the innovation team is racing toward a launch date promised to management, the spigot of objectivity is turned off because reality might get in the way. Innovation initiatives build momentum to the point where nothing will stop the new product from being launched—not even dire news.

Marketing Dishonesty

There are eight recurring errors associated with flawed innovation. The most disingenuous is marketing dishonesty, where the innovation team consciously engages in deception—even though there is a red flag flapping in the breeze, indicating that a new product is ill. Six marketing dishonesty scenarios are outlined here.

Campbell's Souper Combo

Souper Combo was a combination frozen soup and sandwich for microwave heating; it tested extremely well as a concept. The product was test marketed, and national introduction was recommended.

Two forecasts surfaced. The new product team estimated that Souper Combo would be a $68 million business. The marketing research department viewed it differently: It would be a $40 million to $45 million business, due to weak repeat purchase rates. Nobody challenged the optimistic forecast. Senior management trusted what they heard, while being fed a bouillabaisse of marketing dishonesty. The national introduction was a disaster, and Souper Combo died on the altar of blemished innovation in nine months.

Crystal Pepsi

Pepsi's innovation team ignored focus group participants who hated the taste of this clear cola. It was forced through the Pepsi distribution system on its journey to failure. When was the last time you saw Crystal Pepsi on the store shelves?

Apple Newton

The Newton was the first (but flawed) PDA rushed to market, because then-CEO John Scully viewed it as his signature product—knowing that Apple loyalists were dismayed that a "Pepsi guy" was running the company. Scully wanted to establish a technical legacy that endured long after he left the Apple campus.

The first Newtons were shipped to market with more than a thousand documented bugs. Nobody had the courage to tell Scully and the Apple board about this.

Arthritis Foundation Pain Relievers

This was a line of parity analgesics, involving a licensing agreement where the company paid the Atlanta-based Arthritis Foundation $1 million annually for trademark use. This analgesic line was a positioning gimmick destined for a law and order encounter, and that doesn't mean the NBC television program. Nineteen states attorney generals said the proposition was deceptive. The drugs contained analgesics common to other pain relievers, and were developed without assistance from the Arthritis Foundation. The Foundation was paid handsomely for the use of its name.

Although McNeil Consumer Healthcare admitted no wrong doing, the case was settled for close to $2 million.

Pontiac Aztek

This was considered the ugliest car ever, and the research verified this. While the research predicted that the Aztek was a hopeless cause, the project team sanitized the research sent to senior management to make the situation look better than it was. Decisions about the Aztek's fate were based on intelligence that was heavily modified and edited. Get it out became more important than "get it right."

Aztek-type decisions became regrettably common in the General Motors culture. John Scully never heard the bad news about the Newton, and the General Motors executive suite didn't want to hear any bad news about their cars. It is a heck of way to run one of America's largest corporations and a bad deal for General Motors shareholders, when a culture of intimidation fuels marketing dishonesty. No wonder things are grim at GM these days.

Polaroid Captiva

This camera was similar to Polaroid's original goldmine product the SX 70, but with a smaller film format. It was priced at $120, although marketing research indicated it would not sell if priced over $60. In this scenario, marketing sold a bad idea supported with a specious assumption; marketing research couldn't sell the truth.

Captiva's potential sales were inflated with an assumption about high levels of repeat purchases after introduction. Selling cameras is different than selling cookies or shampoo, products that need replacement. Captiva perished in the marketplace, as the company violated its cardinal principle: Make the cash register ring selling film, while offering the cameras at cost.

Ethics Issues

While these new products had varied product deficiencies, they all share a common denominator: an optimistic sales forecast. An innovation team can manipulate the numbers to get any sales level it wants. It's easy to do, use optimistic assumptions. New product teams can, and do, cook the books with creative number crunching.

Most new product failures are heavily researched. It is used to justify moving a bad new product forward. In a recent *Advertising Age* article, Bob Barocci, the CEO of the Advertising Research Foundation, remarked, "There is a general belief that over 50% of the research done at companies is wasted."

Executive Briefing

Jeffery Garten, former dean of the Yale School of Management and *BusinessWeek* columnist, graded business schools with a C+ in teaching ethics. Sweeping bad news about new product initiatives under the rug can be more costly than embezzlement, and it is just as unethical. A *USA Today* survey says that 52% of students working on their master's of business administration degrees would buy stock illegally on inside information. Business schools need to emphasize ethics training far more than they do now, particularly since unethical behavior can be an underlying dynamic in new product failures.

He attributed this to the desire to "support decisions already made." All too often, innovation teams push questionable new products through the pipeline with the support of "justification research."

Another ethical issue is targeting. It is difficult to imagine that ad agencies and their clients did not know Vioxx and Celebrex were overprescribed drugs, sold to consumers with minor aches and pains who could have used less expensive alternatives like Advil and Aleve. Both clients and agencies mutually formulated target strategies with Celebrex and Vioxx as examples. These drugs were developed for senior citizens with chronic pain. But the target segment was too small, so the focus shifted to aging baby boomers with clients and agencies in agreement on the reconfiguration.

Prescriptives

Here are seven recommendations:

1. **Innovation committee.** Boards have finance, audit, nominating and compensation committees. Why not an innovation committee composed of outsiders who are not board members? Their role is to assist the board in assessing innovation initiatives. The board can then decide what action should be taken, including pressing the "kill button."

   Companies sometimes do postmortems after failure. The innovation committee should perform pre-mortems early in the development process, before bad ideas soak up lots of money. There is a rich reservoir of people resources to serve on innovation committees (e.g., academics, retired senior executives, industrial designers, and product and industry specialists). But one thing that they should not be is cronies of professional management.

2. **Find a value-added marketing research department.** The prior case histories illustrate that bad research news often is ignored or rationalized away. Hire a research director who knows how to develop and steward a value-added research department, and that has senior management's respect. The respect factor will protect the function from retribution, should the news be bad. Such a person will not be easy to find. One company's solution was to hire a consultant from McKinsey & Company to steward their research department.

   In the early days, pioneer researchers such as Alfred Politz and Ernest Dichter presented their findings to boards of directors. Marketing research lost it status on its journey from infancy to maturity. Today's market research is frequently unseen by the board. The right person in the function—think one with management respect—gives marketing research an influential voice in the innovation process that it currently does not have.

3. **Reinforce the unvarnished truth.** Senior management needs to embrace skeptics, rather than surround themselves with "yes people." Before management reviews a new product plan, key players—manufacturing, finance, marketing, and marketing research—should sign off that the plan's assumptions, the underlying source for rosy sales forecasts, are truthful.

4. **Ethics boot camp.** Corporations spend millions on employee training, but how much is focused on ethics to help marketers navigate through gray areas? The innovation team should attend an ethics boot camp early in the development process. This should include everybody, including the ad agencies. Manipulating the forecast for a new product is unethical. It cheats the shareholders even more than it cheats the public.

5. **Teaching new product development.** In academia, new product courses are taught with a focus on best practices; a different perspective is required. The abysmal failure rate is due to worst practices. Classroom discussions of best practices aren't doing much to reduce failure. Class lectures should focus on ethics issues, like manipulating forecasts and justification research used to keep bad ideas afloat.

6. **Ethics test.** Business schools screen candidates based on their graduate management admission test (GMAT) scores. But there is another much-needed test that business schools should implement: an ethics test. Ethics scores should carry equal weight with GMATs. This demonstrates to candidates that ethics are important, and represent a significant prerequisite for admission. As evidenced in new product cases, ethics is more than simply the despicable acts of WorldCom's Bernie Ebbers and Enron Corporation's Andrew Fastow. And, most important, this should help business schools turn out students with a stronger moral compass—ones who don't feed management a duplicitous forecast for a flawed new product.

7. **Corporate endowments.** Corporations interact with business schools on many different levels. They make sizable donations, fund basic research and send their executives to workshops and seminars. They also need to endow ethics chairs with dedicated academics who are interested in ethics scholarship. Corporations should not hesitate to open up their vaults of information to these academics. What are the ethical patterns that underscore an endless stream of new product failures?

Final Thoughts

Failure is inevitable in product innovation. Perfect success is impossible, even undesirable, because it impedes reaching for the stars like Apple did with iPhone or Toyota with the Prius. Perfect success would be a dull agenda of safe bets like a new fragrance or a new flavor. This means the company has elected to play small ball.

This was the trap that Procter & Gamble fell into for close to three decades, despite having 1,250 PhD scientists churning out a treasure chest of patents—leading to 250 proprietary technologies. Despite all this patent activity, very few market-place hits that made the company famous—think Tide or Pampers as examples—had surfaced from this scientific capability. The innovation focus had drifted to minor product improvements, until the newly anointed CEO A. G. Lafley came along to change all that.

Lafley mandated that P&G be more aggressive, expect failures, and shoot for an innovation success rate in the range of 50% to 60%. And that means having only 4 out of 10 new products fail at Procter & Gamble, well below the industry norm.

The statistic—nine out of 10 new products fail—has hovered over the marketing landscape for six decades. It is estimated that the food industry loses $20 billion to $30 billion annually on failed new products. Would it not be refreshing to attempt to scale this back with a healthy dose of marketing honesty?

Critical Thinking

1. What is the difference between optimism and lying?
2. In what ways does product innovation lend itself to deceptive practices?

CALVIN L. HODOCK is former chairperson of the American Marketing Association board, author of *Why Smart Companies Do Dumb Things* (Prometheus Books, 2007), and professor of marketing at Berkeley College, based in West Paterson, N.J. He may be reached at calhodock@hotmail.com.

Serving Unfair Customers

LEONARD L. BERRY AND KATHLEEN SEIDERS

1. Changing Focus: From Unfair Companies to Unfair Customers

Ten years ago, we published an article titled "Service Fairness: What It Is and Why It Matters" (Seiders & Berry, 1998). Therein, we argued that poor service is not always linked to unfair company practices, but that unfair company practices are always linked to customer perceptions of poor service. We also argued that companies can pay a heavy price when customers believe they have been treated unfairly because customers' responses to perceived injustice often are pronounced, emotional, and retaliatory. We concluded by providing guidelines for managers on preventing unfairness perceptions and effectively managing those that do arise.

Fairness remains a critically important topic today, for it is essential to a mutually satisfactory exchange between two parties. Perceived unfairness undermines trust and diminished trust undermines the strength of relationships. Perceived unfairness is always a negative development. The focus of our original article was company unfairness to customers. Fairness, however, is a two-way street; thus, our present focus is customer unfairness to companies. This time, we examine how customers can be unfair, why it is important, and what companies can do about it.

We are ardent champions of the customer, but we do *not* believe in the maxim that "the customer is always right." Sometimes, the customer is wrong and unfairness often results. That the customer is sometimes wrong is a dirty little secret of marketing, known to many but rarely discussed in public—or in print. What better occasion to broach this unmentionable topic than *Business Horizons'* 50th anniversary?

2. What Is Customer Unfairness and Why Does it Matter?

Customer unfairness occurs when a customer behaves in a manner that is devoid of common decency, reasonableness, and respect for the rights of others, creating inequity and causing harm for a company and, in some cases, its employees and other customers. Customer unfairness should be viewed independent of illegality because unfair customer behavior frequently is

legal; repugnant, perhaps, but not necessarily illegal. Our focus in this article is legal customer behavior that is unfair, falling in the so-called "gray area" of company response.

When does a customer's bad judgment (or, when do bad manners) cross the line to "unfairness?" Three concepts are particularly useful in considering this question. The first is the severity of the harm the customer causes. The second is the frequency of the customer's problematic behavior. Figure 1 shows increasing levels of these two factors: "minor," "moderate," and "extreme" for severity of harm and "uncommon," "intermittent," and "recurrent" for frequency of occurrence. Customer behavior that reaches either the "moderate" or "intermittent" level would usually earn the unfairness label. At these levels, the customer crosses a threshold.

The third concept is intentionality. The customer who seeks to take advantage and inflict harm, who willfully disrespects the rights of other parties, will almost always deserve the unfairness label. In some cases, customers may seek to harm a company that they believe has harmed them. The customers' behavior in this case is an act of retaliation. When customers blame a company for unfair treatment, there are fair and unfair ways of responding. Intentionally unfair behavior is usually indefensible.

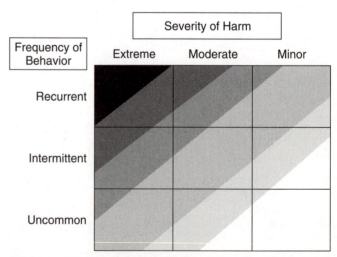

Figure 1 The threshold of customer unfairness. Adapted from Seiders and Berry (1998).

How do companies deal with unfair customers? We contacted executives from a variety of service organizations to solicit their opinions on the topic and to document examples drawn from their experiences. (We restricted our inquiries to consumer services executives based on the assumption that business-to-business services merit a separate exploration.) Our preliminary research reveals that some executives struggle with how to respond to customer unfairness. They don't want to respond in a way that confounds the company's commitment to quality service, which they and others worked hard to instill. Nor do they want to risk offending a still-profitable, albeit problematic, customer. The following comments from four executives illustrate:

- "I think there is a subservient or servant mentality to all service, and to stray from that causes confusion in taking clear and concise action that should be positive for the customer."

- "The lifetime cost of losing a guest exceeds $500, so we go to great lengths to avoid losing them, even when they're wrong. Rather than risk offending guests, we tend to let 'little things' go."

- "My philosophy is that the customer is always right to some degree. It is that matter of degree that determines the action of the company. I believe that if we ever think that the customer is 100% wrong, then we have a high risk of becoming arrogant and not being customer-focused. I know that this may sound crazy, but if we crack open the door to this idea, then I think we can very quickly go down the slippery slope."

- "We are just not used to thinking of guests 'crossing the line.' I don't know that I have ever set up boundaries. I always feel that guests have the right to say what they want and to do what they want, short of inconveniencing another guest or physically harming another guest or employee."

Our position is that companies cannot afford to ignore customer unfairness and should devise a plan to deal with it. Unfair customer behavior can exact a significant toll on employees' job satisfaction and weaken a company's overall service quality. We are not just speculating about this. Recent research by Rupp and Spencer (2006) found that customer injustice increased the degree of effort required for employees to manage their emotions in inter-personal transactions. This increased effort in what is termed *emotional labor* produces added stress, and contributes to employee turnover and overall unwillingness to perform (Grandey, Dickter, & Sin, 2004). Moreover, the injustice of one customer can negatively affect employee behavior toward other customers.

The effects of customer unfairness are often magnified because employees find it difficult to deal with customers who have treated their coworkers disrespectfully, even if the same customers treated them fairly (Rupp, Holub, & Grandey, 2007). Unfair acts are more memorable than typical encounters (Lind & Tyler, 1988), and employees may respond to customer unfairness by discussing incidents with other sympathetic employees, fostering negative word of mouth about customers.

When some customers systematically abuse company policies, such as retail return policies, companies are inclined to either clamp down with tougher rules or increase prices to cover losses. In effect, fair customers are penalized by the actions of unfair customers. Employees are put on the defensive and can become more sensitive to customer manipulation, and more inclined to question the sincerity of customers' communications and the motives that lie behind their actions (Tyler & Bies, 1990). The dynamic can turn adversarial. In short, both employees and customers pay for other customers' misdeeds.

3. Types of Unfair Customers

Over the last 30 years, justice research has focused on three types of justice. *Distributive justice* relates to the outcomes of decisions or allocations; *procedural justice* relates to the procedures used to arrive at those outcomes; and *interactional justice* relates to interpersonal treatment and communication. Interactional justice is demonstrated by interpersonal fairness (i.e., when individuals are treated with dignity and respect) and informational fairness (i.e., when communications are truthful and important decisions are explained) (Rupp & Spencer, 2006). Many studies have found that interactional injustice produces particularly strong responses.

Our exploration of customer unfairness led us to identify distinct types of problem customers. The categories we discuss are neither mutually exclusive nor comprehensive, but describe the most common and problematic types of unfair customers. Each category highlights a different facet of customer unfairness, although some behaviors may logically fit into more than one category. We exclude customers who use stolen credit cards, manipulate price tags, steal merchandise, and stage 'accidents' in service facilities (see, for example, Fullerton & Punj, 2004). The scenarios we consider involve more ambiguity than clear-cut illegality.

3.1. Verbal Abusers

Verbal abusers lash out at employees in a blatantly offensive and disrespectful manner whether in face-to-face transactions, over the telephone, or via the Internet. The verbal abuser capitalizes on the power imbalance commonly present in service encounters: the customer who is 'always right' has the upper hand by default and an opportunity to push the boundaries of fair behavior. One healthcare executive profiled this customer type as "patients and family members who belittle, demean, intimidate, and abuse staff members, and threaten litigation at the slightest lapse in service." Verbal abusers bully front-line employees who typically lack the freedom to defend themselves and, in fact, are expected not to react visibly to unfair treatment by customers. Given the importance of interactional injustice, it is no surprise that the verbal abuser's behavior can have such negative effects on employees.

Customers' verbal abuse of employees is probably more pervasive than most service industry executives would want to admit. There is no accepted protocol for managing a verbal abuse episode, and we suspect that most often this type of incident is not managed. Our favorite story involves the owner of a bicycle store well known for its dedication to customer service. A father was picking up a repaired bicycle for his daughter, who, without telling him, had approved the recommended replacement of both tires (a $40 service). Although the employee patiently and repeatedly explained that the purchase was approved and offered to further verify it, the customer made accusatory remarks and yelled at her angrily, saying at one point, "Either you think I'm stupid or you're stupid. You're trying to rip me off." At that point. Chris Zane, the store's owner, walked up to the customer and said, "I'm Chris Zane; get out of my store and tell all your friends!" After the customer wordlessly slapped $40 on the counter and stormed out, the besieged employee looked at Zane and asked "'. . . and tell all your friends'?"

Zane explained to her, and other employees who had gravitated to the front of the store, that he wanted it to be clear that he valued his employee infinitely more than a rude, belligerent customer. "I also explained that this was the first time I had ever thrown a customer out of the store and that I would not tolerate my employees being mistreated by anyone. . . . I believe that my employees need to know that I respect them and expect them to respect our customers. Simply, if I am willing to fire an employee for mistreating a customer (and I have), then I must also be willing to fire a customer for mistreating an employee."

Verbal abusers can also have a profound effect on other customers. This is illustrated by a customer who, during a lunch rush at a very busy restaurant location, insisted that his steak be prepared rare. Although a manager apologized and explained that each steak is prepared uniformly in order to maintain the best quality (and said there would be no charge for the lunch), the customer continued to voice his disapproval to the staff, creating a disturbance that distracted them and degraded the overall experience of the surrounding customers.

In another incident, two customers in a bar loudly criticized the bartender for assisting other patrons before them and then rebuked the restaurant manager who intervened to try to calm them down. The manager then went to the kitchen to check on the progress of their food; when he returned, the two customers were leaving and shouting obscenities as they walked out. A common device of the verbal abuser is the threat to report employees and/or their facility 'to corporate,' a way to prolong employee unease after the offensive incident is over.

3.2. Blamers

Whereas verbal abusers bring misery primarily to customer contact employees, blamers will indict a company's products, policies, and people at all levels for any perceived shortfall. With blamers, 'the company is always wrong.'

Because customers play a co-producer role in many services, they affect the service quality and final outcome. Blamers, however, never see themselves in any way responsible for the outcome, regardless of the scenario. Causal inferences or attributions individuals use to assess the failure of a product or service performance are based on the locus of blame and whether or not the incident could have been controlled

(Sheppard, Lewicki, & Minton, 1992). From the blamer's perspective, not only is the company always at fault, but the perceived problem is always controllable.

Blamers are not discriminate about where they voice discord, and every service provider is familiar with this type of customer. A tennis coach had been working with an adult student for about six months when the student learned that an opponent in an upcoming match had worked briefly with the same coach in the past. The student asked for and received specific advice from the coach on how to win the match by attacking the opponent's greatest weaknesses. However, the opponent had corrected these weaknesses and much to the student's chagrin, she could find no way to beat her. In the clubhouse immediately after the match, she raged at her coach for not preparing her well, giving her poor information and lousy lessons, and causing her to lose the match.

In another example, a customer called the headquarters of a national casual dining chain to complain about the price of its cocktails. It seems the gentleman had spent $86 in the bar of this restaurant having drinks and appetizers after work the previous evening. He wanted to talk to someone about what he considered the excessive price of the drinks and how unfair he thought the cost. The switchboard operator noted the caller's angry tone and put him through to the president of the company.

The man re-explained to the president and said he could not believe the restaurant had charged him $7.50 for each of the beverages that he ordered. When asked how many he had consumed, the man said that was beside the point. The president asked the number in the man's party, and the man said only two. The president asked the man when he learned that the drinks were $7.50, which he said was after he paid the bill. The president then asked what the company might do to make it right. The customer replied that he wanted all of his money back; the president responded that this was unfair, as the customer and his guest had consumed enough appetizers and drinks to total $86. A full refund would not be equitable.

The customer became extremely angry, threatening to go online and destroy the company, report it to the Better Business Bureau, and picket in front of its restaurants for the next month. He raised his voice and asserted, "You will feel the effects of my negative PR efforts for a long time to come." Frustrated at the angry customer's threats, the president asked the customer how he could resolve this negative situation without giving the customer his money back for the food and drinks he consumed. The customer calmed down, thought about it, and told the president that if the company donated double the amount of the bill to the customer's favorite charity, he would consider the situation resolved. The president agreed to do so in order to move past the situation and end the disagreement.

The blamer is a particularly difficult type of customer for the healthcare industry. Patients who fail to take responsibility for their own health status often are blamers. Many such patients believe that a treatment cure exists for every condition and thus see no need to take measures to improve their own health. In one case, a patient was referred to a hospital's patient relations department after lodging serious complaints with the president's office. The patient claimed that his wound from surgery failed to heal because the staff ignored his complaints. In reality, the patient was non-compliant with recommended diet and wound care, refused to follow his doctor's recommendations for exercise and physical therapy, and failed to return for a follow-up appointment. At each point of contact, the patient threatened to hire a malpractice attorney.

This example may sound extreme, but in fact we heard a number of such stories. One healthcare professional noted, "I have been in patient relations for more than ten years now, and I can attest to the fact that these patients are a huge burden on the healthcare system. They tie up resources that could be used to improve services for all of our patients." An executive from a different healthcare institution expressed a similar view: "I hear from the same patients over and over again, and once a resolution is offered, many times it's a prolonged argument because it's their way or no way. Unfortunately, these cases are no longer rare."

3.3. Rule Breakers

Rule breakers readily ignore policies and procedures when they find them to be inconvenient or at odds with their own goals. Rule breakers generally ignore the honor code by which other customers abide. In chronic cases, a rule breaker may be a mild version of a con artist. Rule breakers are not concerned with equity, which is the first principle of distributive justice. Equity exists in an exchange when participants' rewards equal their contributions; rule breakers seek to optimize their rewards at the expense of the company. This not only harms the company, but also puts company employees in a tenuous and uncomfortable situation as they attempt to protect their employer from customer wrongdoing.

The damage done by rule breakers varies, of course, based on the nature of the rules and polices that are being broken. A restaurant that offers "all you can eat" shrimp entrees encounters some patrons who share with their tablemates, even though the menu clearly states that the price is per person. Managers are not quick to put servers in the awkward position of having to remind guests they are breaking the rule, but will do so if the 'sharing' gets out of hand.

A retailer with a catalog operation is subject to 'customers who bend the facts' (in the words of one executive) when post-delivery complainers assert that a telephone sales associate told them that shipping was free. When this happens, a company representative will listen to a tape of the original call and will usually hear the shipping charges discussed. For smaller transactions with first-time customers, the retailer apologizes, deducts the shipping charge, and restates the shipping fee policy for future transactions. For larger transactions, the customer is told that the call was reviewed and the company is not sure why there was confusion. Once customers realize that a company representative has reviewed the call and knows what actually was said, they rarely demand a shipping refund. "It's a nice way of saying we know what happened without becoming confrontational," explains a company manager.

One type of rule breaker can be termed a *rule maker*. Rule makers expect to be exempted from the rules and demand special treatment because of perceived superior status. Both rule breakers and rule makers demonstrate unfairness to other customers who are behaving according to norms and convention. When certain customers are allowed to break the rules because of their social or financial status, the equality principle of distributive justice is defied (Grover, 1991). A hospital executive describes the rule maker in this way:

"We have had patients who believe that there is some special level of care that we are constantly holding back, and if we knew how special they were that they would get this special executive level care. This is common in the family of trustees and board members. These are families that expect to be cared for only by departmental chairmen. We have coined the concept *chairman syndrome.*"

Often, it is the family-member-turned-advocate who demands to make the rules. For example, a patient's daughter insisted, "I want all of the labs printed out each day and handed to me when I walk in in the morning." A patient's son threatened, "I am an attorney and I demand to know what is going on with my mother!" A corporate chairman transferred his child by private jet to a hospital in another city when his company's physicians (non-pediatric, without privileges to practice in the hospital) were not allowed to direct the team of hospital physicians who were treating the child. These scenarios seem almost amusing until one considers the extent to which medical staff members and other hospital patients may be adversely affected by this disregard for the rules.

3.4. Opportunists

Opportunists have their antennae up for easy paths to personal financial gain. This customer's modus operandi can be demanding compensation by fabricating or exaggerating problems or flaws in a product or service. While this type of opportunist stiffs the company, there is a second type that stiffs 'the little guy.' These penny-ante opportunists, for example, don't tip (or don't adequately tip) service employees because they don't have to; that is, they can get away with it. This behavior is distasteful because, like many cases of verbal abuse, it hurts front-line employees whose tips often represent a significant percentage of their pay.

Opportunists frequently use gamesmanship to optimize their gain. A customer observed a plumbing problem in a restaurant restroom and complained to the manager, who called a plumbing service for the repair, and sent an employee to clean up. The customer contacted the company's customer relations office, complained about the state of the restroom, and requested a refund for his party's $80 meal. In response, the company sent $30 in gift certificates, in addition to an $80 check and an apology. The customer called the company again, stating that $30 was not enough to cause him to return to the restaurant because it would not cover the cost of his dining companions' meals. He was persistent, calling several times to express his displeasure in the amount of the gift certificates. In turn, the company sent an additional $50 in gift certificates, bringing the total compensation to $160, a nice return for encountering a plumbing problem.

The opportunist may not be a chronic gold digger, but rather just someone who recognizes an opportunity to take financial advantage of a company's service failure and recovery efforts. For example, when an ambulatory surgery patient complained to her hospital that her lingerie had been lost, she was offered reimbursement. She claimed that the cost was $400 and, because this was an unusually high amount, the hospital inquired about the value of the items. The patient said she had not kept the receipts. To maintain good will, the hospital paid the $400 and apologized.

The opportunist doesn't require a service failure to take action. Some users of professional services, for example, maneuver to gain pro bono consultation from a prior provider. A communications coach periodically receives 'pick your brain' phone calls from former clients. Because these customers don't intend to pay for this 'informal' advice, the consultant is forced into an awkward position by clients attempting to exploit the relationship.

3.5. Returnaholics

This customer is a hybrid, with traits common to rule breakers and opportunists but engaged in a specific type of activity: returning products to stores. Returnaholics are rule breakers in that they don't adhere to the spirit of the company's return policies, whereby returns are accepted for defective products, a post-purchase change of mind, and gift exchange. In many cases, the returnaholic never intends to keep the product to begin with. Returnaholics are opportunists because they exploit retailer return policies for their own benefit. There are two types of returnaholics: situational and chronic.

Situational returnaholics become active under certain conditions. For example, one retailer's sales of equipment such as snow blowers, generators, and chainsaws would spike just before a major weather event but then fall precipitously shortly thereafter when many customers returned new *and* used equipment, and even products such as ice melt and flashlights, demanding refunds. It was not unusual for a store to see more than half the generators sold the week before a storm returned within two weeks after the storm. This phenomenon was a painful and expensive exercise for the retailer and its vendors. Reluctantly, the company adopted a stricter return policy covering specific items to better manage after-the-storm return rates.

Some situational returners use an item until it is damaged or worn out and then return it for a full refund or new item, claiming it is defective because it 'should have held up better.' They expect the refund to be 100% of purchase price because they believe that retailers carry a manufacturer's warranty for all items indefinitely.

Chronic, or serial, returnaholics are referred to by some store operators as "rental" customers. One customer of a men's shoe and accessories chain started shopping at two of the company's stores in 2001. The customer would often buy a product in store A and return it (after wearing it) to store B, using a different name for the return transaction. He also would complain to upper management about quality or the service he received in hopes of getting discounts on future purchases. The company realized this pattern of behavior spanned six years, once it figured out that all of this activity involved one customer rather than two. In that period, the customer had purchased 23 pairs of shoes and returned 17 for net sales of $381 (which obviously did not come close to covering the cost of 17 pairs of worn and returned shoes). When the customer was contacted about his serial returning behavior, he became angry; he was told it was obvious the company could not please him and that it could no longer afford to do business with him.

Chronic returnaholics can be very crafty. Some purchase expensive items with credit cards to earn rewards or airline points and then return the merchandise during certain periods of the billing cycle when the points will not be removed from their account. Some purchase large quantities of items, try to sell them on the Internet or in private shops, and then return them for a refund if they don't sell. Some interior designers will purchase items for a specific event, such as an open house or a staged model home, and then return the items for a refund. These are but a few examples of how chronic returnaholics operate.

4. What Managers Can Do

Unfair customers need to be dealt with effectively. They can be a big problem for poorly managed companies with customer unfriendly policies and practices that provoke retaliatory customer behavior. Unfair customers also can bedevil well-managed companies that devote considerable energy and investment to serving customers superbly. After all, these companies build their culture on delivering an excellent experience and value to customers. As a long-time operations executive of one of America's most admired supermarket chains told us:

"I think companies that are truly committed to customer service have a difficult time dealing with unfair customers. We always [tell] our store managers that we will give the unfair customer the benefit of the doubt one or two times. The third time, we [will] fire them as a customer."

So, what should managers do about unfair customers?

4.1. Manage Customers to a Standard of Behavior

Companies cannot build a reputation for service excellence unless, in addition to serving customers competently, they treat them with respect and commitment. Treating customers with respect and commitment requires an organizational culture in which employees, themselves, are treated with respect and commitment. Managers that allow customers to behave badly (e.g., to verbally abuse employees, to create a disturbance, to rip off the company) in the name of "customer service" undermine the organizational culture upon which excellent service depends. Appeasing a customer who doesn't deserve appeasement does not go unnoticed within the organization. The bicycle shop owner who ordered an abusive customer out of the store strengthened his culture that day, rather than weakened it.

Just as managers need to manage employees, they should also "manage" customers when the situation warrants. A good manager certainly would intervene if made aware of an employee who treated customers rudely or broke important company policies. Likewise, a manager should be ready to intervene when made aware of customer misbehavior. Effective "customer management," as illustrated by the manager's intervention in the bar ruckus, demonstrated to employees and nearby customers that the disruptive party's behavior was unacceptable and would not be allowed to continue. If the customers did quiet down, the bartender could more easily interact with them because the manager, and not he, addressed their misbehavior.

4.2. Don't Penalize Fair Customers

Companies should design their business operations for the vast majority of their customers who are fair and responsible, rather than for the unfair minority. Firms should not allow unfair customer behavior to instigate needlessly restrictive policies that disrespect the good intentions of most customers. The better approach, for the business culture and reputation, is to deal fairly but firmly with unfair customers specifically.

The retailer experiencing heavy returns of outdoor power equipment following a major storm illustrates this guideline. The retailer could have done nothing, in effect enabling unreasonable customer behavior. Alternatively, the company could have installed a more restrictive return policy for all merchandise, which would have affected all customers, not just returnaholics, and likely hurt the company's reputation for customer service. The company's implementation of a more restrictive return policy for specific products with high afterstorm return rates made returns more difficult for situational returnaholics. The new policy was designed specifically to deal with opportunistic customers.

The goodwill created by *not* treating all customers as untrustworthy is an investment worth making. A supermarket operations executive illustrates this lesson with the following story:

"When I was at [Company X], we had a policy that if customers forgot their checkbook, we would let them leave with their groceries after filling out a simple IOU. The great majority of customers would immediately return to pay the amount. This policy created a great deal of positive goodwill. However, every year we had to write off a significant amount of loss because some customers would not come back to pay off the IOU. I remember one year it was in excess of $30,000. We would make attempts to recover the money, but I don't recall trying to prosecute anyone for it. Our CFO wanted to stop giving the IOUs, but I would not let him. I treated it as a marketing expense because it created so much goodwill. Interestingly, when we started accepting credit, I thought that the loss number would plunge, assuming customers would carry their credit card and use that instead of a check. However, the loss number remained the same. I believe there will always be customers who will take advantage of you. They are very intentional about their unfairness. The loss incurred by them has to be built into your financial model because you should not penalize the great customers for the deeds of a few bad customers."

4.3. Prepare for Customer Unfairness

Companies should strive to both reduce the frequency of unfair customer episodes and effectively manage specific incidents. This requires advance planning. Managers need to determine the kinds of situations that are most likely to produce unfair customer behavior, given the nature of the company's business. Managers can determine at-risk situations for unfairness by: (1) using past experiences to identify conditions in which customer and company goals might conflict; (2) soliciting employee input on causes of customer unfairness; and (3) surveying customers previously involved in unfairness incidents to gain their perspective on what happened and why. Once at-risk exchanges are identified, managers can evaluate the firm's existing practices to consider needed changes. Employee and customer input can again be helpful at this stage (Seiders & Berry, 1998).

Preparing for customer unfairness also involves investing in education and training of front-line employees and managers on how to prevent and manage the most likely types of incidents. Particular emphasis should be placed on the rationale for company policies that respond to customer misbehavior, or that may encourage it. Employees who intervene need to be able to explain the company's position effectively, which makes communications training for dealing with problem customers a priority. Contact personnel (and their managers) would benefit from focused training on the best ways to interact with verbal abusers, rule breakers, returnaholics, and other problem customers. Organizational justice researchers recommend the use of explanation as an impression management strategy (Sitkin & Bies, 1993). Explanations have been found to diffuse negative reactions and convey respect, among other positive outcomes (Seiders & Berry, 1998), although they will not always be effective with unfair customers.

Collecting pertinent information is another way to prepare for customer unfairness. Information can clarify the appropriate company response to a customer incident. The catalog retailer which captures information on every shipping transaction is better prepared to assess post-transaction claims. Has the customer complained about this issue before? If so, did the company explain its policy? What is the customer's purchase history? "Research is a great way to keep things on the up and up," explains a company executive. "It's on a case-by-case basis."

4.4. Don't Reward Misbehavior

As mentioned, companies that take pride in the quality of their service often struggle to satisfactorily resolve acts of customer opportunism. Such companies are so culturally focused on serving customers well and giving them the benefit of the doubt when problems arise that they may offer more than they should to reach resolution. Doing more than should be done for an unfair customer rewards misbehavior and encourages future incidents.

Companies need to respond to customer unfairness with fairness—and firmness. They should respond to unreasonableness with reason. It isn't easy. The case of the restaurant bathroom plumbing problem is instructive. The customer had a legitimate complaint about the state of the restroom, but then used the incident opportunistically to extract as much as possible from the restaurant. The company's first response of a full refund for the party's meal, a small gift certificate, and an apology was fair. The additional gift certificates went beyond fair. The second helping of gift certificates was excessive, reinforcing customer opportunism. Companies need to be willing to cut the cord with unfair customers.

Sometimes unfair customers recant when dealt with appropriately, as shown by a postscript to the bicycle story. The abusive customer phoned the owner to apologize three hours after being told to leave the store, explaining that he had argued with his wife prior to visiting the store. Once he returned home and verified the accuracy of the store employee's explanation, he realized he had been unreasonable. He asked that the store not blame the daughter for his actions and that he be allowed to shop in the store again. He also commented that he respected the owner for supporting his employee, even if it might mean losing a customer. The owner thanked him for the call, welcomed him back to the store, and indicated that the apology would be conveyed to the employee.

5. Rethinking Old Wisdom

Following the old wisdom—the customer is always right—has operated as the basic rule in business for so long that it has become entrenched as an "absolute truth." The practical reality, however, is that sometimes the customer is wrong by behaving unfairly.

Customer unfairness can exact a heavy cost. Company goodwill, employee relations, financial position, and service to responsible customers can deteriorate when customers engage in unfair tactics such as verbal abuse, blaming, rule breaking, opportunism, and "returnaholism."

Companies must acknowledge the unfair behavior of certain customers and manage them effectively. Some customers may need to be fired. Denying the existence and impact of unfair customers erodes the ethics of fairness upon which great service companies thrive.

References

Fullerton, R. A., & Punj, G. (2004). Repercussions of promoting an ideology of consumption: Consumer misbehavior. *Journal of Business Research, 57*(11), 1239–1249.

Grandey, A. A., Dickter, D. N., & Sin, H. P. (2004). The customer is not always right: Customer aggression and emotion regulation of service employees. *Journal of Organizational Behavior, 25*(3), 397–418.

Grover, S. L. (1991). Predicting the perceived fairness of parental leave policies. *Journal of Applied Psychology, 76*(2), 247–255.

Lind, E. A., & Tyler, T. R. (1988). *The social psychology of procedural justice.* New York: Plenum Press.

Rupp, D. E., & Spencer, S. (2006). When customers lash out: The effects of customers' interactional injustice on emotional labor and the mediating role of discrete emotions. *Journal of Applied Psychology, 91*(4), 971–978.

Rupp, D. E., Holub, A. S., & Grandey, A. A. (2007). A cognitive–emotional theory of customer injustice and emotional labor. In D. De Cremer (Ed.), *Advances in the psychology of justice and affect* (pp. 199–226). Charlotte, NC: Information Age Publishing.

Seiders, K., & Berry, L. L. (1998). Service fairness: What it is and why it matters. *Academy of Management Executive, 12*(2), 8–21.

Sheppard, B. H., Lewicki, R. J., & Minton, J. W. (1992). *Organizational justice: The search for fairness in the workplace.* New York: Lexington Books.

Sitkin, S. B., & Bies, R. J. (1993). Social accounts in conflict situations: Using explanations to manage conflict. *Human Relations, 46*(3), 349–370.

Tyler, T. R., & Bies, R. J. (1990). Beyond formal procedures: The interpersonal context of procedural justice. In J. Carroll (Ed.), *Advances in applied social psychology: Business settings* (pp. 77–98). Hillsdale, NJ: Lawrence Erlbaum Associates.

Critical Thinking

1. Which ethical philosophy or perspective underlies the insistence on fairness?

2. Which party has more "right" to fair treatment—the customer or the employee? Under what circumstances would you fire a customer?

Swagland

Where the writers are gluttons, the editors practice ethical relativism and the flacks just want to get their clients some ink.

DAVID WEDDLE

S wagland. It's not a mythical over-the-rainbow realm, an Eastern European country, a theme park. You might call it a state of mind, a wondrous alternate universe concocted by publicists, funded by corporations eager for media coverage of their wares and frequented by journalists who have cast off concerns about conflicts of interest and embraced a new creed of conspicuous consumption.

In Swagland, the streets are paved with freebies, from promotional T-shirts, CDs and DVDs, to designer clothing, jewelry and perfume, to spa treatments, Broadway show tickets and suites in five-star hotels, to cellphones, laptops and luxury sports cars on loan. Travel writers accept free trips to exotic foreign lands. Automotive reviewers take junkets to Switzerland or the sun-dappled hills of Italy to drive the latest high-end roadsters. Entertainment hacks hobnob with stars and directors at the Four Seasons in Los Angeles. High-tech audio and video reviewers max out their home-entertainment centers with LCD HDTV screens, surround-sound systems and five-digit turntables, which they keep for months at a time—for research purposes. Surfing journalists travel to remote South Pacific atolls and stay with supermodels on "floating Four Seasons" luxury cruisers where the champagne never stops flowing.

Fashionistas have long been infamous for raking in the loot—the currency of Swagland. Designers lavish magazine editors with the latest styles because they're "celebrities in their own right," explains an editor at a major fashion daily. "They're gifted quite a bit because they are friends with these designers and they have a lot of access. They may get photographed with those items, and that influences what people buy. All the top editors take free clothes."

In recent years, Los Angeles has become the R&D capital of swag culture. The now-ubiquitous promotional gift bag grew out of Hollywood's plethora of award ceremonies and premiere parties. A gift bag may contain a T-shirt or coffee mug, or it might be crammed with thousands of dollars worth of goods. Whatever it may hold, the gift bag has an uncanny power to bring out the greedy 2-year-old in some members of the media. Many have come to view it not as a perk but a birthright. "When I'm holding an event," says Susie Dobson of the Los Angeles firm Susie Dobson Global PR, "the magazine editors call and ask if there's going to be a gift bag. 'Will there be gift bags?' Yes. 'Will they be good?' Yes. 'Oh, great! I'll be there.'

At some events, journalists are allowed to pack their own gift bags. If the "merch" runs low, things can get ugly. "At the 2003 Environmental Media Awards," says freelance journalist Kyle Roderick, "there was a frenzy at the booth for Under the Canopy, which is this organic fiber fashion line. There was a jostling fight. . . . People were yelling, 'I want my T-shirt!' There were some shoulder blows. The sign was up that said 'Please take one.' People were grabbing three or four or five."

The abundance of swag fuels a thriving underground economy. Writers fence their T-shirts, designer duds and movie and automotive promotional memorabilia to a loose network of used-clothing stores (such as Decades in L.A.), entrepreneurs and Internet vendors. "I have editors calling me all the time and bringing me bags of stuff—designer shoes, jewelry, dresses, everything from Chanel to Gucci," says Keni Valenti, owner of Keni Valenti Retro-Couture, a vintage designer clothing store in New York's Garment Center.

Some journalists steal swag outright from photo shoot sets or magazine fashion closets. "I've had editors call me up and say, 'I have two fur coats here in a bag. I'm at 38th and 7th Avenue, right on the corner. If you can bring me X amount of dollars in cash, they're yours,'" Valenti says. "I said to one editor, 'What exactly are you going to say to the company?' She said, 'I'll just send back the bag empty and blame it on the messenger.' "

Others shake down merchants. Mary Norton, designer of Moo Roo handbags, was flabbergasted when an anchor for a prominent Los Angeles newscast walked into her showroom during the 2003 Oscar season and pointed to three of her creations. He told her that Moo Roo would never be mentioned on his show—ever—if she didn't give them to him.

Anne Rainey Rokahr, director of Red PR in New York, had a similar experience. A magazine writer offered to promote her clients' products on a TV morning show if Rokahr would pay her. "I was shocked and insulted," Rokahr says.

She's not alone. The guardians of journalistic ethics are horrified and dismayed by this subversion of all the values they hold dear. "There are no ifs, ands or buts about it, you put yourself in a compromising position if you accept any gift or free trip or anything from somebody you're writing about," says Edwin Guthman, a Pulitzer Prize-winning journalist and former editor of the Philadelphia Inquirer and national editor of the Los Angeles Times, who is now a senior lecturer at USC's Annenberg School. "It's something that a self-respecting journalist shouldn't do. There isn't any question about it, it's wrong. I'm sorry to hear that it's fairly prevalent."

Ethicists argue that the proliferation of swag has undercut the integrity of the press, blurred the lines between advertising and editorial and encouraged some publications to mislead their readership. "Very few readers have any idea how editorial staffs decide what gets reported on," says Jeffrey Seglin, an associate professor at Emerson College in Boston who writes a weekly column on ethics for the New York Times. "They don't know what the policies are at the magazines about accepting freebies. Readers need to be aware of this issue, especially when they're reading travel pieces and product reviews. There should be a clear distinction between what's advertising and what's editorial. Because when you purchase a magazine, you presume you are buying objective editorial. But that's not always the reality."

The perception that journalists can be bought contributes to an overall distrust of the media. A recent Gallup poll found that only 21% of those surveyed rated newspaper reporters' ethical standards as high or very high. Journalists ranked lower than bankers, auto mechanics, elected officials and nursing home operators. Kelly McBride, the ethics group leader at the Poynter Institute, a training school for professional journalists in St. Petersburg, Fla., laments that the press is "losing ground" in the battle for the public's respect, and believes that swag is a factor. "For people who are concerned about media bias, it is one more straw on the camel's back."

For publicists who practice giveaway marketing, however, such hand-wringing is futile, even a little comical. As far as they're concerned, the battle's already been won. The glittering utopia of Swagland is governed by one supreme precept, and Kelly Cutrone, founder of the firm People's Revolution, sums it up: "Here's the deal: Everything's a commercial."

The Age of Ethical Relativism

The rise of swag culture is no accident, according to McBride. "Corporations are spending a higher percentage of their annual budgets on marketing, and larger portions of those budgets are directed specifically at journalists, because marketing executives realize that ink on any given product is better than advertising," she says. "We've always known that, but they realize now, particularly in this age of an inundation of advertising, that advertising is limited in its ability to reach an audience. It's much more effective to create the elusive buzz about a product that everyone's after."

And the schizophrenic ethics policies of American publications make them an easy target. Many magazines and tabloids either turn a blind eye or encourage their writers to score freebies as a method of cutting expenses. The Robb Report, Motor Trend and Powder routinely send their contributors on junkets. Many others have strict rules against it. Travel + Leisure posts its policy in each issue, stating that its writers do not accept free trips. Most major newspapers and news magazines forbid employees and freelancers to accept merchandise or services from potential subjects, and some high-end glossies—Playboy, Harper's Magazine, Forbes, Fortune—have similar policies.

But even publications that enforce strict ethics policies do not have entirely clean hands. Most, including the Los Angeles Times, commission stories from freelance writers who operate as independent contractors. Freelancers are the migrant farmworkers of journalism—cheap labor that fills the gaps left by editorial downsizing and dwindling advertising revenue. As they scramble from publication to publication to make a living, some practice ethical relativism. If they're writing a story for a newspaper where accepting giveaways is forbidden, they adhere to that policy. But when they're on assignment for a lifestyle magazine that encourages them to accept free hotel rooms and airfare to cut expenses, they shift into high freebie mode. Thus, even the most scrupulous publications end up employing freelancers who may have accepted copious swag on other assignments.

"There is an entire set of problems that comes with freelancers that does not come with staff writers, because there's a limited amount of control you can have over them," observes Stephen Randall, deputy editor of Playboy and an adjunct faculty member at USC's Annenberg School. "You don't know what freelancers are doing on other assignments. You don't know what hidden agendas they might have."

Some editors worry about ethics creep. Rick Holter, arts editor for the Dallas Morning News, points out that if an automaker decides to debut a new model in Germany, "there's no way my paper is going to pay for me to go to Germany." But what happens if five freelancers take the junket and come back with terrific stories, which they then submit to the paper? "If you're the car reviewer at Dallas Morning News, you look bad. Here's a freelancer coming in with a great story that you didn't get. Editors get tempted not to ask the tough questions of the freelancers they're buying something from."

Even more problematic are the pseudo-ethics policies of some publications. "One of the worst things that happens is when there is a policy and the publications don't enforce it," says Seglin. "On paper it may say, 'We will not do this.' But the staff and the freelancers see that everybody takes freebies and no one enforces the ethics code. It sends a message that the code is worthless."

Last month the editorial staffs of Jane, Details, Women's Wear Daily and W were banned from receiving gifts "of value" from advertisers. The New York Daily News reported that rebellious employees of Fairchild Publications planned to circumvent the ban by having publicists mail swag to their home addresses. Fairchild spokeswoman Andrea Kaplan averred that this would be against company policy and was quoted as saying, "We are not aware that this is happening."

Truth in Labeling

Many lifestyle scribes shrug off traditional ethics with the rationalization that they aren't really journalists. Julie Logan, a former editor for Glamour who has written for Self and InStyle, refers to fashion and beauty magazines as "service books." "I don't consider service books to be journalism," Logan says. "I consider it copy writing with a narrative. The function of a service book is to deliver readers to the advertisers. If the advertisers could find a way to put the magazine out without writers, they would. We're there because of their largess, not the other way around."

Yet the mastheads of service books list editors and correspondents and look identical to those of hard news publications. "They have all the trappings of regular journalism," McBride says. "They're doing what passes for consumer journalism—writing about products, places and things that people spend money on." And when consumers purchase a magazine, Seglin argues, "they expect objectivity. They don't expect the magazine to show favoritism. As readers, we want consumer journalists to do the legwork and review all of the available products, not just the ones they got for free."

Logan thinks service book readers could care less about the intricacies of objectivity. "These are people who look at advertorial the same way as they would editorial. These are not rocket scientists."

McBride counters that readers would care if they knew that not all magazines adhere to the same ethical standards. "If you're about to spend a lot of money on a vacation in a foreign country and are trying to decide what hotels to stay at, you would certainly want to know if a reviewer is raving about a place because he got a free room, or because he really did his homework on all the hotels in that area."

Seglin believes the solution is truth in labeling. Magazines should disclose their policies on freebies on the table of contents or masthead. "If editors argue that it's not a big deal to accept gifts and it doesn't affect the integrity of their reporters, then why not tell the reader exactly what your policy is? Then the readers can make an informed decision about how to interpret the magazine's content."

But publications that allow acceptance of gifts have little or no incentive to do any such thing. McBride thinks there will always be a spectrum of publications and writers who take swag, and she sees this as an inevitable byproduct of a free market society. "Part of the beauty of American journalism is it's not licensed. Standards are voluntarily applied. There is no regulation," she says. "So I think the only thing we can do is put as much peer pressure as we can on our brethren and, in the spirit of a free market, give the readers the information they need to make intelligent choices."

The History of Swag

One of the most brilliant tactical breakthroughs in swag culture was developed in Los Angeles. In the late 1990s, publicists realized that the Academy Awards—a fashion vortex that draws the world's finest designers and jewelers and the international press together for one dizzying media-saturated weekend—presented an unprecedented opportunity to raise awareness for their clients' products. Thus the "swag suite" was born. Consortiums of designers rented out entire floors of such chic hotels as the Chateau Marmont, Raffles L' Ermitage and Le Meridien, and filled the suites with samples of their wares. They enticed celebrities and their stylists—and the media—with free champagne, facials, massages, makeup and hair styling, yoga classes and, of course, gift bags. The concept proved fantastically successful.

"Have you ever gone to a 99-Cents store on a welfare payday?" asks Kelly Cutrone. "It's basically like that. [Writers] will try to get four extra gift bags—one for their nanny, one for their sister in Oklahoma and one just in case they need to give it away for a Christmas present."

Cutrone's company, People's Revolution, has organized swag suites during the Oscars and the Golden Globes, and she's seen media greed escalate with each passing year. "It's gotten to the point where the vendors have to nail the stuff down. We've had to create a color-coded gift band system. The different editors and writers won't really know they're a part of it until they arrive. There will be different color codes: a silver bracelet, a gold bracelet and a white bracelet. The gold bracelet would be the highest rank. That means: This person is very, very credible and has a lot of power and you should gift accordingly. The silver one might mean: Give them a T-shirt. The white one is: Don't give them anything. They just need to be in here to feel important and we need their body to fill the space."

The swag suites proved so successful that they soon popped up at the Grammys and New York and LA's fashion weeks. At the Sundance Film Festival the swag suites have exploded into swag lodges, lounges and houses sponsored by Michelob, Skyy Vodka, Mystic Tan, Gap, Chrysler, Diesel, Tommy Hilfiger, Reebok, Ray-Ban and Black & Decker. Last year Volkswagen offered morning yoga classes, treated celebs and select members of the press to, free rides around town in its luxury Phaeton sedan and handed out $1,000 gift bags. The once sleepy main street of Park City, Utah, which used to host a quiet counterculture film festival, has become a gaudy carnival midway where New York fashionistas such as publicist Lara Shrift man hawk their clients' wares and writers for Women's Wear Daily, Us Weekly and the New York Post's Page Six hammer out exultant prose about the swagathon.

Juicy Couture is a textbook example of how swag suite marketing can propel a fledgling company into the limelight almost overnight. Founded in L.A. in 1994 by Gela Nash-Taylor—wife of John Taylor, bass player for Duran Duran—and Pam Skaist-Levy, it started as a T-shirt line and soon became known for low-cut, hip-hugging sweatpants with the words "Juicy" emblazoned across the butt. The product was hip, if no hipper than dozens of other start-up clothing lines that debuted and quickly vanished at around the same time. But Juicy had the marketing savvy of Nash-Taylor and Skaist-Levy.

"They really know how to work it in terms of getting free product into the hands of people," says Rose Apodaca, West Coast bureau chief for Women's Wear Daily. "Early on [in

2001], Juicy did a suite at the Chateau Marmont. It lasted all day. It was crazy chaos. Celebrities, media editors and all kinds of It Girls were there. Most people were given one free outfit. Others got more than that, I'm sure. Their track suits retail for about $175. The cashmere ones go for $500. Advertising Age wrote about the event as a case study. It put their name out there in a big way. They also sent a lot of swag to editors and celebrities and got the Juicy name out there on the people who mattered."

It cost Juicy anywhere from $20,000 to $100,000 to stage swag fests from L.A. to New York, but they proved to be extremely cost-effective. "In the fashion world it is much more impactful to see editorial than to see an advertisement," Nash-Taylor explains. "If you see an advertisement in Vogue, our customer will riffle past that. If the editor says 'Editor's Pick,' you're going to pay attention to that." Juicy's giveaway events generated articles in People, Women's Wear Daily, Us Weekly, the New York Post's Page Six, New York Daily News, Angeleno, OK!, Brntwd, New York magazine, Allure, Elle, Glamour, Harper's Bazaar, InStyle, Marie Claire, Vogue, W, the Los Angeles Times, Los Angeles magazine and the Boston Globe. In 2002 the advertising value equivalency of these articles was estimated to be $41,966,494.

In 2003 Nash-Taylor and Skaist-Levy sold the company to Liz Claiborne for an initial cash payment of $39 million, which may climb to $98 million after a required earn-out payment. And late last year they launched their first Juicy boutique, at the Caesars Palace Forum Shops in Las Vegas—chartering three planes to fly celebs and press to the opening night party.

"I don't know if they gave outfits to people," says Los Angeles Times fashion critic Booth Moore, who covered the opening. "Obviously, I didn't take the plane." (Los Angeles Times staffers and freelancers are not allowed to accept gifts of any kind, including travel, so she drove.) "But a lot of people at the opening were dressed in Juicy, and I don't imagine that they paid for it."

The Prehistory of Swag

Before the swag suite and the gift bag, there was the travel junket. Like D.W. Griffith's perfection of the close-up, the junket was a revolutionary breakthrough in its field. Developed by resorts and travel bureaus after World War II, it has become a surefire way of generating reams of ink.

The junket gives travel bureaus, resorts and hotels the biggest bang for their buck, far more than they could get by taking out ads in major magazines or newspapers. Full-page ads in national magazines run into the hundreds of thousands of dollars. In contrast, it might cost a grand to fly a writer to a hotel or resort for a week-end junket, and the results are far more effective. Kim Marshall, a fanner freelance writer who now runs a PR firm, the Marshall Plan, that organizes "press trips" for luxury resorts such as the Bora Bora Nui and Triple Creek Ranch in Montana, explains that "objective" copy in the form of an article is "seven times more believable. Because an ad is what you say about yourself. A third-party endorsement is far more credible in the mind of the reader."

Publicists refuse to admit that junkets compromise the integrity of participating journalists. "I'm a professional and I work with professionals, and they can't be bought," Marshall says. She claims the correspondents on her junkets adhere to back-breaking schedules to take in all of the sights and activities of the locales she promotes. Nevertheless, she expects at least half of them to get stories into print—"a minimum 50% return rate." Those who don't won't be invited on her next trip.

The spectacular success of travel junkets has led to the "Junketization" of a wide spectrum of industries. Movie studios were the first to realize the potential, and they began flying journalists to exotic locations to schmooze with movie stars. In 1969, more than 500 members of the press congregated on Grand Bahama Island for Warner Bros.' International Film Festival, which was in reality a giant junket to promote the studio's most prestigious summer films, among them "The Wild Bunch" and "The Rain People." The same approach was later applied to the music business.

Today, when auto companies debut their latest models, they invariably fly journalists in for the event. When Acura showed off its 2004 Acura TL in Seattle, dozens attended the junket at the W Hotel, where they were put up for two nights, treated to two dinners and cocktails, attended technical briefings on the car and test drove it. According to Mike Spencer, Acura's public relations manager, only a handful paid their own way. "Hopefully, we'll get at least 100 stories out of it," he says.

Jaguar held a junket in Scottsdale, Ariz., where the freebies included rounds of golf. Rolls-Royce offered reporters a drive up the coast from Santa Barbara to a private winery, where the vino flowed freely. Land Rover has held junkets on a ranch in Colorado and other rural settings where writers could practice skeet shooting, fly-fishing and falconry. According to a PR rep for the automaker—who asked not to be identified for fear that this article would reflect negatively on the industry—this isn't bribery but merely a way of contextualizing the product: "It's not just about what the vehicle physically does, it's also about the culture of the vehicle. The optional activities . . . are everything that you picture someone who ultimately would purchase a Land Rover would do."

Many auto magazines allow or even encourage their writers to take free junkets because, they claim, they can't afford to pay the costs themselves. "An airline ticket or hotel room is not, in this parlance, in our space, in any way a gift," says Matt Stone, executive editor of Motor Trend magazine. "Business travel is a tool necessary for us to do our job."

A veteran freelancer now employed by a major daily newspaper agrees. "To take the high road and accept no freebies is very, very expensive," he says. But, he adds, "the argument that this doesn't affect journalists' judgment is crap. Of course it does. And I'm an old hand at this. I've been to Europe maybe 50 times on product launches. They'll fly us into Frankfurt or Rome, the south of France. It'll be spectacular, right? Then they'll say, 'OK, drive this car. What do you think?' 'Gee, I don't know. Here I am bathed in the warm light of the Riviera. The car looks pretty good to me.' It really takes some doing to resist that tendency to be favorable."

How to Talk Swag

The gift bag, swag suite and junket paradigms have been adopted by almost every conceivable industry. Cosmetic companies fly beauty editors to Paris to present their new product lines. At the 2004 Republican National Convention, journalists received booklets full of discount tickets for New York retailers and were treated to martinis by Time Warner. Chris Mauro, editor of Surfer magazine, and Tom Bie, editor of Powder, say that their contributors accept free travel and product from manufacturers and promoters in the surf and ski industries, but without any guarantee of giving them ink.

"Outdoor writers are the biggest whores in the business," says the veteran free lancer. "I've seen outdoor writers who've had boats delivered to their house from manufacturers. Theoretically they're testing them, but the boat sits in the guy's yard—they just keep it, a 25- to 30-foot boat. There are $50,000 bass boats."

The freebie culture has engendered a sense of entitlement. Publicists love to do imitations of journalists who have tried to scam them. "Our company represents the Tribeca and SoHo Grand hotels," Cutrone says. "I get 10 e-mails a day from journalists who are coming to New York from all over the world. I'm talking about everyone from the Daily Telegraph to the Shanghai Times. They call and say, 'Hi, we're going to do this big, huge blowout story. We can only pick one hotel in New York City. Can you offer a press rate?' As a publicist, this is how I would translate that: 'We're sending this e-mail to every cool hotel in New York. This is a huge [tourist] market for you. We're not going to come out and say that we want a free hotel room.' So what I'm going to say to my client is: 'Can we offer these people a comped room? I think it could turn out to be a great story for us.' "

When fashion writers come to town, they don't stop at taking a free hotel room. 'You ask them to come to an event,' says Kelly Cutrone, founder of the firm People's Revolution, 'and they say, "Can you send me a car?" or, "I don't have anything to wear. I'd really like to wear your designer to the show." You can smell a fashion editor who's looking for a free ride. They'll come to your showroom and they light up, saying, "Ohhhh, loooovvvveee!!! Oh my God, I've got to get one of these. I just love it, love it! Do you think there's any way I can get a deal on one of these?" That's classic.'

When fashion writers come to town, they don't stop at the free hotel room. "You ask them to come to an event," Cutrone explains, "and they say, 'Can you send me a car?' Or, 'I don't have anything to wear. I'd really love to wear your designer to the show.' You can smell a fashion editor who's looking for a free ride. They'll come to your showroom and they light up, saying, 'Ohhhh, loooovvvveee!!! Oh my God, I've got to get one of these. I just love it, love it! You knooooow, we're actually working on this amazing issue, which I think that this would be perfect for. But you know what, I'm going away with my boyfriend for the weekend. We're going to St. Bart's. Do you think there's any way I can get a deal on one of these?' That's classic."

Of course, publicists have no one to blame for this but themselves. They're the ones who addicted journalists to freebies in the first place. Many fashion publicists offer a "media discount" on their clients' products, which can range from 20% to 70%, depending on the client and the writer's clout. (A writer for a national glossy might get a larger discount than a reporter for a regional publication.) And then there's the "gifting" of designer clothing, shoes, purses, jewelry, sunglasses, watches and so on. Again, the status of the byline and the circulation of the publication calibrate the value of the gift. A junior editor at a regional publication might receive a $500 starter purse, while an editorial superstar could receive a $5,000 status bag.

Product is sometimes dispersed as part of a wider campaign to raise public awareness. Cutrone explains: "We'll go to the designer and say, 'Listen, we think that the green leather bag is a very cute must-have item for this season. What I'd like to do is order an extra 35 bags and do a gifting program to the editors.' Then the costs are rolled into production. Then the editors show up at fashion shows wearing it." And a trend is born.

No wonder Juicy Couture's Nash-Taylor proselytizes the virtues of swag. When I interviewed her for this story, I asked if she rewards journalists who write favorable articles with follow-up gifts. "You'd better believe it, David!" she exclaimed. "At the end of the conversation, we always say, 'Do you have Juicy? Do you want something for your wife?' We'll put you on with Kate and say, 'Kate, send David a great box.' Some journalists are not allowed to accept anything." And I was one of them, I informed her. "Oh, you are?" Nash-Taylor groaned. I admitted that my wife and daughter would be angry that I turned her down. She emitted a throaty laugh. "They're bumming. As a journalist, if you were allowed to do that, you'd understand our product better. So why not? That's how I look at it. Why not? I'm sorry I can't send you something for your wife and your daughter. They're going to be saying, 'You should have done it, Dad!' You too, David. We've got great men's stuff."

Critical Thinking

1. How do you define swag?
2. Do you think things have changed since this article was written? Explain.
3. How do you feel about journalists taking freebees? Should there be clear guidelines issued by journalists' employers regarding the taking of freebees? What guidelines would you come up with?

DAVID WEDDLE last wrote for the magazine about his daughter's college course work in film theory.

UNIT 5

Developing the Future Ethos and Social Responsibility of Business

Unit Selections

Learning Outcomes

- In what areas should organizations become more ethically sensitive and socially responsible in the next five years? Be specific and explain your choices.

- Obtain codes of ethics or conduct from several different professional associations (for example, doctors, lawyers, CPAs). What are the similarities and differences between them?

- How useful do you feel codes of ethics are to organizations? Defend your answer.

Student Website

www.mhhe.com/cls

Internet References

International Business Ethics Institute (IBEI)
 www.business-ethics.org/index.asp
UNU/IAS Project on Global Ethos
 www.ias.unu.edu/research/globalethos.cfm

Business ethics should not be viewed as a short-term, "knee-jerk reaction" to recently revealed scandals and corruption. Instead, it should be viewed as a thread woven through the fabric of the entire business culture—one that ought to be integral to its design. Businesses are built on the foundation of trust in our free-enterprise system. When there are violations of this trust between competitors, between employer and employees, or between businesses and consumers, the system ceases to run smoothly.

From a pragmatic viewpoint, the alternative to self-regulated and voluntary ethical behavior and social responsibility on the part of business may be governmental and legislative intervention. From a moral viewpoint, ethical behavior should not exist because of economic pragmatism, governmental edict, or contemporary fashionability—it should exist because it is morally appropriate and right.

This last unit is composed of articles that provide some ideas, guidelines, and principles for developing the future ethos and social responsibility of business. The first article, "Creating an Ethical Culture," discloses how values-based programs can help employees judge right from wrong.

"Outside-the-Box Ethics" discusses five characteristics of an ethical culture. The next article reflects the slow progress for women in the upper levels of the organizational hierarchy. "Hiring Character" presents a look at business leader Warren Buffett's practice of hiring people based on their integrity. The next article, "The Business Case for Diversity," covers how diversity in the workplace has become a competitive advantage for manufacturers. The remaining articles discuss the issues of "Managing

© Stockbyte/Getty Images

Part-Time Employees," the concept of a theoretical basis for diversity, the problems encountered "When Generations Collide," "Strategic Organizational Diversity," employee morale, and employee benefits that vary in different cultures and countries.

Creating an Ethical Culture

Values-based ethics programs can help employees judge right from wrong.

DAVID GEBLER, JD

While the fate of former Enron leaders Kenneth Lay and Jeffrey Skilling is being determined in what has been labeled the "Trial of the Century," former WorldCom managers are in jail for pulling off one of the largest frauds in history.

Yes, criminal activity definitely took place in these companies and in dozens more that have been in the news in recent years, but what's really important is to take stock of the nature of many of the perpetrators.

Some quotes from former WorldCom executives paint a different picture of corporate criminals than we came to know in other eras:

> "I'm sorry for the hurt that has been caused by my cowardly behavior." —*Scott Sullivan, CFO*

> "Faced with a decision that required strong moral courage, I took the easy way out. . . . There are no words to describe my shame."
>
> —*Buford Yates, director of general accounting*

> "At the time I consider the single most critical character-defining moment of my life, I failed. It's something I'll take with me the rest of my life."
>
> —*David Myers, controller*

These are the statements of good people gone bad. But probably most disturbing was the conviction of Betty Vinson, the senior manager in the accounting department who booked billions of dollars in false expenses. At her sentencing, U.S. District Judge Barbara Jones noted that Vinson was among the lowest-ranking members of the conspiracy that led to the $11 billion fraud that sank the telecommunications company in 2002. Still, she said, "Had Ms. Vinson refused to do what she was asked, it's possible this conspiracy might have been nipped in the bud."

Judge Jones added that although Ms. Vinson "was among the least culpable members of the conspiracy" and acted under extreme pressure, "that does not excuse what she did."

Vinson said she improperly covered up expenses by drawing down reserve accounts—some completely unrelated to the expenses—and by moving expenses off income statements and listing them as assets on the balance sheet.

Also the company's former director of corporate reporting, Vinson testified at Bernie Ebbers's trial that, in choosing which accounts to alter, "I just really pulled some out of the air. I used some spreadsheets." She said she repeatedly brought her concerns to colleagues and supervisors, once describing the entries to a coworker as "just crazy." In spring 2002, she noted, she told one boss she would no longer make the entries. "I said that I thought the entries were just being made to make the income statement look like Scott wanted it to look."

Standing before the judge at her sentencing, Vinson said: "I never expected to be here, and I certainly won't do anything like this again." She was sentenced to five months in prison and five months of house arrest.

Pressure Reigns

While the judge correctly said that her lack of culpability didn't excuse her actions, we must carefully note that Betty Vinson, as well as many of her codefendants, didn't start out as criminals seeking to defraud the organization. Under typical antifraud screening tools, she and others like her wouldn't have raised any red flags as being potential committers of corporate fraud.

Scott Sullivan was a powerful leader with a well-known reputation for integrity. If any of us were in Betty Vinson's shoes, could we say with 100% confidence that we would say "no" to the CFO if he asked us to do something and promised that he would take full responsibility for any fallout from the actions we were going to take?

Today's white-collar criminals are more likely to be those among us who are unable to withstand the blistering pressures placed on managers to meet higher and tougher goals. In this environment, companies looking to protect themselves from corporate fraud must take a hard look at their own culture. Does it promote ethical behavior, or does it emphasize something else?

In most companies, "ethics" programs are really no more than compliance programs with a veneer of "do the right thing" messaging to create an apparent link to the company's values. To be effective, they have to go deeper than outlining steps to take to report misconduct. Organizations must understand what causes misconduct in the first place.

We can't forget that Enron had a Code of Ethics. And it wasn't as if WorldCom lacked extensive internal controls. But both had cultures where engaging in unethical conduct was tacitly condoned, if not encouraged.

Building the Right Culture

Now the focus has shifted toward looking at what is going on inside organizations that's either keeping people from doing the right thing or, just as importantly, keeping people from doing something about misconduct they observe. If an organization wants to reduce the risk of unethical conduct, it must focus more effort on building the right culture than on building a compliance infrastructure.

The Ethics Resource Center's 2005 National Business Ethics Survey (NBES) clearly confirms this trend toward recognizing the role of corporate culture. Based on interviews with more than 3,000 employees and managers in the U.S., the survey disclosed that, despite the increase in the number of ethics and compliance program elements being implemented, desired outcomes, such as reduced levels of observed misconduct, haven't changed since 1994. Even more striking is the revelation that, although formal ethics and compliance programs have some impact, organizational culture has the greatest influence in determining program outcomes.

Leadership must know how the myriad human behaviors and interactions fit together like puzzle pieces to create a whole picture. An organization moves toward an ethical culture only if it understands the full range of values and behaviors needed to meet its ethical goals.

The Securities & Exchange Commission (SEC) and the Department of Justice have also been watching these trends. Stephen Cutler, the recently retired SEC director of the Division of Enforcement, was matter of fact about the importance of looking at culture when it came to decisions of whether or not to bring an action. "We're trying to induce companies to address matters of tone and culture.... What we're asking of that CEO, CFO, or General Counsel goes beyond what a perp walk or an enforcement action against another company executive might impel her to do. We're hoping that if she sees that a failure of corporate culture can result in a fine that significantly exceeds the proverbial 'cost of doing business,' and reflects a failure on her watch—and a failure on terms that everyone can understand: the company's bottom line—she may have a little more incentive to pay attention to the environment in which her company's employees do their jobs."

Measuring Success

Only lagging companies still measure the success of their ethics and compliance programs just by tallying the percentage of employees who have certified that they read the Code of Conduct and attended ethics and compliance training. The true indicator of success is whether the company has made significant progress in achieving key program outcomes. The National Business Ethics Survey listed four key outcomes that help determine the success of a program:

- Reduced misconduct observed by employees,
- Reduced pressure to engage in unethical conduct,
- Increased willingness of employees to report misconduct, and
- Greater satisfaction with organizational response to reports of misconduct.

What's going to move these outcomes in the right direction? Establishing the right culture.

Most compliance programs are generated from "corporate" and disseminated down through the organization. As such, measurement of the success of the program is often based on criteria important to the corporate office: how many employees certified the Code of Conduct, how many employees went through the training, or how many calls the hotline received.

Culture is different—and is measured differently. An organization's culture isn't something that's created by senior leadership and then rolled out. A culture is an objective picture of the organization, for better or worse. It's the sum total of all the collective values and behaviors of all employees, managers, and leaders. By definition, it can only be measured by criteria that reflect the individual values of all employees, so understanding cultural vulnerabilities that can lead to ethics issues requires knowledge of what motivates employees in the organization. Leadership must know how the myriad human behaviors and interactions fit together like puzzle pieces to create a whole picture. An organization moves toward an ethical culture only if it understands the full range of values and behaviors needed to meet its ethical goals. The "full-spectrum" organization is one that creates a positive sense of engagement and purpose that drives ethical behavior.

Why is understanding the culture so important in determining the success of a compliance program? Here's an example: Most organizations have a policy that prohibits retaliation against those who bring forward concerns or claims. But creating a culture where employees feel safe enough to admit mistakes and to raise uncomfortable issues requires more than a policy and "Code training." To truly develop an ethical culture, the organization must be aware of how its managers deal with these issues up and down the line and how the values they demonstrate impact desired behaviors. The organization must understand the pressures its people are under and how they react to those pressures. And it must know how its managers communicate and whether employees have a sense of accountability and purpose.

Categorizing Values

Determining whether an organization has the capabilities to put such a culture in place requires careful examination. Do employees and managers demonstrate values such as respect? Do employees feel accountable for their actions and feel that they have a stake in the success of the organization?

How does an organization make such a determination? One approach is to categorize different types of values in a way that lends itself to determining specific strengths and weaknesses that can be assessed and then corrected or enhanced.

The Culture Risk Assessment model presented in Figure 1 has been adapted from the Cultural Transformation Tools® developed by Richard Barrett & Associates. Such tools provide a comprehensive framework for measuring cultures by mapping values. More than 1,000 organizations in 24 countries have used this technique in the past six years. In fact, the international management consulting firm McKinsey & Co. has adopted it as its method of

SUSTAINABILITY	7	Resilience to withstand integrity challenges
SOCIAL RESPONSIBILITY	6	Strategic alliances with external stakeholders
ALIGNMENT	5	Shared values guide decision making
ACCOUNTABILITY	4	Responsibilty and initiative
SYSTEMS AND PROCESSES	3	Compliance systems and processes
COMMUNICATION	2	Relationships that support the organization
FINANCIAL STABILITY	1	Pursuit of profit and stability

© Working Values, Ltd. Based on Cultural Transformation Tools © Richard Barrett & Associates

Figure 1 Seven levels of an ethical organization.

choice for mapping corporate cultures and measuring progress toward achieving culture change.

The model is based on the principle, substantiated through practice, that all values can be assigned to one of seven categories:

Levels 1, 2, and 3—The Organization's Basic Needs

Does the organization support values that enable it to run smoothly and effectively? From an ethics perspective, is the environment one in which employees feel physically and emotionally safe to report unethical behavior and to do the right thing?

Level 1—Financial Stability. Every organization needs to make financial stability a primary concern. Companies that are consumed with just surviving struggle to focus enough attention on how they conduct themselves. This may, in fact, create a negative cycle that makes survival much more difficult. Managers may exercise excessive control, so employees may be working in an environment of fear.

In these circumstances, unethical or even illegal conduct can be rationalized. When asked to conform to regulations, organizations do the minimum with an attitude of begrudging compliance.

Organizations with challenges at this level need to be confident that managers know and stand within clear ethical boundaries.

Level 2—Communication. Without good relationships with employees, customers, and suppliers, integrity is compromised. The critical issue at this level is to create a sense of loyalty and belonging among employees and a sense of caring and connection between the organization and its customers.

The most critical link in the chain is between employees and their direct supervisors. If direct supervisors can't effectively reinforce messages coming from senior leadership, those messages might be diluted and confused by the time they reach line employees. When faced with conflicting messages, employees will usually choose to follow the lead of their direct supervisor over the words of the CEO that have been conveyed through an impersonal communication channel. Disconnects in how local managers "manage"

these messages often mean that employees can face tremendous pressure in following the lead established by leadership.

Fears about belonging and lack of respect lead to fragmentation, dissension, and disloyalty. When leaders meet behind closed doors or fail to communicate openly, employees suspect the worst. Cliques form, and gossip becomes rife. When leaders are more focused on their own success, rather than the success of the organization, they begin to compete with each other.

Level 3—Systems and Processes. At this level, the organization is focused on becoming the best it can be through the adoption of best practices and a focus on quality, productivity, and efficiency.

Level 3 organizations have succeeded in implementing strong internal controls and have enacted clear standards of conduct. Those that succeed at this level are the ones that see internal controls as an opportunity to create better, more efficient processes. But even those that have successfully deployed business processes and practices need to be alert to potentially limiting aspects of being too focused on processes. All organizations need to be alert to resorting to a "check-the-box" attitude that assumes compliance comes naturally from just implementing standards and procedures. Being efficient all too often leads to bureaucracy and inconsistent application of the rules. When this goes badly, employees lose respect for the system and resort to self-help to get things done. This can lead to shortcuts and, in the worst case, engaging in unethical conduct under the guise of doing what it takes to succeed.

Level 4—Accountability

The focus of the fourth level is on creating an environment in which employees and managers begin to take responsibility for their own actions. They want to be held accountable, not micromanaged and supervised every moment of every day. For an ethics and compliance program to be successful, all employees must feel that they have a personal responsibility for the integrity of the organization. Everyone must feel that his or her voice is being heard. This requires managers and leaders to admit that they don't have all the answers and invite employee participation.

Levels 5, 6, and 7—Common Good

Does the organization support values that create a collective sense of belonging where employees feel that they have a stake in the success of the ethics program?

Level 5—Alignment. The critical issue at this level is developing a shared vision of the future and a shared set of values. The shared vision clarifies the intentions of the organization and gives employees a unifying purpose and direction. The shared values provide guidance for making decisions.

The organization develops the ability to align decision making around a set of shared values. The values and behaviors must be reflected in all of the organization's processes and systems, with appropriate consequences for those who aren't willing to walk the talk. A precondition for success at this level is building a climate of trust.

Level 6—Social Responsibility. At this level, the organization is able to use its relationships with stakeholders to sustain itself through crises and change. Employees and customers see that the organization is making a difference in the world through its products and services, its involvement in the local community, or its willingness to fight for causes that improve humanity. They must feel that the company cares about them and their future. Companies operating at this level go the extra mile to make sure they are being responsible citizens. They support and encourage employees' activities in the community by providing time off for volunteer work and/or making a financial contribution to the charities that employees are involved in.

Level 7—Sustainability. To be successful at Level 7, organizations must embrace the highest ethical standards in all their interactions with employees, suppliers, customers, shareholders, and the community. They must always consider the long-term impact of their decisions and actions.

Employee values are distributed across all seven levels. Through surveys, organizations learn which values employees bring to the workplace and which values are missing. Organizations don't operate from any one level of values: They tend to be clustered around three or four levels. Most are focused on the first three: profit and growth (Level 1), customer satisfaction (Level 2), and productivity, efficiency, and quality (Level 3). The most successful organizations operate across the full spectrum with particular focus in the upper levels of consciousness—the common good—accountability, leading to learning and innovation (Level 4), alignment (Level 5), social responsibility (Level 6), and sustainability (Level 7).

Some organizations have fully developed values around Levels 1, 2, and 3 but are lacking in Levels 5, 6, and 7. They may have a complete infrastructure of controls and procedures but may lack the accountability and commitment of employees and leaders to go further than what is required.

Similarly, some organizations have fully developed values around Levels 5, 6, and 7 but are deficient in Levels 1, 2, and 3. These organizations may have visionary leaders and externally focused social responsibility programs, but they may be lacking in core systems that will ensure that the higher-level commitments are embedded into day-to-day processes.

Once an organization understands its values' strengths and weaknesses, it can take specific steps to correct deficient behavior.

Starting the Process

Could a deeper understanding of values have saved WorldCom? We will never know, but if the culture had encouraged open communication and fostered trust, people like Betty Vinson might have been more willing to confront orders that they knew were wrong. Moreover, if the culture had embodied values that encouraged transparency, mid-level managers wouldn't have been asked to engage in such activity in the first place.

The significance of culture issues such as these is also being reflected in major employee surveys that highlight what causes unethical behavior. According to the NBES, "Where top management displays certain ethics-related actions, employees are 50 percentage points less likely to observe misconduct." No other factor in any ethics survey can demonstrate such a drastic influence.

So how do compliance leaders move their organizations to these new directions?

1. **The criteria for success of an ethics program must be outcomes based.** Merely checking off program elements isn't enough to change behavior.
2. **Each organization must identify the key indicators of its culture.** Only by assessing its own ethical culture can a company know what behaviors are the most influential in effecting change.
3. **The organization must gauge how all levels of employees perceive adherence to values by others within the company.** One of the surprising findings of the NBES was that managers, especially senior managers, were out of touch with how nonmanagement employees perceived their adherence to ethical behaviors. Nonmanagers are 27 percentage points less likely than senior managers to indicate that executives engage in all of the ethics-related actions outlined in the survey.
4. **Formal programs are guides to shape the culture, not vice versa.** People who are inclined to follow the rules appreciate the rules as a guide to behavior. Formal program elements need to reflect the culture in which they are deployed if they are going to be most effective in driving the company to the desired outcomes.

Culture may be new on the radar screen, but it isn't outside the scope or skills of forward-thinking finance managers and compliance professionals. Culture can be measured, and finance managers can play a leadership role in developing systematic approaches to move companies in the right direction.

Critical Thinking

1. Whose values should guide an organization? Senior management? Middle management? "Workers"? Investors?
2. What might happen in an organization that switched "resilience to withstand integrity challenges" and "pursuit of profit and stability" on the right hand side of the seven levels of an ethical organization, while leaving the left hand side as is?

DAVID GEBLER, JD, is president of Working Values, Ltd., a business ethics training and consulting firm specializing in developing behavior-based change to support compliance objectives. You can reach him at dgebler@workingvalues.com.

Outside-the-Box Ethics

Take "boring" out of ethics training.

Luis Ramos

In the quest for an ethical culture, leaders are finding that one-size-fits-all ethics training doesn't work. *Right-sizing* behavior starts with messaging that speaks directly to employees about specific ethical issues they are likely to encounter on the job. And it delivers the resources and tools they need to do the right thing when it comes to their own actions and to speak out against unethical activity by others when they see it.

Companies that consistently rank high on the lists of *best corporate citizens* tend to make ethics training part of a company-wide initiative to promote integrity. They look for ways to tackle tough subjects and benchmark results to ensure that people don't just get the message, but understand and apply it. These companies see that an investment in an ethical workplace delivers dividends—including a more unified workforce and stock growth.

Cisco does ethics right. With more than 65,000 employees worldwide, building and sustaining an ethical culture is complicated, but the commitment the company has made to an ethical workplace has earned it the status of "repeat performer" on the *Corporate Responsibility Officer's* (CRO's) 100 Best Corporate Citizens.

Five Key Characteristics

Five key characteristics set apart companies with an ethical culture:

1. Leaders Encourage a Two-Way Dialogue about Business Conduct

The message about ethics starts at the top with support from executives and top management who show their commitment to an ethical workplace by modeling behaviors they want to instill in employees. Words like *trust, honesty, values* are part of the vernacular in an ethical company. Internal and external communications reflect the behavioral expectations for every stakeholder.

2. The Company's Code of Ethics Is a Living Document

A code that's built to satisfy curious investors or to fill new-hire packets underserves the company. A code should represent the centerpiece of an ethical culture and serve as a ready resource. It should also reflect the look, tone, and voice of the company. Although crafters should work with the legal department to review and approve policies, the code should reflect an easy-to-read style that reinforces the company's core values, and guides ethical decision-making.

When Cisco rewrote its *Code of Conduct,* active voice and user-friendly language drove the process. Once topics were defined, each section began with an affirmative statement written in an employee voice—"I Respect Others," "I Protect What Is Ours," "I Follow the Law." The language was conversational in tone, suggestive of one Cisco employee speaking to another. The design was crafted to complement the user-friendly style, with quick-read call-out boxes that helped employees to "Connect with the Code," "Learn More" links that provided more detailed policy and "What If" scenarios that customized the Code to address Cisco-specific issues.

Although Cisco's Code won awards, the real winners were Cisco employees: 95 percent of them agreed that the new Code was easy to read and comprehend. And a code that's easy to read is also likely to be easy to follow.

3. Ethics Isn't a "Program" but a Way of Doing Business

The word *program* suggests a starting and stopping point—not a defining feature of an ethical culture. In its Code, Cisco emphasizes "doing the right thing is part of our DNA." An ethical culture is the result of a continuous, dynamic process that engages every employee; keeping the ethics *message* visible through media keeps ethical *behavior* at the forefront.

Branding enhances visibility—a name makes an ethics initiative recognizable. Then promote it using media that "fit" your workplace and employee demographics. Monthly manager meetings provide great forums for discussing conflicts of interest, proprietary information, or corporate gift policy. A mix of traditional communication vehicles and customized interactive components—translated into every language that employees speak—helps to disperse and reinforce the message about ethics.

4. Training about Ethics Is Relevant, Maybe Even Fun

If the people depicted in an ethics training don't look or sound like its employees or face ethical situations that employees face, the message won't resonate with them. If the messaging is one-way, they will tune out. If the training is long and boring, they will multitask until it's over.

Cisco knew that ethics initiatives needed to appeal to a global workforce that was highly technical. They wanted something dynamic and interactive, easily accessible from desktops and relevant to the Cisco experience.

The result was "Ethics Idol" a series of four, fun modules, each of which introduced an animated "contestant" who told the story of his or her ethical dilemma using action-packed visuals and witty song parody. Once each episode played out, three quirky judges offered their opinion and employees voted on which judge provided the most ethical answer.

The parody of *American Idol* created a buzz about ethics, winning awards and showing that learning about ethics didn't have to be rote, boring, or easy. Scenarios were designed so that the proper course of action wasn't obvious.

5. Employees Are Actively Engaged as Corporate Citizens, Aligned with the Company's Values

A poster on the wall tells employees that ethical behavior is important. A certification program tells employees that ethical behavior is mandatory. Thanks to an effective launch and a multilingual format, Cisco's annual *Code of Business Conduct* certification process was seamless; within the four-week period of the certification campaign, 98 percent of employees certified that they had received and read the *Code* and, within 10 weeks, 99.6 percent of employees certified.

Companies with an ethical culture ensure employees have the resources they need to promote ethics. Leaders have the power to shape and sustain an ethical culture and inspire people to do the right thing.

Critical Thinking

1. How does Cisco's overall approach to ethical business behavior compare with the approach held by your academic institution toward ethical behavior?

2. Describe a situation in own job (or in a job that you have held in the past) that could illustrate how *ethics is a way of doing business.*

Luis Ramos is CEO of The Network, providing ethics and compliance services. Visit www.towinc.com.

From *Leadership Excellence*, April 2009, p. 19. Copyright © 2009 by Leadership Excellence. Reprinted by permission.

Hiring Character

In their new book, **Integrity Works,** authors Dana Telford and Adrian Gostick outline the strategies necessary for becoming a respected and admired leader. In the edited excerpt that follows, the authors present a look at business leader Warren Buffett's practice of hiring people based on their integrity. For sales and marketing executives, it's a practice worth considering, especially when your company's reputation with customers—built through your salespeople—is so critical.

Dana Telford and Adrian Gostick

This chapter was the hardest for us to write. The problem was, we couldn't agree on whom to write about. We had a number of great options we were mulling over. Herb Brooks of the Miracle on Ice 1980 U.S. hockey team certainly put together a collection of players whose character outshined their talent. And the results were extraordinary. We decided to leave him out because we had enough sports figures in the book already. No, we wanted a business leader. So we asked, "Who hires integrity over ability?"

The person suggested to us over and over as we bandied this idea among our colleagues was Warren Buffett, chairman of Berkshire Hathaway Inc.

Sure enough, as we began our research we found we had not even begun to tell Buffett's story. But we were reluctant to repeat his story. Buffett had played an important part in our first book. And yet, his name kept coming up. So often, in fact, that we finally decided to not ignore the obvious.

Perhaps more than anyone in business today, Warren Buffett hires people based on their integrity. Buffett commented, "Berkshire's collection of managers is unusual in several ways. As one example, a very high percentage of these men and women are independently wealthy, having made fortunes in the businesses that they run. They work neither because they need the money nor because they are contractually obligated to—we have no contracts at Berkshire. Rather, they work long and hard because they love their businesses."

The unusual thing about Warren Buffett is that he and his longtime partner, Charlie Munger, hire people they trust—and then treat them as they would wish to be treated if their positions were reversed. Buffett says the one reason he has kept working so long is that he loves the opportunity to interact with people he likes and, most importantly, trusts.

Buffett loves the opportunity to interact daily with people he likes and, most importantly, trusts.

Consider the following remarkable story from a few years ago at Berkshire Hathaway. It's about R.C. Willey, the dominant home furnishings business in Utah. Berkshire purchased the company from Bill Child and his family in 1995. Child and most of his managers are members of the Church of Jesus Christ of Latter-day Saints, also called Mormons, and for this reason R.C. Willey's stores have never been open on Sunday.

Now, anyone who has worked in retail realizes the seeming folly of this notion: Sunday is the favorite shopping day for many customers—even in Utah. Over the years, though, Child had stuck to his principle—and wasn't ready to rejigger the formula just because Warren Buffett came along. And the formula was working. R.C.'s sales were $250,000 in 1954 when Child took over. By 1999, they had grown to $342 million. Child's determination to stick to his convictions was what attracted Buffett to him and his management team. This was a group with values and a successful brand.

Arnie Ferrin, longtime friend of Child, said, "I believe that [Child] is a man of extreme integrity, and I believe that Warren Buffett was looking to buy his business because he likes to do business with people like that, that don't have any shadows in their lives, and they're straightforward and deal above-board."

This isn't to say Child and Buffett have always agreed on the direction of the furniture store.

"I was highly skeptical about taking a no-Sunday policy into a new territory, where we would be up against entrenched rivals open seven days a week," Buffett said. "Nevertheless, this was Bill's business to run. So, despite my reservations, I told him to follow both his business judgment and his religious convictions."

Proving once again that he believed in his convictions, Child insisted on a truly extraordinary proposition: He would personally buy the land and build the store in Boise, Idaho—for about

$11 million as it turned out—and would sell it to Berkshire at his cost if—and only if—the store proved to be successful. On the other hand, if sales fell short of his expectations, Berkshire could exit the business without paying Child a cent. This, of course, would leave him with a huge investment in an empty building.

You're probably guessing there's a happy ending to the story. And there is. The store opened in August of 1998 and immediately became a huge success, making Berkshire a considerable margin. Today, the store is the largest home furnishings store in Idaho.

Child, good to his word, turned the property over to Berkshire—including some extra land that had appreciated significantly. And he wanted nothing more than the original cost of his investment. In response, Buffett said, "And get this: Bill refused to take a dime of interest on the capital he had tied up over the two years."

And there's more. Shortly after the Boise opening, Child went back to Buffett, suggesting they try Las Vegas next. This time, Buffett was even more skeptical. How could they do business in a metropolis of that size and remain closed on Sundays, a day that all of their competitors would be exploiting?

But Buffett trusts his managers because he knows their character. So he gave it a shot. The store was built in Henderson, a mushrooming city adjacent to Las Vegas. The result? This store outsells all others in the R.C. Willey chain, doing a volume of business that far exceeds any competitor in the area. The revenue is twice what Buffett had anticipated.

As this book went to print, R.C. Willey was preparing to open its third store in the Las Vegas area, as well as stores in Reno, Nevada, and Sacramento, California. Sales have grown to more than $600 million, and the target is $1 billion in coming years. "You can understand why the opportunity to partner with people like Bill Child causes me to tap dance to work every morning," Buffett said.

H ere's another example of Buffett's adeptness at hiring character. He agreed to purchase Ben Bridge Jeweler over the phone, prior to any face-to-face meeting with the management.

Ed Bridge manages this 65-store West Coast retailer with his cousin, Jon. Both are fourth-generation owner-managers of a business started 89 years ago in Seattle. And over the years, the business and the family have enjoyed extraordinary character reputations.

Buffett knows that he must give complete autonomy to his managers. "I told Ed and Jon that they would be in charge, and they knew I could be believed: After all, it's obvious that [I] would be a disaster at actually running a store or selling jewelry, though there are members of [my] family who have earned black brits as purchasers."

Talk about hiring integrity! Without any provocation from Buffett, the Bridges allocated a substantial portion of the proceeds from their sale to the hundreds of coworkers who had helped the company achieve its success.

Overall, Berkshire has made many such acquisitions—hiring for character first, and talent second—and then asking these CEOs to manage for maximum long-term value, rather than for next quarter's earnings. While they certainly don't ignore the current profitability of their business, Buffett never wants profits to be achieved at the expense of developing ever-greater competitive strengths, including integrity.

It's an approach he learned early in his career.

W arren Edward Buffett was born on August 30, 1930. His father, Howard, was a stockbroker-turned-congressman. The only boy, Warren was the second of three children. He displayed an amazing aptitude for both money and business at a very early age. Acquaintances recount his uncanny ability to calculate columns of numbers off the top of his head—a feat Buffett still amazes business colleagues with today.

At only six years old, Buffett purchased six-packs of Coca-Cola from his grandfather's grocery store for twenty-five cents and resold each of the bottles for a nickel—making a nice five-cent profit. While other children his age were playing hopscotch and jacks, Buffett was already generating cash flow.

Buffett stayed just two years in the undergraduate program at Wharton Business School at the University of Pennsylvania. He left disappointed, complaining that he knew more than his professors. Eventually, he transferred to the University of Nebraska–Lincoln. He managed to graduate in only three years despite working full time.

Then he finally applied to Harvard Business School. In what was undoubtedly one of the worst admission decisions in history, the school rejected him as "too young." Slighted, Buffett applied to Columbia where famed investment professor Ben Graham taught.

Professor Graham shaped young Buffett's opinions on investing. And the student influenced his mentor as well. Graham bestowed on Buffett the only A+ he ever awarded in decades of teaching.

While Buffett tried working for Graham for a while, he finally struck out on his own with a revolutionary philosophy: He would research the internal workings of extraordinary companies. He could discover what really made them tick and why they held a competitive edge in their markets. And then he would invest in great companies that were trading at substantially less than their market values.

Ten years after its founding, the Buffett Partnership assets were up more than 1,156 percent [compared to the Dow's 122.9 percent], and Buffett was firmly on his way to becoming an investing legend.

In 2004, Warren Buffett was listed by Forbes as the world's second-richest person (right behind Bill Gates), with $42.9 billion in personal wealth. Despite starting with just $300,000 in holdings, Berkshire's holdings now exceed $116 billion. And Buffett and his employees can confidently say they have made thousands of people wealthy.

We often ask business leaders one simple question: Which is more dangerous to your firm—the incompetent new hire or the dishonest new hire? It's the part of our presentation where attendees sit up straight and start thinking.

We always follow the question with an exercise on identifying and hiring integrity. Though it becomes obvious that many of the executives and managers haven't given employee integrity much thought, most of the CEOs in the audiences are increasingly concerned about hiring employees with character.

So, how do you hire workers with integrity? It's possible, but not easy. It is important to spend more time choosing a new employee than you do picking out a new coffee machine. Here are a few simple areas to focus on:

First, ensure educational credentials match the resume. Education is the most misrepresented area on a resume. Notre Dame football coach George O'Leary was fired because the master's degree he said he had earned did not exist, the CEO of software giant Lotus exaggerated his education and military service, and the CEO of Bausch & Lomb forfeited a bonus of more than $1 million because he claimed a fictional MBA.

It is important to spend more time choosing a new employee than you do picking out a new coffee machine.

Job candidates also often claim credit for responsibilities that they never had. Here's a typical scenario:

Job candidate: "I led that project. Saved the company $10 million." Through diligent fact checking, you find an employee at a previous employer who can give you information about the candidate:

Coworker: "Hmm. Actually, Steve was a member of the team, but not the lead. And while it was a great project, we still haven't taken a tally of the cost savings. But $10 million seems really high."

How do you find those things out? Confer with companies where the applicant has worked—especially those firms the person isn't listing as a reference. Talk to people inside the organization, going at least two levels deep (which means you ask each reference for a couple more references). Talk to the nonprofit organizations where the person volunteers. Tap into alumni networks and professional associations. Get on the phone with others in the industry to learn about the person's reputation. Check public records for bankruptcy, civil, and criminal litigation (with the candidate's knowledge). In other words, check candidates' backgrounds carefully (but legally, of course).

We find that most hiring managers spend 90 percent of their time on capability-related questions, and next to no time on character-based questions. In your rush to get someone in the chair, don't forget to check backgrounds and be rigorous in your interviewing for character. Hiring the wrong person can destroy two careers: your employee's—and your own.

Ask ethics-based questions to get to the character issue. We asked a group of executives at a storage company to brainstorm a list of questions they might ask candidates to learn more about their character. Their list included the following questions:

- Who has had the greatest influence on you and why?
- Who is the best CEO you've worked for and why?
- Tell me about your worst boss.
- Who are your role models and why?
- How do you feel about your last manager?
- Tell me about a time you had to explain bad news to your manager.
- What would you do if your best friend did something illegal?
- What would your past manager say about you?
- What does integrity mean to you?
- If you were the CEO of your previous company, what would you change?
- What values did your parents teach you?
- Tell me a few of your faults.
- Why should I trust you?
- How have you dealt with adversity in the past?
- What are your three core values?
- Tell me about a time when you let someone down.
- What is your greatest accomplishment, personal or professional?
- What are your goals and why?
- Tell me about a mistake you made in business and what you learned from it.
- Tell me about a time when you were asked to compromise your integrity.

It's relatively easy to teach a candidate your business. The harder task is trying to instill integrity in someone who doesn't already have it.

Of course, we don't want to imply that it's impossible. Sometimes people will adapt to a positive environment and shine. Men's Wearhouse has certainly had tremendous success hiring former prison inmates, demonstrating everyone should have a second chance.

But integrity is a journey that is very personal, very individual. An outside force, such as an employer, typically can't prescribe it. It's certainly not something that happens overnight. That's one reason many of the CEOs we have talked with prefer promoting people from inside their organizations when possible.

Don Graham, chairman and CEO of the Washington Post Company, said, "There's a very good reason for concentrating your hires and promotions on people who already work in your organization. The best way to predict what someone's going to do in the future is to know what they've done in the past—watch how people address difficult business issues, how they deal with the people who work for them, how they deal with the people for whom they work. You may be able to put on a certain face for a day or even a week, but you're not going to be able to hide the person you are for five or ten years."

Graham tells a story about Frank Batten, who for years ran Landmark Communications and founded The Weather Channel. "Frank is a person of total integrity," Graham says. "Frank once said, 'When you go outside for hire you always get a surprise. Sometimes it's a good surprise. But you never hire quite the person you thought you were hiring.'"

What do you look for in a job applicant? Years of experience? College degree? Specific skill sets? Or do you look for character? If so, you're in good company.

Years ago, Warren Buffett was asked to help choose the next CEO for Salomon Brothers. "What do you think [Warren] was looking for?" Graham asks. "Character and integrity—more than even a particular background. When the reputation of the firm is on the line every day, character counts."

Don't like surprises? Then hire people who have integrity. Want to ensure a good fit with the people you hire? Then hire people who have integrity. Want to ensure your reputation with customers? Then hire people who have integrity.

Are we saying that nothing else matters? No. But we are saying that nothing matters more.

Critical Thinking

1. Describe Warren Buffett's hiring practices that assure he is hiring integrity.

2. What are the top three characteristics that an ethical leader must exhibit (from your perspective)?

From *Integrity Works: Strategies for Becoming a Trusted, Respected and Admired Leader* by **Dana Telford** and **Adrian Gostick.**

The Business Case for Diversity

Far from being just another feel-good initiative, diversity in the workforce has become a competitive advantage for manufacturers.

ADRIENNE SELKO

Having a diverse workforce is a competitive advantage and not merely a human resources initiative, according to Cate Roberts, director of diversity and community affairs at Textron Inc. The conglomerate, which is staffed with 44,000 employees and is comprised of Bell Helicopter, Cessna Aircraft Co. and many other companies, approaches diversity with a strategic objective.

"The three tenets of our business case are: Race for Talent, Need to Globalize and Innovation," explains Roberts. "We believe that diverse work teams create more innovative products and make us more competitive."

How does Textron embrace diversity? One way is through employee network groups, which include African-American, Asian-American, Generation Y, Native American, Hispanic, women and gay groups.

At W.R. Grace & Co., a producer of chemicals and materials with 6,500 employees located in more than 40 countries, diversity takes on a different meaning as the company prefers to move away from the traditional definition of race and gender. Grace's goal is to set up a structure that creates an inclusive environment in which diversity can flourish.

"We established a global diversity council that includes 20 people from 10 countries and 14 functions," explains Alfonso Gonzales, chairman of Grace's Diversity and Inclusion Council and director of Leadership Organizational Effectiveness. "Our goal is to provide a place where everyone feels their voices can be heard. The results of inclusion are increased production and innovation."

The company has developed a Diversity Toolkit as a point of reference to help employees discuss the attributes of diversity and discover inroads to tap into the expansive knowledge that comes with each culture. And these efforts add to the bottom line. Gonzales cites a study in which diverse teams outperformed non-diverse teams by 12% with respect to productivity.

To attract a diverse workforce, companies turn to mentoring and educational programs. At Textron, its year-long TXTConnect program pairs managers with employees—many of whom come from diverse backgrounds—to provide a well-rounded view of the company.

Recruiting efforts have paid off as well for Textron's Engineering Boot Camp Program, which boasts of a 90% hiring rate for its 75% diverse class. The first Boot Camp program took place in January 2008 at Bell Helicopter. Aerospace and mechanical engineering students from the local university, who were assisted by Bell engineers who had graduated less than three years ago, participated in designing a specific project. They toured five facilities and were flown to visit an assembly facility. The company feels this kind of hands-on learning experience appeals to students at the right time in their college experience.

Continually building on this effort, next year the company's Textron University will include in its curriculum a class entitled, "Doing Business Cross-Culturally." The program will address the issue of varying work traditions across different cultures.

Wider Definition of Culture

Although most companies wouldn't categorize military personnel as a separate culture, Advanced Technology Services Inc. (ATS) docs. Over 30% of its 2,200-person workforce is comprised of former military members or current reservists. ATS manages services of production equipment maintenance, information technology and spare parts repair for manufacturers.

> **"Military personnel are a perfect fit for manufacturing. Their technical skills are excellent and their familiarity with a process-oriented system fits right in."**
>
> —Jeff Owens

"Military personnel are a perfect fit for manufacturing. Their technical skills are excellent and their familiarity with a process-oriented system fits right in," says Jeff Owens, president of ATS. The company has hired a dedicated military recruiter, Holly Mosack, who previously served as a company commander for the 82nd Airborne Division in Fallujah, Iraq.

ATS is also looking to recruit the next generation of workers and has created a program called Technical Leadership in Manufacturing. Working with Southern Illinois University's College of Engineering, the company offers 30–40 college students tuition-free scholarships for their junior and senior years. A summer internship, which could be onsite for clients such as Caterpillar, is part of the program. Students receive training in courses as varied as Six Sigma and etiquette.

Convincing today's students that manufacturing is an exciting and fulfilling career is a challenge to many companies. "We demonstrate to students the fast-paced field of automation and show them how its dynamic applications impact factories," Owens says. "We also offer students a career path that includes working at various client sites so they gain different experiences."

Since locating students is yet another challenge, manufacturers need to be tapped into social networks, notes John Hauger, vice president of client services for Global Lead Management Consulting, an international diversity management consulting firm. Job seekers are very sophisticated today, he points out, and companies should be tapped into Facebook and other social networking sites.

Recruiting employees who can connect with the customers and the community is essential, Hauger notes, adding that leadership must have a clear understanding of inclusion. "Cultural dexterity is essential. Leaders and managers must have the ability to move between various cultures and tailor their communication and problem-solving skills in a way that is comfortable for each culture."

For example, when working with a U.S.-based auto parts supplier that was setting up shop in Japan, employees were immersed in cultural activities as a way to learn the norms of the society. "It worked out well and other clients are using this method of cultural dexterity as well," says Hauger.

Widening the Talent Pool

Companies that actively pursue diversity find that the talent pool widens significantly. Non-traditional employees are how Sandra Westlund-Deenihan, president of Quality Float Works, views her workforce. Of her 26 employees, 11 are minorities, four are women and four are veterans. "We bring in non-traditional workers, such as low income people and women from shelters. We provide whatever skills people need to be successful," says Westlund-Deenihan, whose company produces metal float balls for a number of industries.

Quality Floats will hire people who might have disabilities in some areas but are great with their hands and are an asset to her operations. The company provides training for basic skills in math, English and communication and offers on-the-job training as well.

As the company grows and its product line expands, including a product that helps purify water in third-world countries, the workforce must remain constant and strong. For this reason Westlund-Deenihan will assist with the childcare needs of her employees by paying for their children to go to summer camp.

Addressing the needs of employees and providing a supportive environment is one reason that Air Products, a producer of gases and equipment, created a program called Two in a Box. "We look at this program as a personal tutor for our new employees. We find that it helps employees get up to speed very quickly," explains Norma Curby, vice president, strategic planning for the company, which employs 22,000 in 40 countries.

It is the exchange of ideas from a diverse workforce that fuels the future growth opportunities of the company, Curby points out, and to that end effective talent management is key to Air Products' growth.

> **"By bringing together people with diverse backgrounds, who have a variety of experiences, there are more actionable ideas."**
>
> —Norma Curby

"You never know where the next idea will come from," she says. "By bringing together people with diverse backgrounds, who have a variety of experiences, there are more actionable ideas. We find new ways to approach markets, our processes and our business model."

Critical Thinking

1. How would you describe the bottom line value of a diverse work force?
2. Is the bottom line value more or less important than the HR (or ethics) value of diversity in the work force? Explain.

Managing Part-Time Employees

Just because they work fewer hours doesn't mean they can't be key contributors to your organization. To ensure they're as committed as your full-timers, show them you care.

Mark Rowh

Most organizations depend to some degree on part-time employees. After all, part-timers offer one of the best bargains around. They cost substantially less in wages and benefits than most full-time staff and provide needed talent along with flexibility in dealing with business fluctuations. And in the current economic environment, they may be more important than ever.

"The demand for people to work part time is growing dramatically," says Melanie Holmes, vice president of World of Work Solutions at Manpower Inc. "Mature workers, who are at or near retirement age, want time to pursue other interests. Younger workers are interested in work/life balance. As the skills shortage intensifies, employers need to be creative about the ways they attract talent. Providing part-time positions is a key strategy."

At the same time, part-time employees provide special challenges to managers. Some are at least as dedicated as their full-time counterparts. Others work at the margins, with little sense of commitment. In either case, managing part-timers requires attention to their unique situations.

Out of Mind

By definition, part-time employees don't put in as many hours as full-time personnel. But even when they're not physically present, they remain a part of the organization. Don't make the mistake of forgetting about part-timers when they're not working or, especially, when you make plans that could affect them.

"Be careful not to overlook these people for promotion and training and other opportunities simply because they are not around as much," says Heather Gatley, executive vice president of human resource services at AlphaStaff Group, an HR firm based in Ft. Lauderdale, Fla. "Out of sight sometimes really does cause someone to be 'out of mind,' and it is on both the supervisor and employee to make sure that doesn't happen."

From the manager's end, some simple measures can prove helpful. Keeping part-timers' work schedules close at hand where they're visible daily can help keep their names from being overlooked. Developing individualized goal lists for each employee and consulting them frequently can also prove helpful. Other measures might range from including all staff in developing departmental goals, to copying them on memos and e-mails.

"It's important to position part-timers as valuable members of the team," Holmes says. "Include them in meetings, which could mean adjusting their schedules so they can attend. And, include them in all written communications."

Depending on the practices within a given organization, opportunities for substantive feedback might also be expanded. For example, if part-timers aren't included in a formal performance evaluation process at least once a year, making that practice more inclusive could be a worthwhile initiative. Or if this isn't possible because of policy or time constraints, supervisors might take the time to schedule brief, but regular, one-on-one meetings with part-time staff to discuss job expectations, performance, and employee questions or concerns.

This approach might also include professional development activities. If possible, make part-timers eligible for benefits such as support for college classes or attendance at relevant workshops. If budgets or company policies preclude such measures, take a creative approach. Schedule inexpensive in-house workshops or hold brown-bag lunch sessions on topics of professional or personal interest.

"Keep part-timers engaged," Holmes says. "There is always a danger that they might fall off the radar, so you must make them feel like an equal part of the team. It's also important to expect commitment and encourage initiative in your part-timers."

Five Tips for Managing Part-Timers

Joyce L. Gioia-Herman, president of the Herman Group, a management consulting firm based in Greensboro, N.C. (www.hermangroup.com), offers these tips for successfully managing part-time employees:

- Give people specific responsibilities.
- Make sure that part-timers are clear about their days and hours.
- Let them know where they fit in and how critical their work is to the success of the enterprise.
- Make sure that workers understand exactly what is expected of them.
- Focus on results.

The Culture at Hand

In some cases, part-timers simply have a hard time fitting in. Achieving synergy with other personnel can be a real challenge for them. "Because part-time employees are at the workplace for only part of the time, it is more difficult for them to fully understand the culture of the organization," says Billie Blair, PhD, president of Leading and Learning, a Los Angeles-based consulting firm. "It can be hard [for them] to relate to it and to their fellow workers successfully and to lend themselves to the needs of that culture."

Dr. Blair says that workgroups often are made up primarily of full-time employees who tend to overlook their part-time colleagues. Even if they're not overtly rude or uncooperative, they may rely more fully on fellow full-timers and spend a disproportionate amount of their time interacting with one another at the expense of meaningful communication with part-time workers. Rectifying such situations may require managers to focus on bridging gaps between the two groups.

"Managers of part-time employees should spend time sorting out misperceptions and misinterpretations, both of the work needs and the interactions with fellow workers," Dr. Blair says. "Managers must also be ever-vigilant in forming and managing work teams because of the perceived differentiation between full-time and part-time employees."

To supplement involvement in the workplace itself, one simple strategy is to include part-timers in social activities. Keep them informed, and consider their schedules when planning birthday celebrations, showers, or other social events. "Just because someone works part time, a boss shouldn't assume that he doesn't want to attend a weekend seminar or attend an office cocktail hour or holiday party," says Gatley "The need to be 'part of something' remains just as strong as it does for full-time employees."

Different Strokes

Recognizing the differing priorities of part-time employees is key to motivating them, according to Cindy Ventrice, author of *Make Their Day! Employee Recognition That Works*. "Many of the needs of part-timers are exactly the same as [those of] full-timers. They want to receive fair and equitable compensation, do meaningful work, like the people they work with, have their opinions valued, and receive recognition for what they do," Ventrice says. "But they can also have very different needs from full-time staff. An important consideration for motivating them is to understand why they are part time."

She advises asking questions such as these:

- Are they going to school in a related field? Project opportunities that provide relevant experience will motivate them.
- Have they retired and are looking for a way to keep busy? Give these older workers a chance to show off their expertise or make a visible difference.
- Are they part time because they have family obligations that are a priority? Honor that time, and recognize and reward them with time off that they can take when needed.

"The more managers know about individual part-timers, the more likely they are to be successful in motivating and engaging them," adds Ventrice.

The same goes for recognition programs. "Don't ignore part-timers when it comes time to distribute bonuses, rewards, and other forms of recognition," says Francie Dalton, president of Dalton Alliances, a consulting firm based in Columbia, Md. "Part time doesn't mean part mind. Indeed, you may find you net greater productivity from multiple part-timers than you do from a single full-timer."

Providing adequate workspace is also part of the equation. Ruth King, CEO of ProfitabilityChannel.com and author of *The Ugly Truth about Managing People*, recalls an incident where a part-time employee had an office that she used regularly. She reported to work one day and found another person in her office. Management had reassigned her office to a full-time employee, and she had to scramble to find a place to work. "Don't treat a part-time employee as a step-child," King says. "This person should have his regular work area and be treated the same way a full-time employee is treated."

Recognizing Differences

Although efforts to include part-time staff make sense, it's also important to understand the different goals they bring to the workplace. "Managers need to realize that part-timers have different goals in mind," says Nick Vaidya, a partner with the 8020Strategy Group, a management consulting firm based in Austin, Texas. He notes that most part-time employees fall into two types. One prefers part-time status, or at least doesn't mind it. The other wishes for full-time employment.

"To be successful, you must recognize that there is a reason that they are part time, and you must honor that reason and support it," he says. "All else being equal, with such an attitude, you will command their respect and commitment."

For some part-timers, outside interests are major reasons they prefer that status. If you can identify their outside interests, you may be able to link them to workplace performance. "They are part-timers for a reason, which is likely that something else is more important in their lives," says Maryann Karinch, author of *I Can Read You Like a Book*. "You will not effectively manage and motivate a person like that by focusing on the work alone. Find out what is important to the person—family, budding acting career, night school—and link work performance to that important aspect of his or her life."

As an example, she says that a worker who is also a student might benefit if you find a way for him to apply what he's learning at work.

"If he's an accountant or an artist, there's probably a way to make his new skills live at work," she says, "even if it's a matter of asking for his opinion on redecorating your office."

Whatever their motivation, part-time employees are likely to be an important part of any workforce. As a result, efforts to work effectively with them, and to provide the right kind of leadership, are imperative.

"Part-timers are going to become increasingly more common as work/life balance choices by younger workers take precedence over boomer workaholism," says Dalton. "Realize that really smart, highly accomplished people are choosing to work part time. So appreciate them. And work hard to retain them!"

Critical Thinking

1. Were you ever a part-time employee? If so, what do you wish your employer(s) had done differently to make you a more valued employee?

2. Is it ethical for companies to hire part-time employees to get out of paying benefits? Explain why or why not.

MARK ROWH is a frequent contributor to *Office Solutions*.

From *Office Solutions,* April 2008, pp. 28–30. Copyright © 2008 by Office Vision. Reprinted by permission.

Strategic Organizational Diversity: A Model?

FREDERICK TESCH AND FREDERICK MAIDMENT

Using resources, especially human ones, effectively is a key issue facing organizations and their managers, especially the human resource management staffs. Diversity is about the human resources available to an organization, about recognizing and using the breadth and depth of differences in its employees' experiences, backgrounds, and capabilities, and about viewing these differences as assets to the organization (Watson & Kumar, 1992). A key assumption is that diversity in a population should produce a similar diversity in our labor markets and in turn in the workforces derived from those labor markets.

Organizations that pursue workforce diversity are more likely to be successful than ones that do not (Cox & Blake, 1991; Marquez, 2005). Human diversity can actually drive business growth (Robinson & Dechant, 1997). An organization that manages diversity well can, for example, understand its markets better, increase its creativity and innovation, and improve its problem solving, thereby reducing its exposure to risk and increasing its chances of higher returns on investment. Clearly, these effects make workforce diversity a goal worth pursuing.

The major problem encountered in pursuing diversity is the lack of agreement on a definition. A recent study by the Society for Human Resource Management found that "Almost three-quarters of the HR professionals who responded said their organizations had no official definition of diversity. Those who had a definition said it was very broad and included an extensive set of differences and similarities among individuals, such as race, gender, age, etc." (Hastings, 2008, 34). How are we to manage what we have yet to define conceptually or operationally?

Given the potential benefits of workforce diversity, discussion of possible theoretical linkages between diversity and organizational goals has been minimal. What paradigm could account for the range of positive effects? What ideas move diversity from a practical concept to a management principle? Most discussion has focused on the practical matters and applications. Pragmatically, diversity works. Research (Parkhe, 1999) shows that managing diversity well gives organizations a competitive edge and reduces business risk. Given these robust, positive effects, we need not examine nor debate the mechanisms producing them. Do it; don't analyze it!

Unguided diversity, however, might lead an organization to a state of confusion and to actions not consistent with its strategic goals. Much diversity training appears to promote diversity for diversity's sake, often as a moral or ethical imperative. A stance of maximizing all types of human diversity as an end in itself might lead an organization to some dysfunctional thinking and actions. For example, would having recently hired someone from University X with a degree in Discipline Y prohibit hiring another such applicant? Hiring the second, similar applicant could be seen as promoting intellectual and academic homogeneity. Should an applicant be hired because her constellation of skills, knowledge, abilities, and background is unlike that of any other employee, even if her attributes have no relevance to the organization's goals?

Developing a Model for Diversity

Our thesis is that an organization's quest for diversity should be guided by the organization's goals and needs, not by a diffuse concept of diversity as the means to social responsibility or good citizenship.

There are two paths to building a theory. The first path is developing a model to explain the observed events, just as scientists build constructs to explain the phenomena they study (Kuhn, 1970). The second path, typically used by business disciplines, is borrowing a model or paradigm from another discipline and modifying it to the new phenomena. Ideas from economics, psychology, engineering, and mathematics abound in finance, marketing, and management. For example, in finance, portfolio analysis is a tool for managing stock purchases and sales, but marketing borrowed it to use in managing a portfolio of products (Hedley, 1977). Borrowing and using what works is characteristic of the business disciplines and of business people.

Following the second path, there is a theory of diversity in investments that can be applied to diversity in human resources. This application becomes especially clear when organizations view their employees not as an expense but rather as an asset—a view fundamental to human resources, as opposed to personnel, management. Employees, when viewed as an asset, are the equivalent of stocks in a portfolio.

Modigliani's Theory of Diversity in Investments

Franco Modigliani won the Nobel Prize in Economics for this theory of diversity in investments. He began by distinguishing between systematic and unsystematic risks. Systematic risk, also called market risk, is the risk that affects all securities. "Unsystematic risk is the risk that is unique to a company. It can be eliminated by diversifying the portfolio. Thus, systematic risk and unsystematic risk are referred to as non-diversifiable and diversifiable risk, respectively" (Fabozzi & Modigliani, 1992, pp. 154–55).

Building on this difference, he discusses how risk can be reduced or removed. "[U]nsystematic" risk . . . can be washed away by mixing the security with other securities in a diversified portfolio . . . Increasing diversification gradually tends to eliminate the unsystematic risk, leaving only systematic, i.e., market related risk. The remaining variability results from the fact that the return on every security depends to some degree on the overall performance of the market" (Fabozzi & Modigliani, 1992, p. 135).

There will always be some market (systematic) risk: such is the nature of capitalism where organizations compete with one another in the marketplace. Eliminating these risks requires a centrally planned or monopolistic economy.

The case of unsystematic risk is different since it is unique to a company and can be eliminated by diversifying the portfolio. Modigliani's point is that people can control the amount of risk they accept and that the risk can be eliminated if there is enough diversity. The goal is to maximize the long-term results while minimizing, if not eliminating, unsystematic risk. Individually risky stocks remain in the portfolio, but holding a variety of stocks in a variety of industries minimizes risk. Simply stated, "Don't put all your eggs in one basket."

Joe Watson, a diversity expert, captured the argument when he said "Think about diversity in terms of your stock portfolio. If someone came to you and said they were going to put everything you own in Southeast Asian bonds, that's probably not what you would want to do. People want a balanced portfolio with 10% in this and 20% in that because it's understood in business that over time that is what will give you the best possible outcome. Well, how is the workforce any different? It also needs to be diverse to give companies the best possible outcome" (Harris et al., 2008). The organization's goals and strategy should determine the specific securities/people (i.e., differences) in which it needs to invest and which it should ignore.

Human Resources a La Modigliani

Building a parallel from how investors view their stocks in a portfolio, managers should view employees as assets to be managed, not a cost to minimize. With this perspective, Modigliani's concept of diversity for investments becomes a model for human resources diversity. Diversifying an organization's workforce should reduce the unsystematic (non-market) risk unique to the organization's human resources. The greater the diversity, the lower the organization's controllable risk, and the greater the likelihood of higher financial return as a result of the efforts of the employees.

Diversity in an organization's human resources can, for example, reduce the possibility of groupthink (Janis, 1982), "A mode of thinking that people engage in when they are deeply involved in a cohesive [perhaps homogenous] group, when the members, striving for unanimity, override their motivation to realistically appraise alternative courses of action." Groupthink diminishes the group's capabilities to consider, thoroughly, all realistic courses of action. Groups of people with similar backgrounds, experiences, and educations are more likely to fall prey to groupthink than groups having diversity of those factors. Diversity, when properly managed, brings a richer, stronger set of individuals who should be more resistant to the groupthink trap when dealing with organizational issues.

A classic example of the lack of diversity as a tactical organizational weakness is the famous incident of General Motors introducing their "Chevrolet Nova" into the Latin American market (Schnitzier, 2005). In Spanish the phrase "No va!" translates to "No go!," a costly blunder in marketing to the Spanish speaking countries of Latin America. Had the groups involved in this decision at GM contained diversity that was representative of Latin America the episode could have been avoided.

Strategic diversity is not diversity for diversity's sake (i.e., simply maximizing all differences randomly), but is rather diversity aligned to the organization's goals, strategies, mission, and vision (Bonn, 2005). Strategic diversity encourages developing a pool of relevant diversity and not developing differences that are not strategically relevant. For example, an organization doing business in China should probably not hire people from Argentina to conduct its business in Hong Kong. Diversity makes business sense when it is done strategically, not when it is done simply for the sake of diversity or in the name of moral or philosophical agendas. Doing business in the United State of America requires a diverse workforce because it is such a diverse country. To operate in any other way would not only be illegal (e.g., EEO) but also illogical and detrimental to its long-term success.

Similarly, doing business in Norway requires a workforce reflecting the Norwegian stakeholders and having an understanding of Norwegian markets, practices, and laws.

The only sustainable competitive edge that can be unique to an organization is its workforce (Pfeffer, 1995). Most organizations have access to the same technology, transportation and communication systems, and financial markets. Managers exert little influence on their organization's external environments, but do have some control over internal ones. Diversifying the organization's human resources promotes controlling, minimizing, and perhaps even eliminating unsystematic (non-market) risk. This is the theoretical base for workforce diversity.

A strong corporate culture, one that embraces diversity, is one approach to reducing risks. When an organization's operations are scattered across distances, time zones, and cultures, a strong corporate culture is a significant element of the glue holding the pieces together. But no glue can overcome missing pieces. All the cultural variables surrounding the organization must be adequately represented within that organization. Recruiting, selecting, hiring, promoting, training, and compensating must all reflect the drive for diversity. Not doing so would leave the organization vulnerable in an increasingly competitive marketplace and subject to unsystematic risk. Managing diversity well brings the advantage of reduced unsystematic risk in a factor that is controllable and has the most potential for competitive advantage, that is, its human resources.

Human Resources Implications

The HR diversity model based on Modigliani's thinking supplies an additional base, a business justification, to the case for workforce diversity. Arguing for diversity based on legal compliance, ethical posture, or simple cost reduction cannot carry the day. HR executives and managers need the stronger theoretical position this model provides by eliminating or at least reducing unsystematic or non-market risk to the organization in the area of human resources. Let's look at some typical applications.

As organizations go global, those drawing only on their home countries to staff senior positions practice a form of discrimination that severely limits their long-term capabilities. As corporations, for example, become more globalized, their management staff must do the same in order to reduce the unsystematic risks (Bell & Harrison, 1996). One example would be the few non-USA nationals who lead or have led USA corporations (e.g., Ford Motor Company, NCR).

Diversity as a risk management strategy means that we must go beyond simply having people of diverse backgrounds in our organizations. It argues, as does EEO, that the strategy requires offering everyone the same opportunities for movement and advancement within the organization. No department, division, unit, or level can be permitted to be too homogenous, but its diversity must be structural, not random. And that structural linkage should derive from and reflect the organization's strategic goals.

Workforce diversity promotes the achievement of excellence in human resources and the concurrent reduction of organizational risk leading to enhanced competitiveness and performance. Under these conditions of risk management the cream of the organization's human resources can perform exceptionally. The cream of the workforce that rises to the top is made of richer ingredients and is a better grade of cream (Ng & Tung, 1998).

Diversity's Challenge to Human Resource Management

In today's highly turbulent and hyper-competitive environments, organizations simply cannot afford to allow their competitors the competitive advantage of better workers, managers, and executives, that is, better human resources. To do so is to risk becoming second rate—or even becoming extinct (Collins, 2001; Olson & van Bever, 2008). HR professionals need to develop action plans that are strongly linked to the organization's goals and that guide their recruiting, succession planning, career development, and compensation activities. They must create workforces having diversity that is congruent with the organization's strategic goals and that promotes and ensures equitable treatment and opportunities for all employees.

References

Bell, M. P. & Harrison, D. A. (1996). Using intra-national diversity for international assignments: A model of bicultural competence and expatriate adjustment, *Human Resource Management Review,* Spring, 6(1), 47–74.

Bonn, I. (2005). Improving strategic thinking: A multilevel approach, *Leadership & Organizational Development Journal,* 25(5), 336–354.

Collins, J. (2001). *Good to Great: Why Some Companies Make the Leap—and Others Don't,* New York: Harper Business.

Cox, T. H. & Blake, S. (1991). Managing cultural diversity: Implications for organizational competitiveness, *Academy of Management Executive,* August, 5(3), 45–56.

Fabozzi, F. J., & Modigliani, F. (1992). *Capital Markets: Institutions and instruments,* Englewood Cliffs, NJ: Prentice Hall.

Harris, W., Drakes, S., Lott, A., & Barrett, L. (2008). The 40 best companies for diversity, *Black Enterprise,* 38(12), 94–112.

Hastings, R. (2008). SHRM diversity report a call to action: Majority of companies say they haven't defined diversity, *HRMagazine,* 53(4), April, 34.

Hedley, B. (1977). Strategy and the business portfolio, *Long Range Planning,* February.

Janis, I. (1982). *Groupthink: Psychological studies of policy decisions and fiascos,* Boston: Houghton-Mifflin.

Kuhn, T. (1970). *The structure of scientific revolutions,* Chicago: University of Chicago Press.

Marquez, J. (2005). SHRM survey shows diversity contributes to bottom line (Society for Human Resource Management), *Workforce Management,* 84.12, November 7, 8. Retrieved February 26, 2007, from General Reverence Center Gold database.

Ng, E. S. & Tung, R. L. (1998). Ethno-cultural diversity and organizational effectiveness: A field study, *International Journal of Human Resource Management,* December, 9(6), 980–995.

Olson, M. S. & van Bever, D. (2008). *Stall Points: Most Companies Stop Growing—Yours Doesn't Have To,* New Haven, CT: Yale University Press.

Parkhe, A. (1999). Interfirm diversity, organizational learning, and longevity in global strategic alliances, *Journal of International Business Studies,* Winter, 22(4), 579–601.

Pfeffer, J. (1995). Producing sustainable competitive advantage through the effective management of people, *Academy of Management Executive,* February, 9(1), 55–72.

Robinson, G. & Dechant, K. (1997). Building a business case for diversity, *Academy of Management Executive,* August, 21–31.

Schnitzier, P. (2005). Translating success: Network of language experts key to Pangea Lingua's growth, *Indianapolis Business Journal,* 26(21), August 1, 3.

Watson W. E. & Kumar, K. (1992). Differences in decision-making regarding risk-taking: A comparison of culturally diverse and culturally homogeneous task groups, *Journal of Intercultural Relations,* 16(1), 53–65.

Critical Thinking

1. Explain what you think "strategic organizational diversity" means.

2. Come up with weaknesses of "strategic organizational diversity" and explain how these weaknesses can be ameliorated.

FREDERICK TESCH, Western Connecticut State University, USA.
FREDERICK MAIDMENT, Western Connecticut State University, Connecticut, USA.

When Generations Collide

Colleges try to prevent age-old culture clashes as four distinct groups meet in the workplace.

PIPER FOGG

In an office at Western Technical College, the under-30 crowd creates funny, mock videos to reward themselves for a job well done. Or they throw a pizza party to celebrate. That bothers some of their older colleagues who complain that the young folks should be working, not playing.

Denise Vujnovich, who fields those complaints as Western's vice president for student services and college relations, worries that too many baby boomers just don't get it: The younger generations get their work done, she says; they just do it differently.

It's not that the younger set has it all figured out. A twenty-something employee at one university didn't think twice about e-mailing the entire campus when he was trying to sell his car. The problem is, the generations don't always understand one another. And in the academic workplace—where, for the first time in recent memory, four generations have converged—that can create serious culture clashes.

It is happening across college campuses, and it is especially striking in the faculty ranks, where generational challenges have extra significance amid recruiting efforts, tenure evaluations, and the changing definition of what constitutes important faculty work.

As members of Generations X and Y face a workplace dominated by boomers, they are all starting to chafe. Some colleges are having trouble attracting, managing, and sometimes retaining people younger than 35. Members of the younger generations grew up watching their parents sacrifice for their careers, and they want something different: balance and freedom and autonomy. And they won't hesitate to switch jobs or leave academe if it means more-palatable working conditions. Many baby boomers, meanwhile, don't understand why someone would leave the office at 5 P.M. when there is always more to do.

Commitment to Change

How do colleges handle this generational dilemma? As in other sectors of the workplace, where similar issues are festering, good communication can help people better understand one another, say those in the trenches.

"A major leadership gap is coming up," warns Pamela Cox-Otto, a marketing expert and former college vice president who writes about generational marketing in academe. She argues that colleges need to stress flexibility, technology, diversity, and work-life balance. "It's about a real commitment to cultural change," she says.

While stereotypes do not fit every individual, there are traits and preferences that generally apply to each of the generations, say those who have studied different age groups. Members of the oldest generation, born between around 1925 and 1946, are often called "traditionalists." They are known as hard-working, are used to taking direction, and tend to have strict moral codes. In a 2008 survey, "World of Work," conducted by the staffing agency Randstad, 86% of this elder generation described themselves as ethical, compared with 58% of Generation Y respondents.

Baby boomers, born between around 1946 and 1964, dominate today's academic work force, representing at least half of the nation's faculty members. They typically display loyalty to their institution, an assumption that working overtime is a given, and a commitment to making a difference by working together. In the Randstad survey, 78% of baby boomers described themselves as having a strong work ethic, as opposed to 53% of the members of Generation Y and 68% of those in Generation X.

Gen Xers, often noted for their cynicism, tend to care more about autonomy, seek a balance between work and home, and look out for their own interests first. Born between around 1964 and 1982, they have been dubbed the "Me Generation." And finally, just now entering the academic workplace are the oldest members of Generation Y, also known as "Millennials." Born between around 1982 and the late 1990s, they grew up with technology at their fingertips. While similar to Xers, they are known to be more optimistic, fun seeking, and flexible, but they are also the most coddled of all.

Of course, generalizations need to be tempered by recognizing individual workers' actual habits and personalities, which may or may not be directly related to when they were born. But just knowing a few things about each generation can help

One Workplace, Four Generations

Here are some generalizations that, while they may not accurately describe every baby boomer or Gen Xer on a campus, can be used as a rough generational guide.

Traditionalists

aka: the Silent Generation, veterans
Born: between about 1925 and 1946
Cultural influences: Great Depression, World War II, Korean War, postwar boom era, GI Bill
Workplace values: loyalty, recognition, hierarchy, resistance to change

Baby Boomers

aka: the Sandwich Generation (since many take care of both children and aging parents)
Born: between about 1946 and 1964
Cultural influences: popularization of television, assassination of President John F. Kennedy, Beatles, first moon walk, Vietnam War, antiwar protests, sexual revolution
Workplace values: dedication, face time, team spirit

Generation X

aka: the Slacker Generation, the Me Generation
Born: between about 1964 and 1982
Cultural influences: fall of the Soviet Union, women's-liberation movement, MTV, grunge, rise of home video games and personal computers, birth of the Internet, dot-com boom and bust
Workplace values: work-life balance, autonomy, flexibility, informality

Generation Y

aka: Millennials
Born: between about 1982 and the late 1990s
Cultural influences: Internet era, September 11 terrorist attacks, cellphones, Columbine High School massacre, Facebook
Workplace values: feedback, recognition, fulfillment, advanced technology, fun

---

cut down on needless workplace battles, says Patrick Cataldo, associate dean for executive education at the Smeal College of Business at Pennsylvania State University at University Park. He teaches business leaders how to manage across generational gaps.

When a twentysomething in Cataldo's office wanted to buy a Mac computer instead of the office's standard PC, he stopped to think about it. "If I hadn't taught this, the categorical answer would have been no," says Cataldo, a baby boomer whose inclination was to stick to institutional practices. Instead, he asked the young woman to explain her choice—she argued the technology better served her needs—and he found her argument compelling. Cataldo ordered the computer, and everyone ended up happy.

As chief information officer at Lynn University, in Florida, Christian Boniforti, 35, occasionally interacts with senior faculty members. After distributing a campus survey about technology use, he learned that some were having trouble keeping up with changing technologies. He had his staff call them individually and offer assistance, so they wouldn't feel singled out. Among the success stories is one professor who was a complete technophobe but now uses multimedia clips and posts assignments to Blackboard for his classes.

While the twentysomethings in his office don't lack technology skills, says Boniforti, they sometimes have trouble understanding that less is more. For example, they don't hesitate to shoot him a barrage of e-mail messages, while an older staffer will send one well-thought-out memo. Nor can he depend upon his younger staffers to show up on time for meetings, or to dress appropriately. (One employee insisted on wearing his Miami Heat basketball jersey.) Boniforti holds social gatherings so different generations can learn from one another without pressure. Apparently some do. At a recent presentation, one of the younger employees, usually dressed in khakis and a polo shirt, sported a tie.

As members of Generations X and Y face a workplace dominated by boomers, they are all starting to chafe.

Matching Strengths to Tasks

When Marc Camille needed someone to manage the integration of a new software system at Loyola College in Maryland, he chose a baby boomer. Camille, 41, vice president for enrollment management and communications, tries to match generational strengths to specific tasks, while keeping in mind that people's personalities must be balanced into the equation, too. He knew a particular boomer would see the job through to completion, though, no matter what it took. But for a redesign of the college's website, he turned to the office's younger members. "It's easier for them to put themselves in the mind-set of 17- and 18-year-olds," says Camille.

Lillian Selby, a 24-year-old graphic designer at Loyola, proves his point. She recently designed a publicity campaign for a student group that was collecting donated clothing and furniture for charity. She used brightly colored icons and flashy graphics to attract her peers. "We can multitask," she says of her generation, "but we have the attention span of a gnat, so we need bold colors."

Keeping generational quirks in mind when assigning projects is one thing, but some administrators are getting fed up with having to cater to everyone. W. Kent Barnds, vice president for admissions and enrollment at Augustana College, in Illinois, understands that Gen Xers want to know how an assignment will matter to them. But sometimes they just need to get the job done because it's their job. "We can't recraft all our work to make it matter individually to the 'Me Generation,'" says Barnds. That's where the boomers come in, he says: They can model a work ethic. To make that happen, Barnds has broken his admissions-office staff into intergenerational teams.

"I'm forcing a structure where collaboration and conversation have to occur," he says.

The Faculty Challenge

Perhaps most challenging of all is how to bridge generations of faculty members, who set much of the tone on a campus. In departments where senior scholars hold power over new hires and tenure cases, an us-versus-them mentality can develop. Older professors can become disgruntled when they see the comparatively high salaries that newly hired professors demand.

And in disciplines where the intellectual focus is shifting, the old guard can feel it must protect its turf. Take the field of psychology, which has changed dramatically over the last few decades.

Barry Schwartz, a professor of psychology at Swarthmore College for the last 35 years, says that cognitive neuroscience now dominates his field, whereas when he was trained, it was all about behavioralism. Not every department has made the transition smoothly. "There have been some unpleasant battles," says Schwartz. "People tend to get wedded to what they learn. But if you have the attitude you can learn from young people, it creates an open environment," he says.

> ## You've just got to know when to have the good grace to move over and let someone else drive.

Another point of tension is interdisciplinary studies. Cathy Trower, who studies junior-faculty preferences at Harvard University's Graduate School of Education, says boomers are often skeptical of nontraditional faculty appointments. Gen Xers, she says, like the creative freedom of an interdisciplinary institute, where they can easily collaborate with diverse groups of scholars. "They realize breakthroughs don't happen if you talk to the same people," says Trower. This can be a challenge for boomers who want to evaluate faculty members in a specific discipline using traditional parameters, she says.

Schwartz worries that the professoriate is becoming less attractive over all to the younger generations. He is finding that younger people are choosing industry instead. He suggests colleges find ways to create more part-time positions, with reduced expectations, that offer a better work-life balance. Trower says colleges would indeed do well to think creatively about job structures. Since Gen Xers are more comfortable bouncing from job to job, colleges could make it easier to get on and off the tenure track or even in and out of academe altogether.

Short of restructuring faculty positions, colleges can still make their workplaces friendlier to younger academics. Jeffrey Nunokawa, a 49-year-old English professor at Princeton University, is known for connecting with younger people. He believes experienced professors can help younger ones by being approachable and willing to serve as informal mentors. He tries to help junior faculty members with their academic work by "suggesting" rather than "prescribing," and offering practical tips about getting published. "It's our duty," he says.

There is one final responsibility of senior scholars, Nunokawa says, and that is to eventually let the younger generations take over: "You've just got to know when to have the good grace to move over and let someone else drive."

Critical Thinking

1. Explain how colleges' experiences with different generations of employees are unique.

2. If you were a faculty administrator, what would you do to help bring all the generations together to bridge the gaps that exist between them?

PIPER FOGG is a staff reporter for *The Chronicle of Higher Education*.

This Time It's Personal

Work environments that are structurally and culturally designed to facilitate preferred work practices will be rewarded with a positive difference to employee health and sense of well-being, argues Karen Coomer.

KAREN COOMER

The world of work has undoubtedly changed over the last 20, 10, or even five years. Technological developments mean workplaces are now more mobile and flexible, and provide easy access to information via increased team-working, cross-functional work, the growth in call centers, and the move away from hierarchical management structures.

This change in work practices has brought with it a change in the design of workplaces, with open-plan offices now the norm in many organizations. Improvements to physical working conditions have led to expectations, among employees, of comfortable, well-lit workplaces, where the temperature is acceptable, and physically damaging hazards, such as excess noise, are not present.

So, what is the impact on the psychological **health** and well-being of workers in open-plan environments? Do features such as interior plants, matching decor, music, and comfortable areas for relaxation help reduce stress levels and increase productivity, or are generic, clear-desk policies and large, open-plan spaces for everyone—regardless of the type of work that they do—in any way justified?

The Environment and Stress

Occupational stress is a subject that has led to much research and debate. The generally agreed approach to the definition and study of stress is defined by Cox[1] as psychological and takes into account the interaction between the person, their environment, and psychosocial factors. The HSE's stress management standards[2] are an example of a practical tool designed around this definition, with the emphasis on a risk-assessment approach to the reduction of work stressors. In the field of environmental psychology, too, theoretical models have been developed in relation to the effects of environmental conditions on behavior. They can be summarized as follows:

1. Stimulation provided by the environment around us can heighten autonomic activity, such as increased blood pressure and heart rate, and this is known commonly as arousal. How it affects our behavior depends on the source of stimulation, which can be pleasant or unpleasant. Noise is an example of an environmental factor which can increase arousal and affect behavior.

2. When the amount of information received from the environment is exceeded by our capability to process that information, overload can occur, resulting in fatigue, irritability, and frustration. These, in turn, can lead to 'tunnel vision' thinking—ignoring any stimuli that distract from the task in hand. This includes ignoring colleagues and avoiding eye contact or workplace banter in order to get on with the task. Part-time workers are at particular risk of this, for obvious reasons. At the other extreme, a monotonous working environment can lead to under-stimulation, which increases the desire for arousal and excitement.

3. Being able to alter our perception of the environmental stimulus we are exposed to is called adaptation theory. The ability to screen out distractions in an open-plan environment is a good example of this.

4. Behavior constraint relates to the perceived loss of control over the environment, or the anticipation of a factor that may restrict our freedom. If actions to regain control are unsuccessful, learned helplessness can develop, which can affect mental outlook in the workplace and lead to symptoms of stress and depression.

Give Me Some Room

Personal space has two primary purposes: protection, in that it serves as a buffer against feeling the stress response; and communication, in terms of the quality of relationships and the level of intimacy we choose to have with another person. Open-plan offices require employees to work in close proximity with colleagues, so it can be difficult to avoid interpersonal contact, or maintain privacy. Establishing visible territories and personalizing workspaces by displaying personal photographs, children's drawings, cartoons, and other personal objects, is common. This is an important concept, in that such personalization leads to personal attachment, increased personal control, and a sense of responsibility for the workspace or machine. This is worth bearing in mind, given the trend for 'hot-desking', clear desks, and mobile workforces that move from one workspace to another.

Anyone who has been to a zoo recently will have noticed that cages have now largely been replaced with natural habitats, which enable the animals to have some control over their behavior—to be on view if they want, or remain out of sight. The key reason for this change was concern for the animals' psychological and social well-being; zoos were keeping animals alive but were failing to make them flourish. If we liken this concept to an open-plan office, the ability to adjust the workplace to a variety of work environments, e.g. the availability of meeting rooms and zoned areas, has been shown to have a positive effect on both job satisfaction and group cohesiveness—very similar to animals in a zoo.[3]

Interestingly, job satisfaction appears to be an indicator of satisfaction with the work environment. Environmental psychologists have found that the way employees see themselves is affected by the way they judge or evaluate their workplace. Those who perceive themselves as professionally successful show a greater appreciation of the same environment as those who perceive themselves as professional failures.[4] This may help explain why some employees, despite risk assessments and consequent changes, remain unsatisfied with their work environment.

The combination of excessive social interaction, lack of control, and limited personal space can expose employees to over-stimulation. This evokes feelings of irritation and frustration due to overload and arousal, which can ultimately result in employee dissatisfaction and withdrawal. With highly complex jobs, where concentration is crucial, an Australian study[5] found that distraction is a major problem in open-plan offices. Low perceived privacy and the inability to screen out distractions can result in poor performance and negative attitudes. Tactics that employees used to cope included wearing headphones, and relocating to quiet spaces (therefore emphasising the importance of the availability of dedicated private areas). Mundane work, however, which requires little cognitive effort, can benefit from environmental stimulation, such as bright lights, strong colors, and music.

Noise

Health and **safety** professionals are fully aware of the physical effects of noise but what about its effects on mental health? Anyone who has ever travelled on public transport within earshot of loud mobile phone conversations will not be surprised to learn that research has shown that listening to unwanted conversations is a major irritant for workers.[6] Introducing music into the workplace to mask unwanted sound does improve satisfaction, and has been reported in studies[6] to provide a pleasant atmosphere, if the noise was no higher than 48dB. This was recognized during the Second World War, when it was common practice in Britain's factories to pipe music on to the shop

floor through loudspeakers to increase morale and help alleviate the monotony of work tasks. Indeed, there was even a BBC radio programme 'Music while you work', which was transmitted twice a day.[7] However, one person's pleasant music could be another's tuneless cacophony, so personal headphones are routinely used in recognition of this.

As with the issues of personal space, perceived control can reduce the effects of a stress-related response. Not being able to see or understand where the noise is coming from is more annoying than predictable noise—thus, a person who operates a noisy machine but who can control the noise is less annoyed by it than other people exposed to the same noise.

Aesthetics

Many workplaces with open-plan office arrangements have zoned areas for relaxation, eating, and informal meetings. This is beneficial to employees' psychological **health,** especially where there are small spaces provided, as they create a sense of refuge, enabling users to survey the surroundings but still enjoy partial concealment. Indoor plants are often used to create zoned areas, and there is evidence to suggest that they also have a positive effect on human **health** and well-being, particularly in windowless areas.[8]

More than a hundred years ago, Florence Nightingale observed how patients recovered much more successfully when they could see 'nature' out of a window, and there is now a large body of evidence that suggests that the environment in which a patient recovers in a hospital can promote healing and reduce pain and stress.[9] This has led to interest in restorative spaces in workplaces, particularly designed to provide opportunities for rest, recovery and contemplation. Involuntary attention to such design elements as moving water, aquariums, and window views has been shown to facilitate recovery from mental fatigue caused by overload. This is due to stimulation of the parasympathetic nervous system, which gives rise to a calming effect. With the forthcoming ban on smoking areas in England, areas like these could possibly help smokers in the workplace relax.

Window views and being able to see daylight are, as already mentioned, very important, so placing employees who spend the majority of their time at their desks near windows instead of in the middle of a room may result in more satisfied employees. However, individual control over opening and shutting windows, and the provision of blinds to reduce glare, are also considered important.

In relation to space, the layout and design of the workplace also influence the emotional and behavioral response of an **employee.** From a psychological viewpoint physical design is not simply a matter of functional purpose—it also has symbolic meaning. The use of certain colors, textures and furniture can convey messages of care, efficiency, cleanliness and comfort. The hospitality and retail industries are very aware of this, and seek to encourage consumers to not only purchase a product but also to have a positive experience. However, overall tidiness is considered more important than decor with regard to the effect of visitors feeling comfortable and welcome. It appears that an intermediate level of tidiness, with organized stacks of paperwork, has been evaluated as being significantly more welcoming and friendly than overly tidy or untidy offices.[10]

Conclusion

Research on the psychology of the environment indicates that the prevention of stress associated with environmental factors is possible and involves a number of practical options:

- Designated private spaces, use of headphones, and smaller open-plan offices to create environments where the flow of information, noise and other interruptions is reduced. Freedom to choose to work from home (without distractions) can also provide a solution.
- Introducing the concept of nature into the workplace to help employees relax and recover from mental fatigue. This can be as simple as installing plants, or as complex as building a roof-top garden, or a water feature. Obviously, encouraging employees to have breaks away from their work in the first place is necessary to capitalize on these beneficial effects.
- Changing the way the environment and, consequently, the work content is interpreted, and then successfully adapting to the situation, is another solution. Hot-desking may well be a successful way of working for employees who travel, or expect to be mobile, but it may be less successful for employees who expect to work in one place and want to establish a feeling of security by personalizing their work space.

References

1. Cox, T., Griffiths, A., and Rial-Gonzalez, E. (2000): Research on work-related stress, European Agency for Safety and Health at Work—http://osha.eu.int

2. **Health** and **Safety** Executive (2004): Stress Management Standards—www.hse.gov.uk/stress/standards/index.htm

3. Heerwagen, J. (2005): Psychosocial Value of Space—Whole Building Design Guide, National Institute of Building Sciences, Washington—www.wbdg.org/design/psychspace_value.php

4. Fischer, G. N., Tarquinio, C., and Vischer, J.C. (2004): 'Effects of the self-schema on perception of space at work', *Journal of Env Psychology*, vol.24, p. 131–140.

5. Maher, A. & Hippel, C. (2005): 'Individual differences in **employee** reactions to open-plan offices', *Journal of Environmental Psychology*, vol. 25, p. 219–229.

6. Newsham, G. R. (2003): 'Making the Open-Plan Office a Better Place to Work', Construction Technology Update No.60, Institute for Research in Construction—www.irc.nrc-cnrc.gc.ca

7. Korczynski, M., Pickering, M., Robertson, E., and Jones, K. (2005): 'We sang ourselves through that war: women, music and factory work in World War Two', *Labour History Review*, vol. 70, no.2, p. 185–214.

8. Lohr, V.I., Pearson-Mims, C. H., Goodwin, G. K. (1996): 'Interior plants may improve worker productivity and reduce stress in a windowless environment', *Journal of Environmental Horticulture*, vol. 14, no. 2, p. 97–100.

9. Ulrich, R., Zimring, C., Joseph, A., and Choudhary, R. (2004): The Role of the Physical Environment in the Hospital of the 21st Century: A once-in-a-lifetime opportunity, The Centre for **Health** Design—www.healthdesign.org/research/reports/

10. Morrow, P.C., & McElroy, J. C. (1981). 'Interior office design and visitor response', *Journal of Applied Psychology*, 66, pp. 646–630.

Critical Thinking

1. What are some causes of workplace stress? Which of those stressors have you experienced yourself?

2. Apart from the stress-reducing solutions mentioned in the article, what other solutions can you list?

Multiple Choice

Should global employers standardize their employee benefits packages?

LORI CHORDAS

For Informa's employees in India, private health insurance, flexible benefits and dependent coverage are top commodities. But in the United Kingdom, the international provider of information and services sees wellness programs such as gym memberships and health screenings as highly valued benefits.

That's a common theme among multinational corporations: Geography has a huge influence on employee benefits design. But while locales dictate differences, are global companies looking to standardize employee benefits globally?

That's highly unlikely, said Robyn Cameron, who leads Mercer's International Health and Benefits Specialty Group. "It's not a one-size-fits-all approach."

Each country has its priorities when it comes to benefits. "In the United Kingdom, it would be odd not to offer three or four times annual earnings on death-in-service life benefits," said Pam Enright, vice president and director of international benefits for Lockton Benefits Group. "But that would be completely over the top in most other countries. Another example is the dearness allowance, which is a standard part of the compensation model in India, hut as such would not he offered in any other country." (Dearness allowances help offset inflation.)

Multinationals need to look locally when designing benefits programs, Cameron said. "While some companies do set some overarching global guidelines for benefits, most will then take a country-by-country approach for designing benefits, taking into account the local social benefits, and typical market practice."

And, she added, corporations want to have a greater role in understanding what programs are out there, and some central oversight on decision-making on benefit design and financing.

More companies are asking whether their benefits programs are compliant with local laws. In the past, they would have left that to locals to worry about, said Cameron.

Rather than standardizing global benefits, most multinational companies are attempting to prioritize how they approach looking at their benefit programs through transparency of benefit structures, said Christopher Burns, chief executive officer of Willis Group Holdings' global employee benefits practice.

> * **The Trend:** A growing number of organizations are becoming multinational.
> * **The Significance:** Employers are offering a variety of employee benefits to a growing global work force with very diverse needs.
> * **What Needs to Happen:** Multinational employers need to ensure that benefits address local needs and governance concerns.

"Employers need to determine where they want to be in terms of their competition on benefit structures in the local marketplace. Then they can alter the structure of those benefit programs accordingly," he said.

> **"Companies that are just venturing into global markets should follow the simple mantra: Think globally and act locally."**
>
> —Rudy Bethea,
> MetLife

> To India's predominantly young work force, **"retirement benefits aren't as top of mind as health care and flexible benefits."**
>
> —Francis Coleman,
> Watson Wyatt

> Offering the United Kingdom's traditionally generous death-in-service life benefits **"would be completely over the top in most other countries."**
>
> —Pam Enright,
> Lockton Benefits Group

Meeting a Need

The benefits global employees are looking for differ almost as much as cultural and language barriers themselves.

For instance, a U.S. employee would expect an employer to offer private health insurance, but that would be a lesser priority for a U.K. worker, according to a Hewitt Associates report.

Employees in countries such as the United States, India and Mexico continue to value health insurance as a top priority, according to MetLife's 2007 *Study of International Employee Benefits Trends.*

The need of multinational employers to offer benefits, however, seems to speak a more common language: They're concerned about work force shortages and competition for top talent in mature economies, the study found. That's prompted many to reconsider their benefits strategies and find new ways to attract and retain highly skilled workers.

Many of those strategies are focused on emerging markets such as the "BRIC" countries of Brazil, Russia, India and China.

"They're predominantly areas with huge, inexpensive talent pools," said David Martin, employee benefits practice leader for Hub International.

China and India remain two of the biggest markets, largely due to their size.

BRAZIL: This country is quickly becoming a developed benefits environment, said Francis Coleman, international practice leader in Watson Wyatt's West region. Not only have many employers moved to defined contribution plans and enacted pro-employee protection laws, but supplemental health care has become nearly fully saturated among employees. Life, disability and supplemental retirement insurance also are a growing part of many employers' programs.

RUSSIA: There's been an increase in demand for supplemental retirement plans, especially among multinational companies, Coleman said. However, given the declining life expectancy among Russian males, retirement benefits aren't necessarily the highest priority.

INDIA: "India already has a sophisticated benefits structure in place, with most retirement benefits mandated by the government. But we expect the government to cut back more and private enterprise to take over," said Francois Choquette, Aon Consulting's Global Benefits Practice Leader for the Americas.

He said the decades-long monopoly of the insurance sector in the country has virtually dissipated, allowing more carriers to come in and provide choice to employers with Indian operations.

Housing and transportation allowances also are significant benefits offerings in India, Coleman said. "On top of that, a lack of government providers and hospitals has made private health care very popular. Employees there don't get the same choices you find in other countries."

Added to that, there's a predominantly young work force in India, Coleman said. "So retirement benefits aren't as top of mind as health care and flexible benefits among those workers."

Family also is highly revered, so some employers have begun offering deep discounts on health care coverage for dependents.

CHINA: Private health coverage is becoming one of employees' most highly requested benefits, said Coleman. "But any legislation enacted by the Chinese government often has different interpretations in each city, resulting in variations in benefits plans and tax rulings."

Benefits brokers also are keeping a close watch on other emerging markets such as the Middle East and what Coleman calls "the second layer of emerging markets," such as Vietnam and Bangladesh.

Francis Coleman, international practice leader in Watson Wyatt's West region, said it's nearly impossible to design an exact package in every location.

"What country would you base that on? If based on the United States, employers would be providing very rich benefit plans. Most multinationals come up with a set of guiding principles or a philosophy stating what core benefits they should be providing globally and adapt this to each location," Coleman said.

Making It Work

In the current economic environment, multinational employers are focused on using their bulk purchasing power globally to reduce their benefits costs with global insurance providers, said Burns.

Added to that is the need for some flexibility to adjust to each region so employers aren't overpaying on benefits, said Coleman.

He said countries now recognize the need to provide more favorable conditions for supplemental retirement plans, which hasn't always been the case. "Social Security is essentially going out of business in most countries, so they need to incentivize third-pillar savings, whether it be employee or individual savings plus employer. Many countries recently changed legislation to enable companies to set up supplemental plans for individuals or employers on a tax-efficient basis."

Multinationals need to ensure programs are financed as efficiently as possible, said Cameron. "They can do that by taking advantage of things like the use of multinational pooling and captives for risk benefits, and ensuring that consulting and brokerage dollars are being spent wisely."

Multinational pooling works by allowing global companies to spread the risk associated with local benefit plans around the globe, along with offering more favorable underwriting standards, a single point of contact for domestic and international employee coverage, and detailed information on subsidiary insurance plans, said MetLife Multinational Solutions Vice President Rudy Bethea.

MetLife Multinational Solutions' pooling is handled through MAXIS, a global employee benefits network of insurers in more than 75 countries that delivers local coverage to international employees.

One of the biggest trends in global benefits has been the growing switch from defined benefit plans to defined contribution plans.

"Historically, defined benefit retirement plans had been the rule in the United States and much of Europe. But the past several years there's been a switch due to cost rationale and more predictability on the bottom line for companies," said Burns.

The plans also help employers better manage their liabilities, Coleman added. "Switching obligation to defined contribution is easier for employers from a budgetary standpoint, as opposed to having to calculate the widely fluctuating liabilities that come with defined benefit plans."

On the health side, inadequacy of some socialized medical systems in many countries is giving rise to supplemental health plans, said Burns. The challenge, he said, is that health care costs in most private systems now are outpacing the local consumer price index in many countries—a trend he fears likely will continue.

That's where benefit brokers can step in to help. Many multinational employers are turning to outside consultants to help develop a global benefits strategy.

The first step often begins with a benefits audit, said Burns.

"We collect details regarding current benefit programs and costs, along with bringing transparency around compliance and helping clients use their bulk purchasing power to negotiate with global insurance carriers. Then we review the details to ensure they comply with local laws in each country. That helps uncover if a program is out of synch with local regulations; for instance, discovering a company's retirement age of 62 doesn't match up with a country's legal retirement age of 65."

While the need for global benefits continues to grow, multinational employers are feeling the pinch of the global financial downturn.

"That's caused some companies to cut back benefits in some countries or cost-shift to employees," said Cameron.

Clients always are watching their bottom line, said Enright.

"But that can be challenging in industries and markets where a competitive—and expensive—benefits and pay package is necessary," Enright said. "Attracting and retaining the best candidates for key positions usually trumps the need to offer a low-cost benefit plan."

Employers will need to be smarter about how they spend their benefit dollars going forward, said Bethea.

That's where financial vehicles such as captives and multinational pooling can help, he added.

For companies just venturing into global markets, Bethea suggests following a simple mantra: Think globally and act locally.

"Employers start out trying to come up with an overarching program to cover everyone around the globe to make it simple."

But that actually increases the level of complexity, Bethea said.

"They should begin with a global strategy and then allow flexibility to meet the demands of a global, diverse work force."

Critical Thinking

1. Do you feel multinational corporations' employee benefits should be the same regardless of the country (to be fair), or should they be tailored to the culture of the country?

2. What do you believe are the top five requested employee benefits, regardless of country?

Test-Your-Knowledge Form

We encourage you to photocopy and use this page as a tool to assess how the articles in *Annual Editions* expand on the information in your textbook. By reflecting on the articles you will gain enhanced text information. You can also access this useful form on a product's book support website at www.mhhe.com/cls

NAME: DATE:

_____

TITLE AND NUMBER OF ARTICLE:

_____

BRIEFLY STATE THE MAIN IDEA OF THIS ARTICLE:

_____

LIST THREE IMPORTANT FACTS THAT THE AUTHOR USES TO SUPPORT THE MAIN IDEA:

_____

WHAT INFORMATION OR IDEAS DISCUSSED IN THIS ARTICLE ARE ALSO DISCUSSED IN YOUR TEXTBOOK OR OTHER READINGS THAT YOU HAVE DONE? LIST THE TEXTBOOK CHAPTERS AND PAGE NUMBERS:

_____

LIST ANY EXAMPLES OF BIAS OR FAULTY REASONING THAT YOU FOUND IN THE ARTICLE:

_____

LIST ANY NEW TERMS/CONCEPTS THAT WERE DISCUSSED IN THE ARTICLE, AND WRITE A SHORT DEFINITION:

We Want Your Advice

ANNUAL EDITIONS revisions depend on two major opinion sources: one is our Advisory Board, listed in the front of this volume, which works with us in scanning the thousands of articles published in the public press each year; the other is you—the person actually using the book. Please help us and the users of the next edition by completing the prepaid article rating form on this page and returning it to us. Thank you for your help!

ANNUAL EDITIONS: Business Ethics 11/12

ARTICLE RATING FORM

Here is an opportunity for you to have direct input into the next revision of this volume.
We would like you to rate each of the articles listed below, using the following scale:

1. **Excellent: should definitely be retained**
2. **Above average: should probably be retained**
3. **Below average: should probably be deleted**
4. **Poor: should definitely be deleted**

Your ratings will play a vital part in the next revision.
Please mail this prepaid form to us as soon as possible.
Thanks for your help!

RATING	ARTICLE	RATING	ARTICLE
	1. Thinking Ethically: A Framework for Moral Decision Making		18. The Factory That Refused to Die
	2. Business Ethics: Back to Basics		19. Protecting the Whistleblower
	3. Integrating Ethics into the Business Curriculum: The Northern Illinois University Initiative		20. Whistleblowers Get a Raise
	4. Building an Ethical Framework		21. The Parable of the Sadhu
	5. Moral Management Methodology/Mythology: Erroneous Ethical Equations		22. At Work, a Drug Dilemma
	6. Create a Culture of Trust		23. His Most Trusted Employee Was a Thief
	7. Building Trust: How the Best Leaders Do It		24. Trust in the Marketplace
	8. The Ethical Employee		25. Privacy and the Internet: Lives of Others
	9. Employers Are Stung with a Hefty Price When Employees Suffer an Identity Theft		26. The New E–spionage Threat
	10. For Office Romance, the Secret's Out		27. Emerging Lessons
	11. Are You Too Family Friendly?		28. Honest Innovation
	12. High Rates of Misconduct at All Levels of Government		29. Serving Unfair Customers
	13. Under Pressure, Teachers Tamper with Test Scores		30. Swagland
	14. When You're Most Vulnerable to Fraud		31. Creating an Ethical Culture
	15. More Men Make Harassment Claims		32. Outside-the-Box Ethics
	16. Older Workers: Running to the Courthouse?		33. Hiring Character
	17. Cost Reductions, Downsizing-related Layoffs, and HR Practices		34. The Business Case for Diversity
			35. Managing Part-Time Employees
			36. Strategic Organizational Diversity: A Model?
			37. When Generations Collide
			38. This Time It's Personal
			39. Multiple Choice

ABOUT YOU

Name   Date

Are you a teacher? ❑ A student? ❑
Your school's name

Department

Address   City   State   Zip

School telephone #

YOUR COMMENTS ARE IMPORTANT TO US!

Please fill in the following information:
For which course did you use this book?

Did you use a text with this ANNUAL EDITION? ❑ yes ❑ no
What was the title of the text?

What are your general reactions to the Annual Editions concept?

Have you read any pertinent articles recently that you think should be included in the next edition? Explain.

Are there any articles that you feel should be replaced in the next edition? Why?

Are there any World Wide Websites that you feel should be included in the next edition? Please annotate.

May we contact you for editorial input? ❑ yes ❑ no
May we quote your comments? ❑ yes ❑ no

NOTES

NOTES

NOTES

NOTES

NOTES

NOTES

NOTES

NOTES